"Phil Hall's *Independent Film Distribution* is an absolute must-have for anyone and everyone, aspirants and veterans, who produce or want to produce independent films. Although the size of a normal book, *Independent Film Distribution* is a virtual encyclopedia of the many worlds of film distribution. Author Phil Hall's vital information can make the difference between having your films seen or buried."

> — Don Schwarz, *Cinesource* Magazine

"If you've got an independent film taking up hard-drive space, or collecting dust on a shelf, you owe it to yourself to read this book. There may be an audience out there for it after all — this book will help you find it."

> — Matthew Terry, producer/screenwriter/teacher/
> columnist, *www.hollywoodlitsales.com*

"The second edition of *Independent Film Distribution* is still a very informative and enlightening read and will prove to be a great and blunt guide for any self-respecting independent filmmaker intent on making their movie for an audience instead of just screening it for their friends and family."

> — Felix Vasquez Jr., *www.cinema-crazed.com*

"This incredibly focused and wide-ranging book should make the gifted Phil Hall less of a well-kept secret than he's been to date. Here the eclectic critic-scholar-showman tells you exactly what you need to know about so-called indie cinema, blending invaluable new material with historical facts, critical insights, and guest shots by smartly selected professionals. Touching every base from the Edison studio to *Zombie! Vs. Mardi Gras* and beyond, Hall celebrates anti-Hollywood heroes — and chastises the film industry's almighty dollar sign — in words as entertaining as they are informative. Like the movies he celebrates, Hall is beholden to nothing but his own incisive ideas, marching to an indie drummer all his own."

> — David Sterritt, Chairman of the National Society of
> Film Critics and author of *Guiltless Pleasures: A David
> Sterritt Reader* and *The Films of Jean-Luc Godard: Seeing
> the Invisible*

"Phil Hall's *Independent Film Distribution* blows the secrets of getting your indie film on movie theater screens wide open, offering an exhaustive series of interviews with the people who've been there. The secrets are all revealed here!"

> — Christopher Null, editor, *FilmCritic.com*, and author of *Five
> Stars! How to Become a Film Critic, The World's Greatest Job*

"Home run! Well-written, clear, and makes you feel smarter when you're done. It's one of those books that pack info like a tight snowball. This is very, VERY good!"

> — Charles Pappas, film historian and author of *It's a Bitter
> Little World: The Smartest, Toughest, Nastiest Quotes from
> Film Noir*

"WOW! FINALLY! A book on today's film industry that tells it like it is!"

— Ryan Dacko, author, *I Guess the World Could Use Another Ed Wood* and filmmaker (*And I Lived*)

"A comprehensive primer on independent film — from grand debate on the state of the industry to the often-overlooked minutiae of what it takes to market a movie — interspersed with a nice orchestra of voices from the indie film world at every turn. Hall blends DIY aesthetic with an informed approach that makes for an essential read. Anyone with a serious interest in producing a film should take note."

— Dylan Stableford, former editor/producer of MTV News and media editor of *TheWrap.com*

"Calling a book a 'bible of the industry' is normally a cliché. But in this case, it is really true. Phil Hall tells all with humor, honesty, and accuracy. It is a heartfelt look at the highs and lows of the independent film industry by a man who both knows and loves it. This book should be mandatory reading for every filmmaking class in the country! Before you pick up a camera, pick up this book!"

— John Stewart Socha, Relevant Radio Network and *ACPress.com*

"This book takes the aspiring filmmaker on a crash course in practical moviemaking reality through the testimony of those who've been there and know all the traps and detours — filmmakers, distributors, film festival promoters. Phil Hall knows the territory and gives an expert overview of everything it takes to go from wannabe to bona fide filmmaker in a style that reads like a novel, not a how-to. Inside access plus uncommon insight equals the straight dope on today's independent filmmaking world."

— Glenn Erickson, author of *DVD Savant: A Review Resource Book*

"Phil Hall unravels the mysteries surrounding how to get attention for independent films in his enlightening and entertaining new book, *Independent Film Distribution*. Drawing on his considerable expertise in movie PR and as a film critic, Hall offers valuable, up-to-date information for aspiring independent filmmakers in such critical areas as distribution options, helpful organizations and resources, marketing, film festival considerations, and 'what not to do.' If I were making an independent film — or had already completed one — this book would be my bible."

— Betty Jo Tucker, editor and lead film critic for *ReelTalk Movie Reviews*, author of *Confessions of a Movie Addict*, and *Susan Sarandon: A True Maverick*

"A remarkable overview inside the past, present, and future of independent film."

— Christopher Bligh, *Ain't It Cool News* and *DVDAuthority.com*

"Phil Hall knows this business inside out, and offers an insightful, fascinating glimpse into twenty-first-century independent cinema. It's a must read for aspiring moviemakers who want to get their work seen and sold, as well as film aficionados looking for the lowdown on the current state of non-multiplex fare."

— Steven Puchalski, publisher and editor, *Shock Cinema* magazine

"Superb interviews with producers and directors in the new wave of independent cinema, as well as a thoughtful, up-to-date take on the entire process of production — from concept to distribution. As a bonus, Hall offers a much-needed cold, hard look at whether the over-hyped film festival circuit has outlived its usefulness for today's indie producers."

— John Farrell, author of *Digital Movies with Quicktime Pro* and filmmaker (*Richard the Second, Everyman*)

"If you have made, or are even thinking about making, an independent film, you must read this book. An up-to-the-minute, practical guide to the very complex world of film marketing, it moves beyond any narrow definitions of 'independent' to help your movie find its niche. Filled with interviews from industry professionals, it examines the realities and economics of marketing your film and getting it into the hands of the people who will help you get your work seen."

— Jeremy Heilman, *MovieMartyr.com*

"Phil Hall's *Independent Film Distribution* is essential for all true believers of the movie maverick spirit and of cinema's power as a personal art form. Hall's work is entertaining and incisive as it navigates us through the history, inner workings, and market realities of the independent film business. Exuding an abiding love for personal cinema, the book — most delightfully — takes acerbic swipes at those in Indiewood and its marketing cronies who shroud their faux-indie product in the garb of the truly pure."

— Jay Antani, *L.A. Alternative Press / Tokyo Pop / Slant* magazine

"Historical, informative, and entertaining, Hall gives all would-be filmmakers the uncompromising facts about getting their work seen by the public. He cuts through the quagmire of other how-to books to provide clear, concise advice on festivals, networking, and representation. No first-time moviemaker should be without this book."

— Bill Gibron, *DVDTalk.com* and *DVD Verdict*

"Phil Hall's new book is a comprehensive look at independent filmmaking, skillfully combining historical survey, interviews with indie insiders, and practical how-to advice in an entertaining and informative package spanning a broad range of topics and leavened with a healthy dose of humor. Anyone who would even consider navigating the treacherous waters of indie financing, filmmaking, or distribution should pick up this gem immediately."

— Robert Firsching, film critic and historian, *CinemaFacts.com*

"Phil Hall tears down mainstream ideas of what it means to be indie, eschewing Hollywood's so-called independent cinema and holding the magnifying glass over the REEL underground filmmakers, those who truly function independently of the studio system, and thus deserve the term 'independent.' The material is presented with informative readability and displays a mature but passionate take on the subject. An important book for the ever-swelling, truly indie scene."

— Kristofer Todd Upjohn, *B-Scared.com, Fishcomcollective.net*

"Phil Hall's new book is a resourceful and comprehensive look into the indelible psyche of a filmmaking movement — specifically the independent film industry — that deserves the common movie enthusiast's undivided attention. Thoroughly insightful, analytical, and informative, Hall's cinematic tome will have readers appreciating the inner-circle workings pertaining to the chaotic state of independent film distribution. Laced with hearty interviews and other noteworthy anecdotal tidbits, this book will arm observers with a vast understanding regarding the independent film process. Overall, this is an in-depth read for upstart/established filmmakers and ardent film fans alike!"

— Frank Ochieng, *The WorldJournal.com* and *MovieEye.com*

"This is the book that shady distributors don't want you to read! An indispensable guide for producers and filmmakers, Phil Hall demystifies the distribution process in this user-friendly field guide. Featuring insights from successful low-budget filmmakers and straight-shooting distributors, the book poses all the right questions and more than a few tried-and-true answers."

— Jeremiah Kipp, independent filmmaker (*The Pod, Disappearing Act, The Christmas Party*)

"This uncompromisingly accurate road map for filmmakers and producers is, hands down, the best book on the subject I have ever read. Offering priceless insight and invaluable information, the distribution process is laid bare with the precision of a scalpel. If you don't read this book and don't have distribution, you have no one to blame but yourself."

— Mike Sargent, independent filmmaker (*Personals/ Hook'd Up*), film critic for WBAI-FM, cofounder of the African American Film Critics Association

"This is one of the most concise and easy-to-understand books on this topic that I have read. Hall's writing style and the interviews he includes make this an engaging book, while at the same time being very informative. *Independent Film Distribution* is an essential 'must-have' for any microcinema filmmaker. In the ever-increasing complex world of independent film, this book is refreshingly easy to understand, and is a tremendous asset in helping you decide what to do with your film after it's finished."

— Kari Ann Morgan, *Microfilmmaker* Magazine

INDEPENDENT FILM DISTRIBUTION

How to Make a Successful End Run Around the Big Guys

2nd Edition

Phil Hall

Published by Michael Wiese Productions
12400 Ventura Blvd. #1111
Studio City, CA 91604
tel. 818.379.8799
fax 818.986.3408
mw@mwp.com
www.mwp.com

Cover design: MWP
Book design: Gina Mansfield Design
Editor: Paul Norlen

Printed by McNaughton & Gunn, Inc., Saline, Michigan
Manufactured in the United States of America

Library of Congress Cataloging-in-Publication Data

Hall, Phil, 1964-
 Independent film distribution : how to make a successful end run
around the big guys / Phil Hall. -- 2nd ed.
     p. cm.
 ISBN 978-1-932907-85-8
1. Motion pictures--United States--Distribution. 2. Motion pic-
tures--Distribution. I. Title.
 PN1993.5.U6H274 2011
 791.43--dc22
                                          2010030969

Mixed Sources
Product group from well-managed
forests and other controlled sources
www.fsc.org Cert no. SW-COC-002283
© 1996 Forest Stewardship Council
FSC

Dedicated to those
who dream
in celluloid and
digital video

CONTENTS

ACKNOWLEDGMENTS

The writer's greatest fear is not about receiving a negative reaction to published work, but receiving no reaction whatsoever. Fortunately, I did not experience that fear following the 2006 publication of this book's first edition. Almost from the moment the book appeared, I was fortunate to receive a steady stream of positive comments, both from neophyte filmmakers eager to find their niche and established creative artists who appreciated this overview of what is, arguably, the most intimidating aspect of the motion picture industry.

Since 2006, however, there have been a number of changes to the independent film distribution paradigm. The first edition appeared when the U.S. economy was relatively stable. The economic downturn that created considerable havoc during the final stretch of the previous decade left its residue on the independent film world — a number of distributors went out of business. Thus, this book's listing of available distributors needed to be updated.

Furthermore, the rise of so-called social networking media has offered a number of hitherto unknown opportunities for aspiring indie filmmakers to promote themselves and their work. A new chapter on this subject has been added to address this subject.

Thus, this second edition is being offered to catch up where we last left off in 2006. Hopefully, the next wave of filmmakers will be able to use the information here as part of their strategy to build out their careers and reach new audiences.

I would like to acknowledge my publishers, **Michael Wiese** and **Ken Lee**, for giving me this opportunity to update this book. I would also like to thank the supporters of the book's first edition, whose encouragement and positive feedback enabled me to bring this work up to speed.

Special thanks are due to the publishers of *Film Threat, Dark Gallery*, *The Independent* and *Delaware Today* for allowing me to reprint sections of interviews and essays that originally ran in their respective pages.

And extra special thanks are due to **Mark Bell, Matthew Sorrento, Kevin Mark Kline, Randy Pitman, Ben Ohmart, Rory L. Aronsky** and **Nic Baisley**.

FOREWORD

First, if you've managed to complete a feature film, no matter how small, you've accomplished something huge. It's something very few people will ever get to do. Before you worry too much about what happens next, take a breath and celebrate!

Now, please understand, I'm no big distribution guru. All I know are my experiences on my own films, and what I hear from friends. And the rules are always evolving. So take what follows with the appropriate grain of salt.

To me, distribution seems like the oddest and hardest to control part of an odd and hard to control business. It's going to Vegas and rolling the dice. Whether your film is the next *Boys Don't Cry* or is never released has as much to do with luck as it does with the quality of what you made: What are distributors looking for at this moment? Do you fit the hot genre everyone wants this month, or the cold one everyone's avoiding? What critics show up at your screening? Did they just have a fight with their kids? Did the distributor rep who liked your film just get a call from the boss saying, "Buy more films, we need something for spring!" or "Stop buying films, we've spent too much already!"

When people ask my advice about what to do with their film, I always tell them there's no one answer; it depends on the film itself. Is it a genre film? Is it likely to do well in a festival atmosphere? Is it critic friendly? Or is it more "commercial"?

For example, Sundance is often seen as the Holy Grail for indie filmmakers. It's a great festival. I love it. I've premiered two of my films there. But, if you're trying to sell your film, Sundance is only great if your film becomes one of the few each year that get the lion's share of the attention. It can also make things very difficult. If you play Sundance and no one jumps up to distribute it, you now have 2.9 strikes against you. Everyone assumes, "Well, every distributor was at Sundance. If your film was any good someone would have bought it." Now it may well be that the distributors didn't even get to your screenings. Maybe something with a higher profile was playing at the same time. Or it's late in the festival, so a lot of companies have gotten less aggressive, having already made big purchases. But that doesn't stop your movie from being seen as tainted goods if the festival ends and no one's made an offer.

If your film is blatantly commercial and not likely to be a critical hit, I'd probably avoid festivals and go directly to distributors. I haven't tried that approach on any of my own films, but most people seem to feel the best way to do that is to set up a screening or two and invite all the companies, with the hope that several become interested and some sort of bidding war occurs. A bidding war is a long shot, but when it does happen, you can get a lot more money for your film. To be honest, I have no idea if/when distributors will look at an unsolicited film. I do know that a known actor or director certainly ups the likelihood.

If your film is more artistic/critic friendly, then the festival route can be a good way to go. For one thing, it means — no matter what else happens — you'll get to see your film with real (and usually openhearted) audiences, travel with it, and have the fun of sharing it with people. That has a huge value in and of itself for a filmmaker. It's your one chance to really see how all your hard work is affecting people.

And it doesn't have to be Sundance. I like the smaller festivals too (Aspen, East Hampton, whatever), because they aren't markets, so the atmosphere is less "business." The audiences are mostly film fans, not film executives. And yet, some films do get bought out of these festivals (though not usually for lots of money). If your film is good, but modest, you might stand out more at one of these small, intimate festivals.

Then there are terrific big festivals like Telluride and Chicago, which get a lot of attention, press, etc., but aren't quite the marketplace that Sundance has become. There are usually more distributor reps at these bigger festivals than the smaller ones, along with critics from various important publications. So it splits the difference. Less chance of getting lost than at Sundance, but also fewer buyers. There's no formula. You just have to be as clear-eyed as you can about your film and where it has a chance to get attention. Do homework. And then be prepared to be rejected by a lot of festivals anyway! Remember, there are hundreds of other people out there with their films, vying for those same few spots. While the festival route is very tough and there's tons of competition, it still may be your best bet if you have a good film with no easily "sellable" elements (e.g., star actor, famous novel as basis of film, lots of sex and/or violence). Tough as the festival world is, the competition for distributor attention and money is a whole lot tougher.

Remember, distributors aren't just worried about whether your film is "good." They're more worried about whether they'll be able to find a way to sell it and make a profit on their investment. I've been at plenty of festivals where a film everyone thought was terrific didn't get bought by anyone because no one could think of what the poster would look like. Or where a film that no one thought was all that great got the big sale because people thought they could make money with it.

People ask me if it's worth taking on outside help to get your film sold. My feeling is, if you can find a sales rep or an agent or a publicist who really loves your film — who will be there if it all doesn't just fall into place right away — then that's someone you want on your team. That might mean not going with the biggest "name." But who cares if some world-famous agency represents your film if they never do anything to help sell it?

Remember, passion can be feigned. These people make a living repping lots of films, and it's in their interest to throw yours on the pile, just in case it hits. So just because someone says you're the next Martin Scorsese doesn't mean they necessarily believe it. You have to listen very closely and not just jump at the first compliment you get. It's like being on a date: Is someone saying they think you're great because they mean it, or because they want to get you into bed only to forget you the next day?

One way to get a better bead on the reality beneath the wooing is to talk to other filmmakers who've been with that rep, or agent, or publicist, or whomever. Were they happy? Did the person hang in when the going got tough, or did they suddenly stop taking phone calls? And talk to as many sources as you can. Any one person might have had a great or terrible experience. But is there a trend when you talk to three or four?

Also, look at the history. Has that person or company taken a number of indie films to success? A yes isn't a guarantee that they'll do the same for you (some places take on such a high volume of films they're bound to hit on some), but a no might make you think twice.

Another thing young filmmakers ask me is, "How do I deal with my distributor once I have one?" Remember, distributors are as different as people. Some are very filmmaker friendly and want you to be part of the process every step of the way. Others act like you're the annoying kid they have to find a way to get rid of, no matter what you do.

But I find that staying open and listening can help. Don't just assume they're the enemy. They've bought your film. They've put their careers at least a little on the line for your work. Yes, they have other films if yours dies, so it's not as important for them as for you. Yes, they may screw you over if they suddenly have another project that they think they can make more money on. But if you go in defensive, with a chip on your shoulder, you won't avoid the bad stuff anyway (face it, they hold the cards), but you might alienate people who could be on your side. It's a lesson I've had to learn more than once. For example, soon after Paramount Classics bought my film *The Singing Detective* at Sundance, they asked me to come in to discuss some possible changes. I felt very defensive and angry ("They bought the film saying they loved it. Now they want to change it?!"). But I calmed myself down and went to the meeting with an open heart and mind. Lo and behold, almost all their notes were things that actually bugged me about the film, too — but I thought it was too late to change. And I was thrilled that they were willing to pay to make those minor but important changes. And because I was so open to some of what they were saying, they backed down on the points I didn't agree with.

Similarly, keeping a somewhat realistic attitude about the process will help your relationship. Every filmmaker wants his or her film to be that rare breakthrough film that makes a lot of money, gets tons of attention, etc., etc. But there are hundreds of films released every year and only a few that catch that wave. You need your distributor to do what they can to give you a shot at that kind of success, position your film for it, but *nothing they do can guarantee your film will do well. Statistically it probably won't, even if they try hard*. If a distributor senses that you are going to be dissatisfied with everything they do no matter what, they'll quickly start shutting their ears to you. But if you pick your battles, and keep them reasonable, you're a lot more likely to get a fair hearing.

If you start bitching because they're not spending as much money on your odd, dark first film with unknown actors as they are on the new A-list cast light comedy they're also distributing, they'll tune you out pretty quickly. But if you make reasonable requests ("Can't we spend a bit more on ads for the weekly alternative paper? Why not use this particular quote from critic X? What about some screenings at colleges to raise awareness?"), you're more likely to get a thoughtful response, and even win sometimes.

And what if your film comes and goes quickly, or doesn't get great reviews, or even never gets bought at all? Be aware: *Everyone* faces rejection. It's part of the nature of art. It doesn't mean you made a bad film. Tons of films that we now think of as great films (*Memento, Bonnie and Clyde, Harold and Maude, The Stunt Man*, etc., etc.) almost didn't get distributed at all.

And maybe you did make a flawed or weak film. Think of your favorite filmmaker. Look at their filmography. Pretty likely there's a film or two on there that just didn't "work." Stanley

Kubrick literally bought back his own first film to take it out of circulation because he was so embarrassed by it.

I've directed five films and produced another. Each one has gotten some great reviews and some awful reviews. If the *New York Times* loves your film and the *Des Moines Register* hates it, does that really mean you've made a better film than if those reviews are the other way around? Yes, it matters in terms of commercial success, but not in terms of whether you made a "good" film (whatever that is). Almost *every* film made from the heart will communicate with *someone*. Beyond that, it's a numbers game. Yeah, better to have a million people love your film than a thousand, I guess. But if you can touch one person in the world with what you've created, you've done something rare and important and worthwhile. I've seen many, *many* terrific films that never got distribution, or that barely saw the light of day. One (*La Ciudad*) was my favorite American film the year I saw it. And we've *all* seen plenty of not-so-good films that get tons of attention.

It's unfair, it's dumb, and it's completely out of your control.

And in 500 years your film will be forgotten whether it never comes out or it wins the grand prize at Sundance. And you won't care. So let yourself feel the heartbreak and disappointment. Weep and yell a bit. Then go look in the eyes of someone who loves you, shrug, and start to work on the next one.

Keith Gordon, Filmmaker

Keith Gordon first came to notice in the early 1980s as an actor in such hit films as Dressed to Kill, Christine, *and* Back to School. *In the late 1980s, he shifted gears and gained attention as a director of such complex and original independently financed productions as* The Chocolate War *(1988),* A Midnight Clear *(1992),* Mother Night *(1996),* Waking the Dead *(2000), and* The Singing Detective *(2003). He is one of the most highly regarded creative talents in today's independent cinema.*

A BRIEF AND POTENTIALLY DISTURBING OVERVIEW OF THE STATE OF INDEPENDENT FILM IN AMERICA

For the dreams come, always they come.
— R. S. Thomas

1

Irving Berlin once wrote a song that proclaimed there was no business like show business. In a way, Berlin was only half correct.

Admittedly, the entertainment industry is the most visible corporate sector, thanks to its roster of larger-than-life personalities, its emphasis on glamour and glitz, and the seemingly endless hype that surrounds it. Indeed, for many people it is easier to identify all of Elizabeth Taylor's ex-husbands or recite the entire *Star Wars* screenplay verbatim than it is to identify their local elected officials.

But where Berlin erred is in the fact that show business is very much like any other business: It is a profit-fueled industry controlled by a powerful elite who are less than enthused over the prospects of ceding their domain to edgy, independent up-starts with an overwhelming hunger to slice themselves a piece of the proverbial pie.

And this, more than anything, is the greatest problem facing independent filmmakers today. When it comes to the concept of "show business," they know everything about the "show" but not as much (if anything) about the "business." For this sole reason, there are thousands of independently produced films that never find their way into commercial release. It is not because the films are inadequate — quite frankly, most of them are actually superior to the muck you'll find playing at your local multiplex. The reason these films don't get seen is because the filmmakers do not understand the complexities of the independent film distribution business.

Let's not put all of the blame on the filmmakers, since the majority of them have little opportunity to get a glimpse at how independent film distribution really works. Film schools focus on the nuts and bolts of the filmmaking process itself; the business side of cinema is either ignored or receives a brief, desultory summary. The general entertainment media prefers to skim the surface of the movie world — their concern is who's wearing what and who's divorcing whom. The film trade media, with very few exceptions, also prefers surface-skimming to an in-depth analysis of how to snag a distribution deal.

But at the same time, we need to be reasonable and honest. Nobody makes independent films for the sake of making independent films. At least no sane person does. While an independent film can be considered as the artistic, intellectual, and emotional statement of its filmmaker/creator and the artists who supported this filmmaker in the endeavor, it must also be viewed as a commercial product. Energy, imagination, labor, and (most importantly) money are invested in the making of the film. What possible purpose can be achieved if all of these investments, especially the last, are for naught?

The strategy here and throughout this book is to gain an understanding of how the independent film distribution business works, with the goal of getting your film picked up for commercial release. Admittedly, it will not be an easy mission (and you'll learn more about that in due time). But it is not impossible, as long as the subject is approached with maturity, professionalism, tenacity, a good sense of humor, and an even stronger sense of grace. Independent film distribution is not for the weak or the silly. But for those who have the drive and can persevere in the face of rejection and a decidedly less than level playing field, the challenge can be invigorating.

INDEPENDENT FILM 101

Let's pause for a few minutes and ponder this thought: Just what, exactly, are we talking about when we use the expression "independent film"? Thanks to the way the film industry operates, the answer has become increasingly fuzzy during the past few years. Even those who are well connected with the industry cannot help but express confusion over the definition.

"For me, the line between studio and independent has been blurred so much over the past 15 years that sometimes I can hardly tell the difference," says Jordan Hiller, editor of the online magazine *Bang It Out*.

Films that wrap themselves in the notion of being independent (or allow themselves to be wrapped by an eager media that too often plays along with the charade) have also obscured the notion of genuine independence. A rather prime example of this was the 2003 release *Lost in Translation*. Anyone looking for independence from the Hollywood scene might have problems there, considering it was directed and scripted by Hollywood insider Sofia Coppola (the daughter of the legendary Francis Ford Coppola and wife of A-list filmmaker Spike Jonze), it boasted major stars Bill Murray and Scarlett Johansson in the leading roles, and it was released amid multi-million-dollar hype by Focus Features, a division of Universal Studios.

"The concept of 'independent' is tricky and not all that clear, and I don't imagine I am alone in thinking that," comments Donald J. Levit, senior critic for *ReelTalk Movie Reviews*. "Technically, it should imply made-directed, financed-produced and/or distributed outside the big studio system, that is, free of the usual monetary pressures and thus perhaps more artistic or daring. Maybe during the '80s and the home video surge, 'independent' films did better, though their talents were eventually gobbled up. But today, hardly anything is truly outside the money net. No reason to dismiss Joan Didion's 1973 'delusion that studios have nothing to do with the making of motion pictures in modern times. [Ordinary people] have heard the phrase *independent production*, and have fancied that the phrase means what the words mean.' As an example, I'd be surprised if Sofia Coppola could've made 'independent' *Lost in Translation* without daddy's and hubby's influence, much less got major distribution and advertising and gone on to become lots of people's darling."

"Well, the *Star Wars* prequels are all 'independent' too," adds Christopher Null, editor of *FilmCritic.com* and an independent filmmaker. "I can accept that there are various degrees of independent film, but there are limits. Just because George Lucas didn't take any money from Fox for production doesn't *really* mean he's making an independent film. And just because a studio buys a movie it sees at Sundance doesn't make it independent either. (I'm thinking of vanity-type projects made by bored actors sitting on loads of cash and set up with production deals around Hollywood.) There's no good line to draw, but no, I wouldn't refer to *Lost in Translation* as independent in the true spirit of things — whereas I would argue that *Napoleon Dynamite* definitely is an indie and *Garden State* probably is as well."

However, some can make an argument that films such as *Lost in Translation* and other recent commercial successes that were made by plugged-in Hollywood types (such as *My Big Fat Greek Wedding* and *Sideways*) deserve to be considered as independent productions.

"I believe so," states Dustin Putman, editor for *TheMovieBoy. com* online review magazine. "All of the mentioned films, while owned by the studios, were never guaranteed financial success or big release patterns. Made on low budgets, they were passionate creations conceived by writers and directors more concerned with telling a good story than pleasing Joe Moviegoer. That they were, ultimately, successful at the box office is a testament to how good they were. Had they been pieces of crap, they would have failed miserably. In comparison, big-budget, special effects–laden studio fare like *The Day After Tomorrow* or any of the Jerry Bruckheimer–produced action films can be pieces of crap and still be assured to make money."

Putman's observation is especially cogent. After all, today's film world is not going out of its way to make room for independent films. As stated before, the "business" half of "show business" is ruling the roost for those who occupy the seats of film industry power. And, honestly, if financing is coming from a Hollywood insider, what filmmakers in their right mind would hold up their hand and turn up their nose in scorn?

"Remember what Balzac wrote? 'Behind every great fortune there is a crime,'" says Charles Pappas, film historian and author of *It's a Bitter Little World: The Smartest, Toughest, Nastiest Quotes from Film Noir*. "Behind every independent film is a trust fund. Or a grant. Or investment capital. With the average cost of a Hollywood-produced movie going north of $63 million, if an indie is even a tenth of that, it's still way beyond the average means of a Starbucks 'but I'm really a screenwriter' barista. When you have that much money at stake, your survival instinct commands you to make movies that are about as dangerous as T-ball. There will always be a money train somewhere. It doesn't matter who's paying — if it's a stogie-smoking Louis B. Mayer type or a Perrier-sipping Harvey Weinstein type, dollars are dollars. Not only is a rich man's joke always funny, but a rich man's movie will always be whatever he wants it to be. Without the money, you're just Dieter Sprocket in a black turtleneck."

Besides, Pappas adds, defining "independent film" is equivalent to playing a game with no rules and no end.

"Independent film means *Monster a-Go Go* to some, *American Beauty* to others," he says. "Or it might be something you sip a nice Pinot Noir to, smug in the knowledge that you and maybe three other Upper West Siders are privy to its existence — even if it only takes up less space on the cultural landscape than theoretical subatomic particles. For others, it's a hipness that's parsecs ahead of the cultural curve. For me, it means the kind of movie that makes you exclaim, 'My, Grandma, what big teeth you have.' There's no Platonic Ideal of the independent film. There's no Missing Link from which all the rest descended. It didn't have a golden age when the sun beamed behind its makers' shoulders and doves alit on their shoulders while they taught toga'd film students in marble temples how to deconstruct Kurosawa and Ringo Lam."

And here comes another point that tends to get lost in the shuffle: Just where did independent film begin and how did it evolve into today's indie scene? In fact, you cannot make your way through the independent film distribution orbit without knowing where it all came from.

OUTSIDERS FIGHTING BACK

The independent film world actually stretches far back to the nascent years of the motion picture industry in America. During the first decade of the twentieth century, movies evolved from a sideshow novelty into a surprisingly popular form of mass entertainment. By the end of that decade, an actual film industry was beginning to coalesce as the most successful film production companies began to explore ways to secure their dominance of their field.

Key in the attempt to maintain corporate control of film distribution was none other than Thomas A. Edison. Many people are aware of the pioneering technological work that Edison and his team accomplished on behalf of filmmaking, but often overlooked is Edison's crucial work as a producer and distributor. In fact, the most famous American movie of this era, *The Great Train Robbery* (1903), was an Edison production (so was the first horror movie, the 1910 version of *Frankenstein* — which was also the first film brouhaha, as local censorship boards successfully had the film yanked when some audience members complained it was too scary).

Edison initially attempted to grab hold of the film business for himself by suing his competition for violation of his patents relating to filmmaking and film projection. When it became obvious this would be a costly pursuit without the ironclad hope of judicial success, Edison abruptly shifted gears in January 1909 and brought his competition to his corporate bosom via a new organization: the Motion Picture Patents Company. Edison sought out the leading American film companies (Biograph, Essanay, Kalem, Kliene, Lubin, Selig and Vitagraph) and the two major French producers (Méliès and Pathé) in a partnership that determined these companies alone had exclusive rights for motion picture production under American and European patent laws. Furthermore, they invented the General Film Company as the source for distributing their combined output. Exhibitors, who were basically independent businessmen running their own stand–alone venues or small chains of theaters, were informed they could only book films made by the companies in the Motion Picture Patents Company and distributed through the General Film Company. But in order to do that, the exhibitors would be required to pay an annual license of two dollars a week to the General Film Company.

This action did not sit well with most exhibitors, but it was especially outrageous to a man named Carl Laemmle. A German immigrant, Laemmle ran what was known as an "exchange," basically a wholesale operation that purchased films from producers and rented them out to the individual exhibitors. Laemmle challenged the Motion Picture Patents Company in private negotiations, and then took his case public by printing the group's threatening letters in the film trade journals. Angry at this upstart's actions, the Motion Picture Patents Company then ceased to provide Laemmle's exchange with movies. In response, Laemmle created the Independent Motion-Picture Company (known as IMP) — and unknowingly gave birth to the independent film distribution business.

Laemmle happily turned producer, making his own films under the IMP banner and sending them out to exhibitors. Laemmle also did something his competition never dreamed of doing: He identified the performers who appeared in his movies. At that time, acting in movies was considered a déclassé occupation (even in the performing arts), and no serious thespian would dare agree to be identified in screen titles. Likewise, the producers of the Motion Picture Patents Company were not eager to give their actors star billing, for they feared that star salaries would soon follow. But audiences were curious to know just who they were watching on the screen. Laemmle gave particular attention to a pretty young starlet named Florence Lawrence, whom he lured away from Biograph for an exclusive contract with IMP. Laemmle even created a publicity campaign that fervently denied rumors that the lovely Miss Lawrence had been killed in a streetcar accident — a rumor, it was later revealed, that was invented by Laemmle's office.

While Laemmle invented his own rules, a hitherto unknown exhibitor saw the opportunity to make his own jump into independent film distribution. Adolph Zukor acquired the U.S. rights to the 1912 film production of *Queen Elizabeth* starring Sarah Bernhardt, the world's most famous actress. This was a major coup and the members of the Motion Picture Patents Company found themselves unable to invent any intelligent reason why Zukor's prestigious acquisition could not be shown in American theaters. *Queen Elizabeth* was released to unprecedented commercial success, and many Broadway legends were suddenly eager to work with Zukor: If Bernhardt could make films, they theorized, it was only right that they too should be immortalized on screen. Zukor launched the *Famous Players in Famous Plays* series in 1913 with James O'Neill (the father of Eugene O'Neill) in a film version of his stage success *The Count of Monte Cristo*. Again, the Edison cabal could not halt these films from being shown due to the obvious prestige associated with their productions.

Zukor actually overplayed his hand somewhat, for the *Famous Players in Famous Plays* series proved to be a considerable commercial flop (the films were rather awful, and even *Queen Elizabeth*, truth be told, was something of a dud). But the fact that he was able to knock down the monopolistic barriers set up by Edison and his cronies helped to seal the doom of the Motion Picture Patents Company. By 1915, this group and its General Film Company subsidiary were killed in the courts. Edison quit the film business for good in 1918, angry and confused over his failure to master its intricacies. The other companies in the Motion Picture Patents Company eventually went out of business or were swallowed up by their faster-moving competition.

Ironically, Laemmle and Zukor would succeed Edison and his partners as the power brokers of Hollywood: Laemmle as the founder of Universal Pictures and Zukor as the force behind Paramount Pictures. The original independents became the first generation of movie moguls.

By the end of the 1910s and the beginning of the 1920s, the American film industry as we know it today began to take further shape in the Los Angeles suburb of Hollywood. A studio system evolved that concentrated all aspects of film development, production, and distribution — all from within the studios' gates. Independent filmmaking continued, but distribution for these films was haphazard at best. Some smaller distributors crashed and burned under the financial strain: Chadwick Pictures, which pegged an excess amount of hoped-for success on Larry Semon's 1926 comedy feature version of *The Wizard of Oz*, went bankrupt right before the film was slated to open, forcing the film to be yanked from theaters without being seen (and, as a by-product, killing the momentum in Semon's career).

But one well-moneyed clique prospered. The creation of United Artists by the combined forces of Mary Pickford, Douglas Fairbanks, Charlie Chaplin, and D. W. Griffith in 1919 gave independent producers the opportunity to have a well-financed distribution company available to send their films out into the nation's theaters. We'll look into the United Artists story later in this book as we explore self-distribution. But for now, we can say that for many years United Artists was the prime source of American independent film distribution, and many of the top independent film producers brought forth their work under the United Artists banner.

And here is the key to understanding independent film distribution: The independents were originally considered to be the producers, not the directors. Admittedly, Chaplin and Griffith were directors, but they were also their own producers (Griffith would abandon being his own producer in 1924 after a series of expensive film failures and sign with Paramount Pictures). As the silent cinema of the 1920s gave way to the talkies of the 1930s, the independent filmmakers were the producers who ran their own mini-studios and held talent under contract. Samuel Goldwyn,

David O. Selznick, Howard Hughes, and Walter Wanger were the most visible and powerful of these Hollywood independents during the 1930s and 1940s (Hughes was the only one who occasionally tried his hand at directing). By the 1950s, Stanley Kramer and Otto Preminger were the primary independent forces in Hollywood (Kramer took to directing later in his career, while Preminger was the rare studio director who took the opposite path by branching into independent producing).

But beyond this sphere were other independent film scenes that played to niche markets Hollywood didn't bother to acknowledge. In fact, most audiences were unaware these films existed until they were rediscovered many years after their initial theatrical runs. All of these have been detailed in great length elsewhere, but they deserve some mention here for historic purposes.

The largest and (perhaps) the most entertaining of these independent niches were the exploitation films. Created on shoestring budgets, they sought to navigate their sordid way around Hollywood's self-created censorship codes on taboo subjects including drug addiction, prostitution, and various forms of moral perversion. The films were, for the most part, terrible on every possible artistic and intellectual level. Yet the salacious nature of their subject matter and the incessant marketing push behind them drove moviegoers to the grind house theaters that played them for "adults only" audiences. Occasionally a real movie somehow wound up in this mix, including a rerelease of MGM's banned *Freaks* and a truncated and dubbed import of Ingmar Bergman's serious *Summer with Monika* under the zany new title *Monika: The Story of a Bad Girl* (which carried the advertising slogan "a picture for wide screens and broad minds"). This niche market thrived theatrically until the demise of the grind houses and the drive-ins in the 1980s, but it continues in the direct-to-video market today.

Perhaps the most remarkable of the niche markets, from a sociological standpoint, were the so-called "race films" featuring all-black casts. These low-budget movies were produced solely for exhibition in segregated theaters across the United States. Some of the films were made by African American filmmakers, most notably the legendary Oscar Micheaux (who will be profiled later in this book) and the long-overlooked Spencer Williams (who directed, produced, wrote, and starred in a series of Texas-based features throughout the 1940s). These films were significant in giving African American performers the chance to play roles of a wider variety than Hollywood was offering. But, truth be told, the bulk of these films were poorly made and plagued with unimaginative direction, formulaic screenplays, and acting that frequently ran the gamut from bad to terrible. While they serve historic value in tracing African American artistic expression during the reign of state-sanctioned segregation and in offering opportunities for black performers to take on roles beyond the Hollywood restrictions of menial servants or nightclub performers, these films are often difficult to sit through today viewed purely as entertainment.

The race films expired in the late 1940s as the civil rights movement saw African Americans demand equal access to mainstream activities — including the right to go to the cinema of their choosing. In a way, the race films reemerged in the early 1970s with the blaxploitation genre, with all-black or predominantly African American casts and (in many cases) African American talent behind the camera as well. Many of these were also independently produced and released, although the best known of the genre (*Shaft*, *Superfly*, and their inevitable sequels) were studio productions.

Another niche indie genre playing to a particular audience was the Yiddish-language cinema. This was a little different since many of the films were American-financed productions made in Europe, often with American actors, with their distribution for the global Jewish diaspora (their American release was relatively limited to immigrants, as most second-generation Jewish Americans had jettisoned Yiddish and mostly could not understand the dialogue in the movies). World War II ended this market, and the postwar Jewish diaspora either sought further assimilation around the world (which meant losing Yiddish as their primary language) or emigrated to Israel, where Yiddish was intentionally discouraged in order to promote the revival of the Hebrew language. As with the race movies, this cinema was rediscovered years after its films' initial release.

Even smaller niche markets also existed, consisting of film-makers creating avant-garde, experimental movies. They were initially short films, although some were grouped together into feature anthologies; feature-length productions came about in the 1960s. Later dubbed "underground" cinema, these films used unusual camera techniques, offbeat editing, and frequently disturbing images to relate the artistic expression of their creators. Filmmakers such as Rudy Burckhardt, Maya Deren, Kenneth Anger, Stan Brakhage, and Shirley Clarke were among the key figures here. Their popularity was (and is) primarily with critics and selected audiences who enjoyed access to film societies that presented their work — mainstream audiences never saw them, and average moviegoers today are unlikely to even know who these filmmakers are.

And finally, floating on the periphery of this world, were isolated dreamers, schemers, and a few genuine artists who made movies on shoestring budgets and found their movies picked up by tiny distribution companies including Producers Releasing Corporation, Distribution Corporation of America, and Astor (the last company actually upgraded itself from releasing race films and cheapo horror such as the 1953 lunar gorilla romp *Robot Monster* into bringing high-grade art films such as *La Dolce Vita* and *Last Year in Marienbad* to American cinemas). There were also many fly-by-night distributors who ceased operation after dropping one or two movies into release. Over time, some of the films made in this sector found their way into belated classic status (most notably Herk Harvey's 1962 chiller *Carnival of Souls* and the delightfully warped anti-classics of Edward D. Wood Jr.). But for the most part, these films were obscurities in their day and remain so today. The concept of successfully creating and releasing an independently financed film was, on the whole, an elusive notion.

From this chaos, it would seem that independent film-making as we know it today could not take root. Incredibly, it did. It took three men, curiously all based in New York, to stake out independent film distribution as a commercially viable enterprise. It also took a film festival to plant the dream with independent filmmakers that a distribution deal required a single screening with the right people in the audience.

The first of these men is, ironically, the least known today: Morris Engel. In 1953, working on a budget of only $30,000 and using a special lightweight camera that he designed, Engel crafted a charming feature film called *The Little Fugitive* about a seven-year-old Brooklyn boy who runs away to Coney Island after he mistakenly believes that he killed his brother. Engel's handheld camerawork was highly unusual for its time, and it provided a rare documentary-style intimacy for its Coney Island sequences. *The Little Fugitive* caught many people off guard with its charm and style, and the film won the Silver Lion at the Venice Film Festival and an Academy Award nomination for Best Original Screenplay. No less a figure than François Truffaut cited Engel's film as the inspiration for both his 1959 landmark *The 400 Blows* and the French New Wave that followed.

Even more remarkably, the film was a major commercial success via its distribution by the independent Joseph Burstyn Inc. This distributor primarily handled European fare, including *Miracle in Milan* and *Umberto D.*, but occasionally picked up American independent ventures such as Stanley Kubrick's independently produced 1953 feature debut *Fear and Desire*.

Unfortunately for Engel, lightning never struck again. He helmed two other independently financed films, *Lovers and Lollipops* (1956, distributed by the small company Trans Lux, which released Fellini's *La Strada* and the Raymond Burr version of *Godzilla* the same year) and *Weddings and Babies* (1958, distributed — incredibly, since it was decidedly non-Hollywood in style and substance — by 20th Century-Fox). Neither film found the critical or commercial adoration that *The Little Fugitive* enjoyed. Engel dropped out of sight from the movie world, focusing on commercial photography. He made a few low-budget features later in his career, including *I Need a Ride to California* (1968) and *A Little Bit Pregnant* (1993), but they were never released. Engel was virtually forgotten until a 2001 retrospective of his films in

New York, followed by the DVD premieres of his first three features from Kino on Video. Engel died on March 5, 2005, and by the time of his passing he was finally recognized for his achievements in independent filmmaking.

For many independent filmmakers, the first true icon of the genre was John Cassavetes. He was also a fairly unlikely icon: Cassavetes was primarily known as the star of "B" movies and the so-so TV series *Johnny Staccato* when he borrowed $40,000 and began shooting a mostly improvised feature called *Shadows* (1959). With its harsh and unsentimental view of the Beat generation spiced with a mature view of race relations, *Shadows* was unlike any film made in its time. And unlike the so-called underground filmmakers, Cassavetes was determined to have *Shadows* seen in mainstream theaters. Through the virtue of his name recognition and the intensity of his devotion to the project, Cassavetes pushed *Shadows*, and kept pushing until critical and commercial recognition began to register.

Even Hollywood noticed, and Cassavetes was hired to direct two studio-financed films: *A Child Is Waiting* and *Too Late Blues* (both released in 1962). Neither film was successful, due primarily to severe miscasting (Judy Garland's sincere but misguided performance in the former film, Bobby Darin's and Stella Stevens' unsatisfactory performances in the latter), and also due to the fact that Cassavetes lacked the control to make films similar in the rambling style that made *Shadows* so effective.

After earning money by acting in such films as *The Killers* (1964) and *The Dirty Dozen* (1967, for which he received an Oscar nomination), Cassavetes withdrew to his home and used the location to shoot what would become *Faces* (1968). The emotional power of *Faces*, with its story of a married couple's parallel infidelities, was shattering. Cassavetes self-released *Faces* to wide success, even earning Oscar nominations for his screenplay and for the performances by Seymour Cassel and Lynn Carlin; the Oscar nominations were no mean feat, given the money and marketing machinery required to generate such industry-stamped acclamation.

Again Hollywood called Cassavetes, and again he made two films under a studio banner that were not particularly successful: *Husbands* (1970) and *Minnie and Moskowitz* (1971). Yet again he went home to create his own self-financed film that would be self-released: *A Woman Under the Influence* (1974), which many people consider to be his masterpiece. And yet again he received Academy recognition, with Oscar nominations for his direction and for Gena Rowlands' performance.

Sadly, the Cassavetes story took a turn for the worse. Lightning did not strike for a third time and his attempt to self-distribute his self-financed feature *The Killing of the Chinese Bookie* (1976) left him bankrupt. He was able to raise funds to complete *Opening Night* (1979), but he could only manage a one-week theatrical run in a few markets. Despite critical acclaim and Golden Globe nominations for its stars Gena Rowlands and Joan Blondell, the film did not have a full theatrical release until after his death in 1989. Cassavetes' subsequent films, *Gloria* (1980), *Love Streams* (1985), and *Big Trouble* (1986, in which he replaced Elaine May as director midway through production), were for-hire jobs that had their respective moments of glory but that, on the whole, lacked the artistry and intellectual power of his earlier work.

While the quantity of his films was relatively limited, Cassavetes' inspiration to many independent filmmakers came from his ability to create small, compelling, language-driven features that made up for their lack of big budgets with an emotional power that rarely finds its way onto the screen. His success in self-releasing *Shadows*, *Faces*, and *A Woman Under the Influence* helped to inspire a new generation of filmmakers to explore self-distribution as an option to get their movies seen (we will discuss this later in the book).

The third prominent figure in the development of independent film distribution was both the most famous and (from a cinematic consideration) the least talented of the trio: Andy Warhol. The brilliantly self-promoting Warhol was a typical underground filmmaker in his scope and style, and he had a tendency to create wildly non-commercial and often incomprehensible movies (most notably *Empire*, a 485-minute single shot of the Empire State Building viewed during the course of a day). His films were often monotonous in content and amateurish in technique, with inaudible sound and shaky camerawork (which, in a way, is a blessing since clear sound and visuals would only further magnify the inadequacies of their horrible performances).

Not unlike Cassavetes, Warhol was able to parlay his name recognition to advance his films. For better or worse, it worked. In 1964, he received an Independent Film Award from *Film Culture* magazine. He set up his own distribution outlet via Andy Warhol Films and began securing commercial engagements. His 1965 *My Hustler* offered an unapologetic portrait of gay life (a rarity for that era). His 1966 *Chelsea Girls* created a minor controversy with its challenging use of the split screen presentation. Although his own directing efforts were curtailed after a 1968 assassination attempt, Warhol had already achieved something never before done: His name was a recognized brand on a truly independent line of films. With Paul Morrissey taking the wheel as director, films released under the Andy Warhol aegis were among the most successful independent offerings of the late 1960s and early 1970s, and served to inspire a wave of wonderfully offbeat filmmakers who dared to push boundaries of good sense and good taste (most notably John Waters and David Lynch, who arguably would never have found their audiences had Warhol not been there first).

A special honorable mention needs to be given to the 1954 feature *Salt of the Earth*. Made by blacklisted Hollywood filmmakers in New Mexico under grueling and frequently disruptive circumstances, the film did not immediately influence independent filmmaking in the United States since it was barely seen here — it played in a grand total of ten theaters for its initial release, with two of those venues in New York, and the media was not accommodating (no less a figure than Pauline Kael dismissed it as Communist propaganda). But the film did have a wide European release — in Paris it ran for more than a year and, not surprisingly, it was a commercial success in the

Soviet Union — and it helped to bring global audiences closer to American indie efforts. The film's American reputation was not strengthened until many years after it was completed, when the change in the sociopolitical climate from the McCarthyist 1950s to the free-spirited 1960s allowed it to be considered and appreciated as a significant work of art. The belated praise for *Salt of the Earth* is a tribute to the tenacity of its creators to work under trying circumstances in order to produce an independent film of significant social and intellectual value.

While Engel, Cassavetes, and Warhol showed the economic viability of independent filmmaking, it took an annual event to inspire a rush of filmmakers to grab their cameras. The Sundance Film Festival began in 1978 as the United States Film Festival. The festival was not originally conceived as a buyers-and-sellers exchange, but over time it evolved into a venue where independent films could be seen and bid upon by distributors. In 1989, the festival was the center of media attention when an unknown filmmaker named Steven Soderbergh screened his film *sex, lies, and videotape*. The film received rapturous reviews and won the Audience Award at Sundance. More importantly, it was acquired at Sundance by a small but hungry distributor called Miramax, which played incessantly on the positive hype the film received at the festival. Miramax's vibrant marketing campaign turned Soderbergh's film into a commercial success. Miramax repeated this formula with minor variations when it later went on to hype up previously unknown independent filmmakers such as Kevin Smith and Quentin Tarantino.

Ironically, people forget that *sex, lies, and videotape* was not the Grand Prize Award winner at Sundance in 1989. That honor went to Nancy Savoca's *True Love*, which was picked up for release by United Artists. But Soderbergh's film (and Miramax's aggressive genius for promotion) was the one that independent filmmakers recalled. *True Love* was nowhere near the commercial theatrical hit of Soderbergh's film and it is barely recalled today. Likewise, Savoca's career never reached the success that Soderbergh enjoyed.

Thanks to the 1989 event, the frenzy for getting a movie into Sundance grew throughout the 1990s. This culminated in the arrival of *The Blair Witch Project* in 1999, which left Sundance with a $1 million acquisition deal from Artisan Entertainment. Never mind that *The Blair Witch Project* didn't win a single award at Sundance (Tony Bui's *Three Seasons* was the big award winner that year). The $1 million acquisition was *the* news story of that festival, and that whet the appetite of more indie filmmakers to seek out distribution for their flicks.

Engel, Cassavetes, and Warhol are no longer with us. Sundance, as we will see later in the book, is still around, albeit in a very different configuration. But today, independent filmmakers work in an environment that is decidedly different from anything that came before. In many ways, it's not the best environment to be in if you're an independent filmmaker.

INTERVIEW
RICK CURNUTTE, EDITOR, *THE FILM JOURNAL*

One of the most influential advocates of contemporary independent cinema is Rick Curnutte, editor of the quarterly online magazine *The Film Journal* (*www.thefilmjournal.com*). Curnutte's magazine provides a scholarly approach to film commentary, particularly in its celebration of younger and up-and-coming independent filmmakers who are striving to make inroads within an industry that is not entirely welcoming of their presence.

Curnutte's *The Film Journal* also provides considerable focus on classic filmmaking, especially groundbreaking independent films that laid the foundation for today's indie scene.

Curnutte, who is also a cofounder of the Central Ohio Film Critics Association and a member of the Online Film Critics Society's Governing Committee, is not one to approach the subject of film commentary in a carefully diplomatic way. His vibrant and cerebral focus on cinematic studies has resulted in a refreshing blast of intellect and wit that has helped revitalize the notion that film criticism can go beyond the banality of upward or downward thumbs and snappy blurb-ready gushing.

Q: What does the phrase "independent film" mean to you?

RICK CURNUTTE: Nothing really, not anymore. "Independent film" has come to be as meaningless a term as "alternative music." It no longer refers to a work ethic or work aesthetic; rather, it refers to a perception of an aesthetic. Presenters at the Independent Spirit Awards get $30,000 gift bags. Every major studio has a "boutique" division, used to release "artsy" movies that the studios proper can't — or more likely, won't — release under their own banners. A true independent filmmaker is an individual who takes the tools at his/her disposal and, rather than subcontracting the work out to the studios and workhouses, does the work him/herself. This independent filmmaker toils under a more pure artistic ideology. Just because a film stars lesser-known stars and is helmed by an idiosyncratic director does not mean it is an "independent" film.

Q: Some recent hit movies such as My Big Fat Greek Wedding, Lost in Translation, *and* Sideways *were talked about as independent films, even though all were made by Hollywood insiders with Hollywood money. Can a production genuinely be called an independent film even if there is relatively little independence from Hollywood in its creation?*

RICK CURNUTTE: Absolutely not. Alexander Payne, Sofia Coppola, Wes Anderson, et al. … these are not independent filmmakers. Their films are conceived and produced in the same manner as Hollywood films. In fact, the way so many films have contracted talent, they've come to resemble the old studio system more than ever before. Real independent filmmakers — like James Fotopoulos, Simon Tarr, Apitchatpong Weerasethakul, Andrew Repasky McElhinney — take complete control of their work and take most, if not all, of the process on as their own.

Q: What have been the most significant and memorable independent films, both features and documentaries, that you've seen in the past few years? And what makes these films stand out from the Hollywood fare?

RICK CURNUTTE: I must use the same definitions of "independent" that I've been using thus far. There are a number of supremely talented, true independent filmmakers working today. My favorites are the aforementioned: James Fotopoulos, Simon Tarr, Apitchatpong Weerasethakul, Andrew Repasky McElhinney. I would add to that list the wonderful experimentalist Sadie Benning — she works solely with the Pixelvision camera — Ian Kerkhof, and two film critics-turned-filmmakers, Bilge Ebiri of *New Guy*, not the Hollywood one featuring D. J. Qualls, and Dan Sallit, whose *All the Ships at Sea* is one of the best films I've seen in the last five years. McElhinney's *A Chronicle of Corpses* and *Georges Bataille's Story of the Eye* are masterworks. Tarr's Rubicon is an ethereal experimental work. Fotopoulos, one of this country's most prolific talents, has at least two great works to his credit: *Back Against the Wall* and *Migrating Forms*. All of "Joe" Weerasethakul's films are flawless.

Q: What does it take for an independent film to make the jump into mainstream consciousness?

RICK CURNUTTE: Who knows? If you're talking about what most of the movie-going world calls independent film-making, then I suppose it all comes down to good marketing and industry buzz. If referring to true independents, then the task is much more wrought with frustration and failure. Self-distribution is expensive, though DVD burning and the Internet have helped make great strides toward making that a bit easier.

Q: Can smaller boutique distributors of independent films such as Zeitgeist, Wellspring, Palm Pictures, or Strand Releasing, just as examples, successfully compete against the Hollywood crowd in getting their films the level of attention and box office to make them commercially viable?

RICK CURNUTTE: Those guys will never be able to bring their films Hollywood-style media attention. A single, midrange studio film probably costs more than an entire year's worth of two or three of those indies' rosters combined. All they can really do is keep doing what they're doing, which is filling an audience niche that the studios ignore.

Q: What do you see as the potential downside — from an artistic and/or commercial viewpoint — of today's independent films?

RICK CURNUTTE: Artistically, the Sundance model independent film has become just about the most dry, nausea-inducing type of movie. I'm referring to films such as *Sideways*, *Shakespeare in Love*, *American Beauty*, *Chocolat*, etc., all films which are considered, or were, "independent." This is terribly counterproductive to the artistic process, because the perception of "independent" films became meshed with that of studio films. I should also note here that I don't have any preference between Hollywood and independent films.

Q: From your experience, do you feel that today's film festivals offer a viable launching point for independent films?

RICK CURNUTTE: Sure, but they've become so acquisition-based that many of the festival programmers out there are now programming their festivals to cater to the PR and distributor wants and needs, rather than those of the festival film-going public. But festivals can still offer unknowns a great opportunity to get their work seen.

Q: What advice would you give aspiring creative artists who want to get into the independent film business?

RICK CURNUTTE: Mostly, to know what they are doing before they get started. It's easy to get caught up in the allure of being a filmmaker. It's not so easy to do it successfully.

Q: How do you look upon films that are self-distributed by the film-maker? Does that factor in to your consideration of the film?

RICK CURNUTTE: I'm delighted to get access to films like these. I get sent films all year long, as the editor of *The Film Journal*. Granted, much of it is pure junk, just kids shooting themselves with Mom and Dad's camcorders. But I've also been sent some pretty ambitious stuff from seriously talented independent filmmakers. I'd definitely advise independent filmmakers to approach critics directly, especially if they're having troubles getting in the distributors' doors.

Q: How would you compare the independent films being produced today with the independent films produced in previous decades?

RICK CURNUTTE: I wouldn't contrast them. I don't really think quality gets better or worse, by that big a degree, over time. For every Cassavetes, there was, I'm sure, a failed hack with no talent who tried to do the same thing as Mr. Cassavetes. The biggest difference, I'd imagine, is in the tools available. No longer do independent filmmakers have to work with the super-expensive medium of film. Digital video inspires the process to no end.

Q: What films would you classify as being among the important independent films of all time, and why?

RICK CURNUTTE: A great question. Cassavetes' *Shadows*, because it reinvented the shape of the cinematic landscape. Welles' *Chimes at Midnight*, because it is what cinema was, is, and can be. Gibson's *The Passion of the Christ*, because it possesses one of the most singular visions in all of cinema. Van Sant's *Gerry* and Joe Weerasethakul's *Tropical Malady*, because they represent the rebirth of a new world cinema.

Q: Do you feel the entertainment media as a whole is genuinely supporting of independent cinema?

RICK CURNUTTE: I think they do a good job of selling the "independent" films the studios and boutiques want them to push. Other than that, they are worthless to the art form.

Q: Or would it be fair to state the media prefers to rally around a handful of specific titles while ignoring the vast majority of independent output?

RICK CURNUTTE: Yes.

Q: Do you feel the online media is doing an adequate job of covering today's independent cinema?

RICK CURNUTTE: Not really, but I think it's only because they are indicative of everyone else in this country. It's all a great big flavor-of-the-minute mentality.

Q: As a film reviewer, do you find yourself cutting smaller-budget independent films more slack when compared to the big-budget Hollywood productions?

RICK CURNUTTE: Absolutely not. I view all films through the same goggles. However, I do think I have a better tolerance for the things that many critics and, certainly, Joe Moviegoer can't tolerate — amateur production values, nonprofessional acting, etc. Americans especially are used to the Hollywood/ Indiewood model of film presentation. When they see something like Fotopoulos' *Back Against the Wall*, they may be put off by the mannered, naturalistic acting. But, for me, these are aesthetic virtues, not impediments.

Q: Or would it be intellectually unfair not to hold the smaller indie films to the same standards as the big-ticket Hollywood fare?

RICK CURNUTTE: Yes, it would be not only unfair, but unprofessional and hypocritical.

Q: Recent African American-focused independent films such as Woman, Thou Art Loosed *and* Diary of a Mad Black Woman *caught a lot of people by surprise with uncommonly high box office grosses. Do you believe these films will herald a new wave of independently produced African American cinema, or are these just unrelated flashes in the pan?*

RICK CURNUTTE: I've not seen these films, but they certainly seem to be filling an as-yet-untapped niche. There have been other, less-popular black-themed films recently, such as *Brother to Brother* and *Unknown Soldier*. Hopefully, those films will be embraced in the future as well. But anything's better than another *Barbershop* film.

Q: Films with a gay and lesbian subtext seem to exist solely in the indie orbit — Hollywood is not making movies with gay or lesbian love stories. What is your opinion of today's gay and lesbian cinema? And do you think Hollywood will try to tap into this market with its own gay and lesbian films?

RICK CURNUTTE: GLBT [gay, lesbian, bisexual, and transgender] cinema often falls into the same traps as other cinemas. Hollywood will never fully embrace gay-themed cinema until the gay culture itself starts accepting the independent offerings. Eventually, both will come around.

Q: Besides African Americans and gay and lesbian filmmakers, independent cinema has also been the focal point for creative artists of other demographics: Latinos, Native Americans, Asian Americans, and even Mormons. Do you feel independent cinema runs the risk of ghettoizing minority communities? Or is Hollywood so close-minded to adequately representing these voices that they have no other choice but to go indie?

RICK CURNUTTE: This may be an unpopular viewpoint, but I think the filmmakers themselves are often just as responsible for said ghettoizing as the studios. They often come across as making their work as "for us, by us" — to borrow a popular clothing label's motto — art, meant solely for them and those like-minded individuals they pre-approve. Right now, nearly all cinema is ghettoized in some shape or form. Documentary films, foreign films, animated films, dramatic films, comedy films, art films and, of course, independent films. To me, cinema is cinema is cinema. There's no need to ghettoize.

Q: Where do you see the independent film industry heading in the coming years?

RICK CURNUTTE: The same place it's been going since its inception in the Edison/Lumière/Méliès/etc. years: onward into creative, artistic dementia.

DIFFERENT VOICES:
OUTSIDERS ON A CELLULOID PLATFORM

In the mid-1990s, somewhere between the *sex, lies, and videotape* conquest of Sundance and the madness surrounding *The Blair Witch Project*, I had an office in New York where my neighbor was Dominick J. Daniels, an independent film producer. Daniels was in the midst of making a gangster film called *Made Men* and the production was anything but smooth. Every day, he would stop by and recount the various struggles, indignities, delays, and hassles that arose. If Sisyphus had been condemned to make movies instead of rolling a boulder up a mountain, he would have been in a situation similar to what Daniels was facing.

One day, after recalling the seemingly endless problems he was facing in the production, Daniels said with a laugh, "If it was easy, everyone would be doing it." Then he paused, considered what he'd said, and added, "Come to think of it, everyone is doing it."

What Daniels meant by that remark has more accuracy than flippancy. In the independent film world, there is a severely lopsided imbalance between supply and demand. The scale is tipped far into the realm of supply, which means there are just too many films being made today and not enough opportunities for them to be seen.

The concept of independent film production being too easy has become extremely pervasive. This has been built up by two key elements. The first element is the proliferation of low-cost digital video equipment, which enables anyone to shoot films on the cheap. With the right camera and software, it is not impossible to create a handsome, professional-quality motion picture. Of course, owning tools and using them correctly is not one and the same.

The second element is the propaganda of the indie distribution dreamland, which suggests that all you need is good luck and a clever backstory to get your foot in Hollywood's door. There's no lack of great stories, which have become legendary thanks to endless media repetition, insisting that neophyte filmmakers can strike gold on their first spin of the wheel. Actor Robert Townsend maxed out his credit cards to make *Hollywood Shuffle*, Kevin Smith sold his comic-book collection to make *Clerks*, Quentin Tarantino created his own film school by working at a video store before creating *Reservoir Dogs*, TV production assistant Edward Burns spent a mere $20,000 to make *The Brothers McMullen*, aspiring auteur Robert Rodriguez spent an absurdly low $7,000 to make *El Mariachi*, actor Jonathan Caouette spent an obscenely low $219 to make *Tarnation* and, of course, there was that sinister website that put *The Blair Witch Project* on the cybermap.

It all seems easy, doesn't it? Perhaps a little too easy, no?

"The economy of filmmaking, especially for independent film, has vastly changed the job of filmmaking and the career of the filmmaker," notes Matthew Seig, independent producer and executive director of the Rivertown Film Society in Rockland County, New York, and the former programmer for the Two Boots Pioneer Theater, a leading New York indie cinema venue. "What was once the realm of the 'professional' is now accessible to almost everyone. A great deal of experience isn't necessary to make something startlingly original and in touch with the zeitgeist. But the effect of these technological advances is also that budgets, wages, and technical quality are depressed and the length of a filmmaker's career is often very short. Filmmaking has become similar to writing, with a huge range of quality and content available, the acceptance of highly personal stories, a greater interest in nonfiction, and a lot of people working for low wages. A great many people attempt it, many people stick with it for a while, few people make a living at it, and fewer people make a decent living at it."

But Seig adds that all is not glum. "The upside is that when so many people have access to the means of telling stories we get stories that were unavailable before, and that is a good thing for society," he says.

Seig's latter insight is especially astute, considering that independent film is often the only medium available today for giving a voice to those who don't have access to the Hollywood machinery. And this is not just about film artists working outside of the studios. From a sociological standpoint, independent film has been crucial in recent years for giving voices to different demographic groups that are either ignored completely by Hollywood or are treated with condescending stereotypes (even at this late date). Let's take a few minutes to consider this in depth.

Independent film, which gave African Americans a chance to shine in the race films of the 1940s and the blaxploitation of the 1970s, has also given talented African American filmmakers the ability to move beyond Hollywood stereotypes. Charles Burnett tapped into this market with his classic *Killer of Sheep* (1977), the gritty cinema verité–style drama of a working class Watts family surrounded by crime and violence. Julie Dash framed a black feminist portrait in a Gullah environment with her wonderfully iconoclastic *Daughters of the Dust* (1992). Sadly, neither filmmaker's subsequent work (which included both independent films and Hollywood-financed work) captured the spirit and imagination of their breakthrough movies. More successful was Spike Lee, whose *She's Gotta Have It* (1986) heralded a distinct and eclectic cinematic voice. Lee, unlike Burnett and Dash, was able to build a body of work that enjoyed the financial support of Hollywood, European, and independent American money sources while keeping his own voice and vision (especially his voice, since Lee is among the most talented filmmakers when it comes to self-marketing). He is, of course, a singular exception to the Hollywood rule.

More recently, independent film is providing another wave of meaningful celluloid portraits of African American issues in a manner that is far removed from the lowbrow hip-hop comedies or violent gangsta thrillers that seem to dominate today's black-oriented Hollywood output. Recent features such as the aforementioned *Woman, Thou Art Loosed* (2004) and *Diary of a Mad Black Woman* (2005) caught many industry people by surprise in racking up substantial box office returns, even though they carried mixed to negative feedback from the critics (especially *Diary of a Mad Black Woman*, which carried an uncommonly high quantity of harsh reviews).

Both films also provided a cinematic platform for genuine Hollywood outsiders who were previously unknown to the studios (and even to most white Americans): Bishop T. D. Jakes, a charismatic television evangelist, adapted *Woman, Thou Art Loosed* from his book and played a major supporting role in the film. Playwright/actor Tyler Perry brought the characters of his regional theater productions (including the sassy matriarch Madea, which he played in drag) to *Diary of a Mad Black Woman*. If white audiences were asked to identify either gentleman before their respective films were released, the overwhelming reaction would have been a blank stare.

Perry has continued to enjoy filmmaking success. Yet the failure of Hollywood and the mainstream independent film industry to predict the initial success of either Perry or Jakes did not come as too much of a shock to a leading film journalist who covers the black film world.

"Hollywood consistently underestimates the African American audience," observes Kamal Larsuel, editor of the influential *3BlackChicks* online magazine. "Especially women and older folks. The 55-plus age group is totally underserved. Rarely is there a black movie that my 77-year-old grandmother can enjoy with her church friends. Hollywood just doesn't understand that market. Secondly, it's about the money. The African American film genre is fueled by the millions of dollars that the younger generation pays for the subpar movies that are presented to us. Hopefully seeing a movie like *Diary of a Mad Black Woman* make four times what it cost will help to open the door for other movies. In fairness, I will point out Queen Latifah, Ice Cube, Halle Berry, and Wesley Snipes (to name a few) all have production companies and are trying to put decent movies out there. We just have to give them a little time to put out more culturally responsible movies. And we in the African American community have to do our part. We need to start supporting our independent films. The more money these movies make, the better chance more will be made."

However, filmmaker Kevin Fitzgerald (creator of the documentary *Freestyle: The Art of Rhyme* and the force behind the Hip-Hop Film Festival) sees the issue as going beyond black and white.

"Racism still exists, you can't deny that," he says. "And not only from whites, but from all races — including minorities hating on their own peo-

photo courtesy Magnolia Pictures

ple. Also, nobody trusts anyone. I cut my dreads in the early days of making *Freestyle* because no foundations or companies would work with us. I think people thought we were going to buy drugs if they gave us money and at one point this actually was not far from the truth. But after I cut them it was like magic. Friends and family started helping us with some film here and there or a lab hookup or a few hundred or a G or so to buy stuff and pay for travel to follow our characters. You really have to be on point with your shit to make sure it gets done. You can't half-step a bit this way or that way because people will see it and you won't get shit. But in the end of the day, it comes down to if your film is good. And a lot of times it's not and it doesn't matter if you're white or black. But sometimes if you're black and your film is bad then it can be worse. But I would say being a wack white filmmaker is pretty bad, too!"

African American independent filmmakers are not the only ones fighting against being marginalized. Even more prevalent within the independent film circuit are movies focusing on the gay and lesbian communities. In fact, that's the only place where such films are being made in volume. Why isn't Hollywood touching this subject?

"Temporary oversaturation," says David Foucher, editor of *EDGE Boston*, a gay-oriented entertainment and culture

Twana (Debbie Morgan) and Michelle (Kimberly Elise) share a church moment in Woman, Thou Art Loosed, *one of the most successful independently produced African American films in recent years.* "Hollywood consistently underestimates the African American audience," *observes Kamal Larsuel, editor of the influential* 3BlackChicks *online magazine.* "Especially women and older folks. The 55-plus age group is totally underserved. Rarely is there a black movie that my 77-year-old grandmother can enjoy with her church friends. Hollywood just doesn't understand that market."

magazine. "The big studios don't care a whit for one genre over another, so long as people pay money to sit in a dark theater and watch their movies. Because films take many months to produce, the studios are involved with the unenviable job of predicting the appetite of audiences eight to 16 months into the future. The advent of GLBT (gay, lesbian, bisexual, and transgender) culture into the entertainment mainstream — *Will and Grace*, *Queer Eye for the Straight Guy* — has led directly to the realization that being gay is no longer a 'fad' to be exploited. It is entirely appropriate that we do not have exclusively GLBT-themed films. Instead, we should have films in which gay people are present on all levels in non-stereotypical ways."

Foucher, however, does not believe in embracing this niche market simply because it exists. "The days where a 'gay' movie might be an anomaly for which millions would shell out ten bucks purely on merits of its sexually distinct subject matter are blissfully behind us," he says. "The GLBT population must now seek to retain the fine balance of cultural identity in a world that will increasingly attempt to assimilate us into the norm, while preserving our attachment to the baser tenets of human existence. As a people, we must learn to celebrate that which makes us similar, while not discarding that which makes us diverse."

Other markets are somewhat more difficult to navigate. Asian American films, for example, are less common in commercial release.

"I suppose that Asian American films are a developing market that is perceived to be too niche or narrowly commercial for Hollywood," says filmmaker Quentin Lee, who helmed and self-distributed the Asian American-focused independent films *Shopping with Fangs* (1998, co-directed with Justin Lin) and *Ethan Mao* (2005). "The Asian American market is still at its nascence. Hollywood is interested in making films that make a lot of money, not a little money. So it's really just a matter of economics."

Latino films are also more difficult to predict for commercial purposes. The Latino population is not homogeneous, and films made about a specific community will probably find little support in other communities. Not surprisingly, some of the most visible independently produced films with Latino themes (including *Maria Full of Grace*, *Real Women Have Curves*, *El Manito*, and *Luminarias*) were marketed as art films and not targeted to the overall Latino population or to individual Latino ethnic groups.

From a personal example, I recall doing the promotion I helped to coordinate on the 1996 import *Nueba Yol*, which was made in the Dominican Republic. The film opened in New York to huge commercial success, as the local Dominican community turned out in full force to enjoy the film. The film was not sold as an art movie, but rather was booked in neighborhood theaters where there was a significant Dominican population. But when the film was taken to other Latino centers around the U.S., it bombed — the predominantly Mexican population in Los Angeles and the predominantly Cuban population in Florida had no affinity with *Nueba Yol* and its distinct Dominican flavoring. Even though the film was in Spanish, these communities wanted nothing to do with it and it found no audience beyond the Dominican communities in the United States.

photo courtesy Margin Films

Jun Hee Lee as the troubled youth whose traditional Chinese American family reacts with hostility to the news of his homosexuality in Quentin Lee's Ethan Mao. "The Asian American market is still at its nascence," says Quentin Lee. "Hollywood is interested in making films that make a lot of money, not a little money. So it's really just a matter of economics."

Even more elusive are films by and about Native Americans. While filmmakers Chris Eyre (*Smoke Signals*, *Skins*) and writer-turned-filmmaker Sherman Alexie (*The Business of Fancydancing*) have been able to bring their motion pictures to commercial release, other American Indian filmmakers are still ghettoized within specialty film festivals focusing on Native-related films. The output of this community of filmmakers is vast, including features and shorts and documentaries, but unless one has access to these specialized festivals these films remain an unexplored territory to most filmgoers. (Ironically, a report in the April 25, 2005, edition of the *New York Times* noted that 12 tribes financed a $1 million independent feature called *Black Cloud*, about a Navajo boxer— but the film was made by a non-Indian: blond actor Rick Schroder, the former star of *NYPD Blue*.)

One of the more surprising communities to emerge within the independent film world is filmmakers who belong to the Church of Jesus Christ of Latter-Day Saints, also known as Mormons. Most of these films have some religious element to them, albeit of an LDS orientation, and not surprisingly these films are barely known beyond Mormon audiences (such as *The Book of Mormon, Volume 1: The Journey* and the missionary drama *The Best Two Years*). But then there is also Mormon filmmaker Jared Hess, who helmed the 2004 hit comedy *Napoleon Dynamite*. The Hess film, made for only $400,000, had nothing to do with Mormonism and everything to do with commercial success. It will be interesting to see whether other Mormon filmmakers keep Joseph Smith's theology off the screen in order to pursue filmmaking success.

THE VIEW FROM TODAY:
WHO IS DISTRIBUTING MOVIES?

So where do we stand today in regard to film distribution? At the moment, there are seven distribution options for filmmakers today. They are, in descending order based on their financial power and clout:

1. THE HOLLYWOOD STUDIOS. If you're an independent filmmaker, forget it. This is an enclosed orbit where projects are greenlighted from within. Indie filmmakers who build cred and hits from the outside are occasionally welcomed inside. But if you are a first-time filmmaker without a track record and you're not related to a Hollywood mogul or power broker, you will not get your phone calls returned.

2. THE "CLASSICS" DIVISIONS. Every now and then, the studios decide to spin off so-called "classics" divisions to acquire smaller flicks. More often than not, these divisions have taken to financing small-scale films as well. As of this writing, the distributors in this category include Paramount Classics (a division of Paramount), Fox Searchlight (a division of 20th Century-Fox), Sony Pictures Classics (a division of Columbia), Warner Independent Pictures (a division of Warner Bros.) and Focus Features (a division of Universal). Miramax was intended to be a "classics" division of Disney until it grew into being something much bigger and (truth be told) more independent than Disney expected.

3. THE MAJOR INDEPENDENTS. These are the well-financed companies working beyond the studios, but they are still powerful enough to matter when it comes to drumming up attention, awards and box office. Lionsgate Entertainment, Artisan Entertainment, THINKfilm, IFC Films, and (until its acquisition in 2005) Newmarket Films are the players in this sphere.

4. THE BOUTIQUES. These are the smaller, edgier distributors who only put out a handful of titles annually. Their focus is entirely on the art house circuit; if you find their flicks in a multiplex, it is either a mistake or an anomaly. A few of these boutiques have been ambitious in trying to grow beyond their means into wide-scale release, most notably the subscription-driven American Film Theatre in the mid-1970s and the Shooting Gallery Film Series in the late 1990s, but financial problems derailed their plans and forced their premature demise. Among the boutiques still thriving are Zeitgeist Films, Wellspring, Kino International, Strand Releasing, Palm Pictures, First Run Features, Avatar Films, Milestone Film & Video, New Yorker Films, Empire Pictures, TLA Releasing, and Pathfinder Pictures.

5. THE NONTHEATRICAL DISTRIBUTORS. These companies avoid the commercial theatrical channels completely and go straight to the so-called nontheatrical venues, including

schools, colleges, libraries, film societies, museums, and nonprofit groups. They offer both film rentals and video rentals and sales. Among the companies here are First Run/Icarus Films, California Newsreel, Bullfrog Films, and Films for the Humanities and Sciences. (Some theatrical distributors also operate their own nontheatrical subsidiaries, most notably New Yorker Films, and on occasion a nontheatrical distributor will get a film into limited theatrical release.) We'll see more of them later in this book.

6. THE DTV ORBIT. DTV means "direct-to-video" and their mission is rather self-evident: avoiding theatrical release completely and going straight into the home video market. The more notable companies here include Troma Entertainment (which began as a theatrical distributor but is strictly DTV today), MTI Home Entertainment, SRS Cinema, New Concorde, and Kultur. We'll also pursue this subject in greater depth later.

7. THE DIY ORBIT. DIY means "do-it-yourself " and this covers self-distribution. Some filmmakers, such as Henry Jaglom, Arthur Dong, and Quentin Lee, have repeatedly and successfully put out several of their own titles via self-distribution. Mostly, however, filmmakers do this for a single title. We'll also pursue this subject in greater depth later.

Now that we know where independent film came from and where it is today, we can move forward into penetrating the marketplace and getting your film into release.

INTERVIEW
GREGORY HATANAKA, DISTRIBUTOR/FILMMAKER

Gregory Hatanaka has overseen the distribution of close to 250 films in the U.S. marketplace, including works by the likes of Satyajit Ray, Andre Techine, John Woo, and even Edward D. Wood Jr. Today, Hatanaka is focusing his attentions on a new director: himself!

In 2004, Hatanaka presented a film that he wrote and directed. It is called *Until the Night*, an emotionally complex drama about parallel relationships that are fraying to disaster. In one couple, a struggling writer obsesses with various vices to escape the burden of his self-destructive relationship with a jealous and troubled woman. In the second union, a successful young career woman lives the perfect public image as her marriage to a failed actor grows increasingly oppressive.

Until the Night culminates Hatanaka's remarkable career. At the age of 17, while struggling to get his directing career off the ground with an aborted romantic drama entitled *Women*, he got his first job working for Headliner Productions, a company that had produced exploitation films in the 1950s. Hatanaka oversaw the distribution of such films as Ed Wood's rediscovered cult classic *The Sinister Urge* and *God Is My Witness*, the first Bollywood epic to be screened in American art houses. During this period, Hatanaka also theatrically booked films for Circle Releasing — under the guidance of George Pelecanos (now an acclaimed crime noir novelist) — a production and distribution company known most for producing the Coen brothers' *Blood Simple*, *Miller's Crossing*, and *Barton Fink*. Among the films Hatanaka worked on was John Woo's *The Killer*, which he rereleased in a series of successful midnight runs on the art-house circuit. During a brief stint at Filmopolis Pictures, he oversaw the release of Andre Techine's *My Favorite Season* and the final films of Satyajit Ray.

In 1996, Hatanaka formed distribution company Phaedra Cinema, which specialized in bringing the works of indie directors to the screen. Over a five-year period, the company distributed close to 100 films in the U.S. marketplace, ranging from acclaimed French titles such as *La Separation* and *L'Ennui* to U.S. indies including *Sudden Manhattan*, *Ratchet*, *The Next Step*, and *Men Cry Bullets*. Hatanaka is the founder and president of Cinema Epoch. Recent highlights include a series of classic films from Claude Chabrol, the theatrically restored cult hit *Master of the Flying Guillotine*, plus indie flicks like Abel Ferrara's *R'Xmas* and *Schlock! The Secret History of American Movies*.

Ironically, working as a distributor did not mean his film *Until the Night* would be assured of theatrical release. But let's have Hatanaka tell his story.

photo courtesy Margin Films

Norman Reedus and Kathleen Robertson share a heated moment in Gregory Hatanaka's Until the Night. *"Being an educated filmmaker is top priority," says Hatanaka. "Study the marketplace, study which companies are releasing what types of films, how did those films fare at the box office and on DVD, solicit companies who you feel might be best suited to handle your film."*

Q: *Do you recommend that film-makers approach distributors with unsolicited inquiries? Or is there more clout if they come recommended by a third party, such as a producer's rep, agent, publicist, etc.?*

GREGORY HATANAKA: With the distribution marketplace being extremely competitive, acquisitions execs are taking a harder look in every corner and keep an eye on what is out there. Acquisitions execs are more accessible and it isn't as difficult getting them to take a look at your film as it used to be.

That being said, with the dozens and dozens of films that an exec may view during a month, having an established producer's rep can definitely help in expediting the evaluation process and getting your film to the top of the pile. Producer's reps can help immensely in creating a higher visibility for your film, as well as negotiating the best deal for you.

Even though I was myself a film distributor, I still felt it necessary to hire a producer's rep for my film to help in getting the word out there. My rep was Alex Nohe, who was an exec at IFP/West, and through his various IFP Screening Events, he had relationships with the acquisitions execs at the various distributors.

I am convinced that whatever deal an indie filmmaker can get on his own, a producer's rep can still improve upon it.

Q: *In trying to sell a film to a potential distributor, what are the key considerations that filmmakers need to focus on?*

GREGORY HATANAKA: Being an educated filmmaker is top priority. Study the marketplace, study which companies are releasing what types of films, how did those films fare at the box office and on DVD, solicit companies who you feel might be best suited to handle your film. Also, try to create a buzz about your film before approaching a distributor. Get your film screened in some festivals and obtain reviews that can be included as part of your press kit. Launch a website for your film that distributors can visit for more information and that will hopefully generate further excitement and anticipation.

Q: Conversely, what are the key mistakes that filmmakers need to avoid when trying to get in touch with distributors?

GREGORY HATANAKA: Definitely do not over-saturate yourself with distributors. Do not call every week, do not send email after email announcing every single update on your film. I recall one filmmaker who won something like 40 festival awards and every time he won, he would send a mass email to everyone, 40-plus emails in all. In the end, I feel it was very counterproductive for his film and still to this day, he doesn't have distribution. If you have made a good film, the word will get around and distributors will be contacting you.

Q: How important is it for an independent film to be on the festival circuit prior to the filmmaker's contact with distributors?

GREGORY HATANAKA: I think that unless you are making a genre-type film — i.e. horror, action — it is absolutely crucial to have your film screened in some festivals before you try to lock down distribution. Playing festivals helps to create buzz and up the awareness level for your film. Also, you want to get as many distributors as possible to see your film in a festival environment as opposed to sending out screener cassettes or DVDs to them.

Q: What do you consider the most important festivals and film markets for independent filmmakers to seek out for their films? If you have any input on the Cannes market, please share it here.

GREGORY HATANAKA: The top festivals are Cannes, Toronto, Sundance, Berlin, and Venice, which everyone dreams of screening in. But don't give up if you don't get into any of those because there are numerous other festivals that can help give exposure and build a buzz for your film. And these festivals are fast-growing, and sport some highly original programming. Some of these include Slamdance, South by Southwest (SXSW), Tribeca, Hamptons, Seattle, San Francisco IndieFest, Hawaii, and Fort Lauderdale.

And, if your film is appropriate, there are also some fantastically run and programmed niche festivals such as Outfest (L.A.), VC Filmfest (L.A.), Urbanworld, and NAATA (San Francisco). Then there are the film markets, most notably the American Film Market and the Cannes Film Market, which aren't really environments for filmmakers but rather for the various foreign sales companies representing the filmmakers. A lot of business occurs at these markets and the sale of your film at these markets is crucial to recoup your budget.

Q: Should filmmakers opt for direct-to-video deals? Or should they try to hold out for theatrical pickup?

GREGORY HATANAKA: Everyone who makes films — including me, and I am familiar with the realities of getting distribution — hopes to have their work seen on the big screen. But ultimately theatrical pickups are few and far between and unless you've made a big splash in a festival or have strong name actors, it will be very hard to find a distributor to release your film theatrically. If you find you are not being offered a theatrical deal, then you must make a decision of what fork in the road to take: either to distribute the film yourself theatrically or to take a straight-to-video deal. Now, there are some good examples of self-distributed hits, such as Gene Cajayon's *The Debut* and Greg Pak's *Robot Stories*, and if you stretch it, Mel Gibson's *The Passion of the Christ*, the distribution of which was self-financed by him. But realize that self-distribution will take up a year and half of your life, when you could be writing or making that next film, and it is a territory that can be exciting but at the same time very demoralizing and depressing.

And realize that this is at a time when, during the past year, films with Gary Oldman, Jackie Chan, Gene Hackman, Christina Ricci, Sylvester Stallone, amongst many other noted actors, have gone straight to video. Take as an example Lionsgate Films: They acquire maybe 100 or so films a year, and of these maybe 25% get a theatrical release and the rest are DVD premieres.

But if you truly feel that you have a film with a strong theatrical audience and are willing to put the immense amount of time and money into promoting it theatrically, then by all means you should do everything you can to realize that vision.

Q: What organizations and resources would you recommend to aspiring filmmakers so they can get better connected within the film world and gain a better understanding of how the industry works?

GREGORY HATANAKA: Well, the IFP is a terrific place to start to make contacts, network, and get a feel for things. And if you live in Los Angeles, the Filmmakers Alliance is another terrific place to meet fellow indie filmmakers.

Q: Let's shift gears and talk about your first foray into filmmaking, the feature Until the Night. *When* Until the Night *was completed, what was your release strategy? And over time, did you stick closely to it or did you deviate from it as things progressed?*

GREGORY HATANAKA: Well, anyone who makes a film hopes that a studio or ministudio might pick up the film. We knew going in that the subject matter would make this a tough sell so never really expected that would happen unless the film got accepted into a major film festival such as Sundance or Cannes. The film premiered at the CineVegas Festival, which is run by Trevor Groth, who programs Sundance, and it went on to show in other festivals including the Hamptons, Denver, and San Francisco IndieFest. Once the festival rounds were complete, we had to now make a choice as to its distribution future.

Until the Night was produced by Pathfinder Pictures, a domestic distribution company, and Pathfinder was certainly capable of releasing the film theatrically, but being that the film was never transferred to 35mm (a $50,000 additional expense) and that the theatrical release would have cost much more, it was decided that the film should be set up as a DVD premiere. It was a difficult choice to make because the ultimate gratification would have been to see the film play in some sort of limited theatrical run across the country, but the marketplace for indie films has changed considerably over the past ten years and there are serious financial considerations that need to be made. I think that filmmakers need to rethink their goals on distribution and understand that there are no longer traditional ways to distribute films.

But having the film as a DVD premiere enabled it to get into the Hollywood Video chain on a national level, as well as other major retailers such as Borders Books, Barnes & Noble, and Tower Records, and so in the end, I feel the film has received a terrific amount of exposure.

Q: Some people may not be familiar with CineVegas. What is special about that festival?

GREGORY HATANAKA: The CineVegas Festival is the fastest-growing festival in the country. It was cofounded by Dennis Hopper and programmed by Trevor Groth, who also programs the Sundance Film Festival. I felt that CineVegas was a good showcase for the film because it was invited as one of nine films in competition and not simply as a featured selection, so I felt that it would receive a certain amount of good exposure, which it did.

After CineVegas, the film was shown in the Starz Denver, San Diego, Hamptons Film Festival, and the San Francisco IndieFest — all terrific venues for screening independent films.

Q: Was Until the Night *turned down from any festivals? If so, was any reason given why?*

GREGORY HATANAKA: The film was turned down by Sundance, although as mentioned before Trevor Groth programmed the film subsequently in his CineVegas Film Festival. It was also turned down by Cannes and Berlin. But these are the crème de la crème of festivals, and considering that each receives a minimum of 3,000 film submissions per year, it's really a case of having talent and luck.

Q: Did Until the Night *get any commercial theatrical play dates?*

GREGORY HATANAKA: It screened at the Egyptian Theater/American Cinematheque in Los Angeles as part of the Alternative Screen series programmed by Margot Gerber, who is also one of the founders of the Slamdance Film Festival. Not having transferred the film to 35mm pretty much ruled out any sort of conventional theatrical release for the film.

Q: Until the Night *did not get a commercial play date in New York, even though it came with the well-respected Pathfinder Pictures as its distributor. What was the reason given by the New York exhibitors for not showing the film?*

GREGORY HATANAKA: *Until the Night* was shot on digital and had never been transferred to a 35mm print, a high-cost item for an indie film, so it was difficult to get any theaters to screen the film. Since then, strong advocators of the digital format such as Steven Soderbergh and Mark Cuban (owner of the Dallas Mavericks and Landmark Theatres) have made a goal to get as many theaters equipped to screen digital as they can. In fact, Soderbergh plans on making films specifically to be shown in digital theaters (his first, *Bubble*, was released in early 2006). This is very promising news as this will eliminate almost the final barrier in getting digital filmmaking to be shown to a wider audience.

The cost of running a theater in New York is so exorbitant that it is very hard for exhibitors to take chances on the smaller indies and that is perhaps why the exhibitors may have chosen not to show *Until the Night*, which is admittedly a challenging film.

Q: You recently completed your second film, yes?

GREGORY HATANAKA: My new film is *Mad Cowgirl* and it is a drama about a dying woman with a brain disorder (perhaps mad cow disease) who goes on a surreal journey that quickly descends into insanity and violence. It stars Sarah Lassez, who I worked with previously in *Until the Night*, James Duval, Devon Odessa, and Walter Koenig (from *Star Trek*). It's similar to but yet quite a different film from *Until the Night*. I am also taking a different approach to the planned distribution of the film: I have raised enough money to include the transfer of the film to a 35mm print, so I will have more choices when considering screenings in festivals. This will also allow me to distribute the film myself into a limited number of theaters once the festival circuit has been complete.

LISTEN TO WHAT THE MAN SAYS

Okay, so how can you put the information in this chapter to practical usage? Here is some practical advice for you to take and run with.

1. Do not buy any of the happy-hype surrounding the independent film business. This is a tough, highly competitive field. It also not a world where people are tossing bushels of dollars skyward while singing "We're in the Money!" I've had two very prominent distributors confide to me that they are uncertain how or if anyone is getting rich via indie movies — and these were distributors who released films that gained national attention and Oscar nominations! Even distributors who seem to be riding the crest of success can abruptly disappear and leave their creditors splashing in red ink (have you ever heard of Shooting Gallery?). When approaching indie distribution, it doesn't hurt to be a little bit cynical.

2. Stay informed on what is happening with the film industry. Avoid the gossipy media, which is just a bunch of gush and mush. Instead, subscribe to the trade journals that offer honest and insightful coverage of the motion picture business. *Variety* and *Hollywood Reporter* are the main dailies and their coverage has long been valued for its insight and honesty. *Film Journal International* and *Boxoffice* magazine place a greater emphasis on the distribution and exhibition side of the business, and both magazines are extremely well researched. The Internet has no shortage of information resources with news and cogent opinions: *IndieWire*, *Film Threat*, *FilmJerk.com*, *Box Office Guru*, and *Movie City News* should be bookmarked and checked on a daily basis.

3. See the indie films in theatrical release. For some people, this may require driving significant distances since these films are primarily booked on single screens in metropolitan art house venues. If that is the case, make the most of it and try to catch two or three indie films in a day. But it is important to get to these venues and see for yourself what is considered good enough for the big screen. Also, don't be shy about asking the theater manager about the audiences for these films: the demographics, the promotion surrounding them, the distributors' level of support, the box office, etc.

4. Budget yourself wisely. Learn from poor John Cassavetes' lesson after the failure of *The Killing of a Chinese Bookie* — you can go broke in this business, even if you are a prominent individual working with a significant source of funds. And as you read through this book, you will see that your wallet is going to be open on many, many occasions.

5. But if you find yourself reaching the financial saturation point, hit the brakes hard! Forget those stories about filmmakers maxing out their credit cards in pursuit of

Hollywood contracts. For every Robert Townsend who milked his credit cards and was rewarded with success, there are hundreds (if not thousands) of unknown auteurs who did the same thing and wound up with blighted credit reports or a date in bankruptcy court.

6. Again, don't buy the happy-hype! Be responsible in how you conduct your business. Remember, there is no such thing as a sure bet. Dustin Putman said it best earlier in this chapter when, citing films like *Sideways*, *My Big Fat Greek Wedding*, and *Lost in Translation*, he noted: "All of the mentioned films, while owned by the studios, were never guaranteed financial success or big-release patterns." Whatever their merits as artistic achievements, would we ever consider talking about them had they not been financially viable? For every *Sideways* that packs theaters and scoops up awards, there is an endless number of indies that come and go with nary a penny of profit or praise to show for their efforts. This business is not for the weak or faint of heart!

BEFORE YOU EVEN THINK OF
CONTACTING A DISTRIBUTOR...

If you don't know where you're going, you'll wind up somewhere else.
— Yogi Berra

2

San Francisco–based filmmaker Erica Jordan is responsible for helming two of the most remarkable independent features I've seen: *Walls of Sand* (1994), a touching drama about a young Iranian woman trying to obtain a green card, and *In the Wake* (2001), a powerful emotional odyssey about an aspiring sculptor's attempt to find new meaning to her life. While it is difficult not to appreciate the filmmaker's talent, even Jordan herself laments her inability to get the films picked up for release.

photo courtesy Erica Jordan Productions

"I don't feel I've done justice to either *Walls of Sand* or *In the Wake* in my attempts to obtain distribution through a company or through self-distribution," she says. "One of my downfalls, as I know many filmmakers and artists can relate to, is I purely enjoy the creative aspects and dread the business aspects of making a film. Though I've been making films for a long time, I continue to feel out of touch with the business of distribution. Often before pursuing all the distribution options I have for a completed film, I begin

A trio of Iranian women face the world in a scene from Erica Jordan's feature film Walls of Sand. *"One of my downfalls, as I know many filmmakers and artists can relate to, is I purely enjoy the creative aspects and dread the business aspects of making a film," says Jordan.*

making a new one. There is always the thought that maybe my next film will receive greater recognition and then my past work will become more widely recognized. I'm now making a documentary and when asked about my previous films, I think: 'Oh yes I really should continue working on distribution for those past, all-encompassing labors of love.'"

Erica Jordan is hardly an exception to the rule. In fact, she is typical of many creative artists seeking to get their work seen and appreciated. Yet the ultimate goal of filmmaking is to put one's work out into the world. Admittedly, it is a hostile world to go into — especially the distribution side of it.

Let's take this hypothetical situation and run with it: Now is the time to take your independent feature film and send it out into the world. How do you proceed?

Actually, let's backtrack for a moment. Are you genuinely ready to deal with distributors? There are many considerations that need to be addressed before you begin to shop your film around. Some of these considerations are based in the physical, others are rooted in the intellectual and emotional. All told, they need to be in place before you can seriously shop your film.

Before you start knocking on doors, run the following checklist to determine if, indeed, all systems are functioning properly. If there is something amiss, you will need to stop and make some adjustments.

1. Ask yourself: Is this film really good enough for release?

Veteran film distributor Peter M. Hargrove categorizes films in a blunt but honest manner. "I put films into four categories: award-winning, good, sellable, and burn the negative," he says. "Most, alas, fall in the last category."

Hargrove's notion of filmmaking might seem harsh to some people, but having screened literally thousands of unreleased films in pursuit of distribution deals, he can afford to be less than sympathetic.

In recent years, Hargrove and his fellow distributors have seen a glut of new films. Many of these were shot on digital video.

While the ease of being able to make films on low-cost digital video equipment has increased the quantity of independent movies being made today, it has had an opposite effect on the quality of such films. To be frank, there is a lopsided ratio of quantity to quality.

"The fact that any schlub can walk into a Wal-Mart and buy a digital video camera for a couple of hundred bucks means that anybody can make their own *Blair Witch* later that day, in their backyard with their drunk friends," observes Jon Popick, editor of the popular *Planet Sick-Boy* online magazine. "Ten years ago, the only people who would try something like this were pretty serious about what they were doing. It's possible a few revolutionary filmmakers might get their big breaks this way, but it's mostly going to produce a whole lot of garbage. I picture film festival programmers putting guns in their mouths after a few weeks of watching these movies."

Stop for a moment and use Popick's remarks as the basis of judging your own production. If presented to a motion picture industry professional, would your film inspire peals of rapture and amazement? Or would your film inspire guns being placed in the mouths of those poor film people who became brain-fried from watching too many very bad flicks?

No one wants to acknowledge they made a bad film. But before you contact anyone about distributing your movie, be very honest with yourself. Can you see your film playing at the local multiplex, or the major art house in your area? Are you genuinely able to imagine it screening on the Sundance Channel or the Independent Film Channel? Does it fulfill the basic tenets of what professional filmmaking is all about?

If you can sincerely answer "Yes!" with no qualms or hint of unease, then proceed.

2. Which distributor are your considering?

Diana Ross fans will recall the theme song from her campy 1975 movie *Mahogany*: "Do You Know Where You're Going To?" Indeed, it is a song that too many filmmakers need to hear when it comes to contacting distributors.

Dennis Doros, president of Milestone Film & Video, is more than cognizant of the lack of homework on the part of many new filmmakers trying to get a distributor. Doros' company has been honored by the New York Film Critics Circle and twice by the National Society of Film Critics for its restoration and release of forgotten classic films, yet such honors are unknown to many of the filmmakers who come knocking at his door.

"First and foremost, get to know the company you are approaching," says Doros. "And approach those that are a good fit. It is annoying to have someone come to us insisting that we are the perfect distributor for their teenage serial-killer comedy horror film shot on a camcorder when we have done nothing remotely like that in the past."

If you need immediate assistance in learning who's who and who does what in the distribution sphere, skip over to Chapter Eight in this book and you will get a crash course in the subject. Otherwise, keep reading and Chapter Eight will pop up soon enough.

3. Are all of the elements in place?

What are we talking about by the "elements"? Well, this can include the following considerations:

The title. Yes, the title. Believe it or else, a crummy title can short-circuit a film even before a potential distributor views it.

"A movie with a bad title turns me off immediately," says Ron Bonk, president of SRS Cinema LLC. "It might seem funny to the filmmaker but usually doesn't go over well in the market-place. I hate to dumb down the marketplace, but sometimes a single-word title sells better."

The screener. This is the video or DVD that is sent to the distributor to evaluate the film. The screener should include the finished film (and by "finished" I mean the film is 100% completed — no works in progress, work prints, or non-color-corrected offerings, please!). A lousy screener will sour the distributor and scream "Amateur Hour" in loud, shrill tones.

"There was one screener I received last year, a very funny sci-fi comedy with great costumes, good acting, and really decent effects for its very low budget," recalls Edward Havens, former director of acquisitions for Troma Entertainment. "But the entire film was just a bit out of focus and inexplicably hard-matted to a 2.40:1 ratio when it was clear the shots were not composed when shot to be presented widescreen." Needless to say, Havens passed on the work based solely on the sloppy screener.

"Send a full screener," adds Ron Bonk. "I can never make a decision from a trailer and often get so busy that I prefer to sit down, watch the whole movie, and make a decision."

Artwork from the film. Do you have publicity stills from your film? If not, you're not alone — too many independent filmmakers fail to take still photographs of their actors while the film is in production. In fact, when I was compiling my previous book, *The Encyclopedia of Underground Movies*, the biggest problem to arise during the production stage was locating publication-worthy photographs from the contemporary underground movies being featured. Most of the pictures provided were low-res screen captures, which could not be used for publication.

"Take great pictures — it is key here!" continues Ron Bonk. "Make some slick artwork using what you see on the shelves in Blockbuster as a starting point and include it with the screener. I like seeing a title that comes in with good artwork potential or a good basic idea that we can expand on and make a good impression on our buyers with. Bad artwork on the submission can be a turnoff — and I tend to pop the more interesting-looking titles in first to screen for distribution."

What happens if you don't have photographs from your film? There are two choices: Either gather the actors again and take new photographs, or take screen captures from the film. To be frank, screen captures are rarely satisfactory: They were moving images designed to be viewed in motion, and inevitably there will be problems with the visual clarity of the images when they are frozen out of their natural motion. Of course, it may not be possible to gather the cast together again to snap new photographs, so screen captures may be your only choice. But keep in this mind when you are shooting your next movie!

If you are in the process of making a film, by all means get a photographer to come to the set and take publicity stills.

"As photographers, we have the ability to stop and capture a moment in a hundredth of a second," says Andre Michel Landeros, New York photographer (*www.arealanderos.com*). "This is what we are best at. Count on us to nail down that one shot, that one image that will speak for the larger body of work. Stealth is our approach; we are able to work without costly disruptions, thus allowing each scene to take shape and remain fluid."

Landeros adds that having a photographer taking still photos, rather than the filmmaker, ensures peace of mind in the photographic process. "A photographer frees the filmmaker to focus all energies on filming rather than recreating each scene expressly to capture stills."

But where can a filmmaker find a professional photographer, especially for a low-budget (or no-budget) movie? "I would try all kinds of inexpensive ways of finding a publicity still photographer," advises Lawrence Grecco, New York photographer (*www.grecco.com*). "You can go to the career center or internship departments of art/design schools with a photography department, or you can place inexpensive ads on sites like Craig's List (*http://craigslist.org*), or do simple Web searches for people who do film stills who may be willing to work for less, so long as they are given proper credit in the film."

The music rights. Do you have full clearance to use the music for your film? If your film was scored by outside musical artists, you may need to double-check to determine that your music clearance rights are in order. Without this, you will not be able to release your film.

I can speak from personal frustrations on two separate occasions when I was hired to promote music documentaries that faced acute distribution disruptions because of music clearance concerns. In 2004, the documentary *MC5: A True Testimonial* was going into theatrical release when Wayne Kramer, a member of the legendary band at the center of the film, declared that the filmmakers did not clear the music licensing rights for the songs in the film (Kramer's former bandmates disagreed). Many theaters were agitated over the potential for legal problems, as Kramer made highly publicized declarations against the film and its producers, and the film was yanked from several screens before it was set to be shown.

But at least *MC5: A True Testimonial* received some theatrical play dates. Less successful was Penelope Spheeris with her 2001 documentary on the Ozzfest tour, *We Sold Our Souls for Rock 'n' Roll*. The film was pulled out of release literally days before its premiere when it was discovered that Sharon Osbourne failed to clear the rights for the Black Sabbath songs used in the film. The film never had a theatrical release (the Osbournes subsequently went on to MTV reality programming fame) and at this date is still unavailable for commercial screening.

Steve Kaplan, president of Alpha Video, has also been down this bumpy road. "The biggest problem we've encountered repeatedly is in the use of previously existing music or sound elements, or so-called 'stock footage' that is perceived (through wishful thinking or lack of information) to be in the public domain," he says. "It turns out that it just cannot be cleared for use… or can be cleared for a large amount of money. Several times we have asked the filmmakers to rescore offending scenes (an old record by the Ventures or Tony Bennett playing subliminally in the background is enough to cause a major hassle). One indie director included songs by a well-known group. The soundtrack had re-recordings and re-interpretations of songs originally included on their major label LP. The songs were owned by the label. Clearance on the songs led us on a wild goose chase and I finally had to pass on the film because I couldn't deal with the hassle."

Other rights issues. The improper usage of copyright-protected material beyond music is also an issue that filmmakers overlook. Steve Kaplan, however, did not overlook this.

"We had a filmmaker who included a scene in which actors watched an actual CBS news report on TV, not realizing that the news show was the property of CBS," he recalls. "We had to redo the scene just as we went into DVD authoring."

The waivers. If you made a documentary, you need to have a signed waiver from the subject of your film. A waiver is basically a contract stating that the person in the film agreed to be in the movie and is aware of how the footage of them will be used. I am aware of at least one well-known documentary filmmaker who had to withdraw his film from release because of questions regarding the lack of a waiver from the subject of the production.

Even the Hollywood set finds itself stuck with footage that cannot be shown when waivers are not signed. The popular MTV reality show *Punk'd* set up separate videotaped pranks involving baseball star Alex Rodriguez and actors James Vartan and David Spade, but none of the men being "punk'd" agreed to sign waivers allowing the footage to be aired. Without the waivers, the footage cannot be seen publicly — and, to date, it has never aired (creating quite a waste of time, energy, and money).

The available talent. If your film has a recognized name in the cast (even if it is a second-tier star), be certain that the talent would be available to help promote the film. Do not ignore the possibility that this star might be either unavailable or even uninterested in assisting your promotional efforts.

One person who learned this the hard way was David Nagler, a former film publicist who was hired in 1999 to promote an indie film called *Men Cry Bullets*, which found its way into a New York theatrical engagement.

"One of the leads of the movie *Men Cry Bullets* was Jeri Ryan, then of TV's *Star Trek: Voyager*," recalls Nagler, who is currently editorial coordinator for digital media at Comedy Central. "When I was trying to arrange publicity for the film, her publicist was not particularly responsive, despite the filmmaker's assurance that Jeri Ryan would be available for any and all interviews. Basically, Jeri Ryan had no reason to publicize the film, so she — or her publicist, perhaps more so — didn't want to anything to interfere with her Borg duties."

When Ryan was not being as cooperative as initially promised, the filmmaker offered Nagler the chance to promote Ryan's costar in the film, a little-known actress named Honey Lauren. Alas, Ms. Lauren was viewed as an inadequate substitute by the media outlets who wanted to speak with her better-known costar.

"Honey Lauren, on the other hand, was more than happy to talk at length about *Men Cry Bullets*," says Nagler. "Or anything else, for that matter."

Realizing that Ryan's star power (even as a TV star) was the main selling point for media attention, Nagler persisted in trying to get her publicist to make her available. "If I remember correctly, after numerous requests, Jeri Ryan ended up being available for exactly one interview in conjunction with *Men Cry Bullets,*" says Nagler. "It was for *TV Guide Online*, appropriately enough."

Having a recognizable name talent in a film can certainly help raise awareness of a film. Producer/actor Tommy Lee Thomas realized that when he was able to secure Eric Roberts to star as the miscreant correctional officer in his 2002 prison-based thriller *Con Games*. While Roberts' star power may not have been where it was some years earlier, he still possessed enough stellar wattage to call attention to the project, which in turn helped to secure the film's release in the United States and overseas.

"I think it is very important to have a name talent in the movie," says Thomas, who costarred opposite Roberts in *Con Games*. "But it is not the most important element, as I have learned through the school of hard knocks. First and foremost you need a strong sales team and of course most importantly you need a great movie, otherwise even if you have the biggest star in the world your movie may still fail financially."

4. The Passover principle

In the Jewish faith, the holiday of Passover is celebrated by a family gathering at a special meal called a seder. At the start of the meal, the oldest male in the family asks a traditional question that is meant to signify the importance of the celebration: "Why is this night different from all other nights?"

The answer, of course, is the celebration of Passover and the flight of the Israelites from Pharaonic Egypt. But take that Passover question and apply it to your movie. Why is your film different from all other films? What makes it unique from all of the other flicks on the market?

In selling a film, the filmmaker needs to clearly and succinctly differentiate his product from the competition. The industry, admittedly, is not the best place for mavericks and creative thinkers to plant a flag.

"Success doesn't beget success," comments film historian Charles Pappas. "It cuts and pastes it, ad infinitum. If an independent makes money, all the other independent filmmakers rush to make the same picture. If that picture is all very Lars von Trier, then expect *Dogville* to be imprinted on your corneas and cortexes for the next few years."

In fairness, however, it is not just independent American filmmakers who fall into this trap. David Nagler notes that certain imported films also tend to fit into a template. "For instance, there are a couple of standard British comedies that inevitably hit the art houses here in the States," he says. "Either outlandish things begin happening to a nebbish young Englishman who eventually comes into his own, gets the girl, and reconnects with his family, or else some sad old folks defy their age by doing something truly outlandish, getting in touch with their sexual or rebellious side."

In selling your film, maintain the Passover principle and stress the difference and originality of the concept and execution. In doing so, you will stand out from the growing crowd.

"The key to jumping into mainstream consciousness is not in the budget or the talent — it is in the telling of the story," says independent filmmaker Ryan Dacko, director of the award-winning feature *And I Lived* and author of the book *I Guess the World Could Always Use Another Ed Wood*. Dacko notes, "In the film business, original stories are elusive commodities. And while it is human nature to attempt to emulate a successful formula done elsewhere, one needs to realize that there are probably hundreds (if not thousands) of other aspiring filmmakers seeking to do the exact same thing."

5. The press kit

"It is helpful to think of a successful press/media kit as nothing more than a well-organized and comprehensive sales brochure for the filmmaker," says Nate Towne, president of the public relations/marketing consulting group Xanadu Communications. "After all, the publicity game is all about selling a commodity — oneself — to the press. Therefore, it pays to have a wealth of materials to draw on that summarize the professional

photo courtesy Ascension 3 Productions

Filmmaker Ryan Dacko scouting a location for his award-winning feature And I Lived. *"In the film business, original stories are elusive commodities," says Dacko. "And while it is human nature to attempt and emulate a successful formula done elsewhere, one needs to realize that there are probably hundreds (if not thousands) of other aspiring filmmakers seeking to do the exact same thing"*

accomplishments of the filmmaker. Remember, the press kit is intended to save journalists time — think of it as a one-stop shop for the press. By making background information readily available, filmmakers are saving journalists research time and presenting themselves as trustworthy professionals."

The killer press kit does not have to be elaborate, nor does it require fancy packaging and gimmicks. All it needs is basic, clear content providing the right amount of facts and background. Let's go page by page and see what it takes to make the perfect press kit.

Part one: the cover. This obviously starts with the title of the film, plus the name of the production company, the director, and (if applicable) name-value cast members. If the film has won awards or was an official selection at an A-list film festival, you can list those facts on the cover. If the film snagged a knockout quote from a major film critic or media outlet, you can also include that. The bottom of the page should list the contact information for the production company and (if applicable) the film's sales rep and press contact.

Part two: the credits. This is devoted to the cast and crew data. And yes, it is only a single page. If the film has recognizable actors, lead with the cast listing. You don't need to cite every performer in the film. The actors playing the major eight to ten characters are sufficient for citation. For the crew, include the director, producers (including executive and associate producers), screenwriter, cinematographer, editor, and the composer of the film's music score. If the film has a special technical hook, such as funky makeup or innovative special effects, then the names of the artists responsible for these achievements should also be present. This page should also include some other key data: running time, MPAA rating or lack thereof, aspect ratio, format the film is currently in (don't be shy to say it was made in 16mm or DV), the production company, and the film's website.

Part three: the plot summary. This is devoted to the synopsis of the film. Do not give a short, one-paragraph synopsis followed by a longer in-depth summary — what is the point of telling the same story twice? Just stick with a single synopsis that runs no longer than a page and includes enough information to whet the reader's appetite — but do not give away the entire story. If the synopsis runs over a page, edit it down to fit a page.

Part four: the backstory. This is an optional page, but many filmmakers like to include it. If the film has an unusual, dramatic, or amusing production history, then write a single page detailing it. You can call it "Production History" or "On the Making of ..." or whatever. But remember the aforementioned Passover principle — what makes this story truly different from all others? If yours is another case of a filmmaker maxing out credit cards or spending a year's worth of Sundays to put the film together, you're entering "been there, done that" land.

Part five: about the talent. This is for the biographies section, highlighting career achievements of cast and crew. Like part two, this section starts with the cast. Biographies should not be more than a single paragraph (unless there is a major star here with an illustrious career), and should not include cute notes that have nothing to do with the film (stuff along the lines of "the actors lives on a boat in Egg Harbor, New Jersey, with three cats"). Whether you choose to list all of the actors in part two or just the leading players is your call. Likewise, you may choose to include only the director, producer, screenwriter, and cinematographer for the crew biographies. On a separate sheet at the end of this section should be the biography of the production company behind the film. If this is the production company's first film, it should be stated (after all, everyone has to start somewhere).

Part six: media coverage. This is for press coverage and reviews. This section should not be packed with every single article or review. Only include reviews, features, and interviews from well-regarded media that praise the film. Believe it or not, I've seen press kits with mediocre reviews of the films! Coverage from obscure or amateur media is generally not a good idea, no matter how sincere their write-ups might be.

If you are photocopying newspaper or magazine articles, make sure the copies are clear, easy to read, and include the names and dates of the publications. If the photocopies are of poor quality, it is okay to use online versions of the same coverage.

Part seven: the digital edition. "Arrange to have electronic copies of the press kit available, as more often than not, reporters on deadline will ask filmmakers to email press kits (if available) to save on time," advises Nate Towne.

What to avoid. Do not include a director's statement — the film is the director's statement. Also avoid press clips from other projects involving the filmmaker or the cast — these are not relevant to the film being presented.

And most important: Run a spellcheck and then have several people proofread the press kit before handing it out. Spelling errors, missing words, and improper English in a press kit do not give the impression of professionalism.

There is your press kit. Either staple it neatly or arrange it nicely in a folder with the film's logo and artwork on its front, and you are ready to hand out press kits.

6. The Website

Contrary to popular misconception, the notion of using a website to promote a film did not begin with the 1999 monster hit *The*

Blair Witch Project, since other films had websites before that. But no film prior to *The Blair Witch Project* ever used the Internet as imaginatively. Dustin Putman, who was among the first critics to see *The Blair Witch Project* long before it became a phenomenon, does not believe other films have surpassed *Blair Witch* in terms of aggressive and imaginative Internet-based marketing.

"Honestly, no," he says. "*The Blair Witch Project* was a one-of-a-kind occurrence. Had it not been for the film's and the directors' official websites and the early Internet reviews, it would have come and gone in theaters in a flash. The key to the marketing — and it was a genius idea that hasn't been done nearly as successfully before or since— was that it captured the audience's imagination. So many people were convinced that it was a real documentary (even after they had seen it), and the summer the movie was released I was inundated with emails insisting it was nonfiction! The film's marketing offered something a little different to potential viewers, and created an excitement that was unprecedented for something that only cost like $150,000. There hasn't been another film since then that has done that under those circumstances."

The website is a crucial marketing tool for a movie. And not unlike the movie it is highlighting, it should not be static or stagnant. If anything, it needs to generate three key responses: (1) draw and keep the attention of those who visit it; (2) ensure that the people who visit it spread the word on the film to others; (3) ensure those who visit it come back again.

"It is always best when there are some valuable, intriguing digital assets — viral spot, plot line — that can connect with consumers and draw them in to learn more, pass to a friend, etc.," says Darren Paul, managing partner with The Night Agency LLC, a New York viral- and guerrilla-marketing agency. "*Blair Witch* was great because it sparked the ever so valuable marketing debate 'Is this real?' and 'What the f★★★ is this?'"

Paul notes that films with hot-topic issues make for natural website buzz generators. "Also, controversy is always good to get pass-along," he says. "The other valuable and impact-worthy components of an online buzz campaign are to incorporate sex, shock value, and humor."

While we are on the subject of websites, it would help if you registered the film on the Internet Movie Database (*www.imdb.com*). If you've never done that before, remember to be patient — it is not the most user-friendly online resource to navigate. Also, the IMDb has become more particular in recent years about the films it agrees to list. The glut of movies being produced clearly doesn't help matters much, so the IMDb is requiring that independently produced films without theatrical distribution in place at least have some confirmed festival play dates and/or reviews in place that can be accessed via the Internet. Without either element, the IMDb will not rush to put the new films into its database (and, truth be told, they rarely rush even when those elements are present!).

INTERVIEW
ERIC ROBICHAUD, CEO, 401 CONSULTING

Back in the 1990s, Eric Robichaud was among the pioneers creating interactive computer programs based on hit movies and cult television shows. His work included best-selling products such as screensavers for *Terminator 2*, *Star Trek Voyager*, and *Saturday Night Live* and interactive CD-ROMs for *Batman and Robin*, *Free Willy 2*, and *The Land Before Time*. Today, Robichaud is the CEO of 401 Consulting, the Woonsocket, Rhode Island–based marketing/communications/new media agency (*www.401consulting.com*). His clients range from the U.S. government and Fortune 500 companies to small businesses and local nonprofits. When it comes to understanding how to work the Internet, few people possess his know-how and insight.

Q: What are the key elements that you recommend having on the home page of the website?

ERIC ROBICHAUD: I'll try to break down and demystify the process of professional website development. First and foremost, I find it extremely important to communicate that if you're going to develop a website for commercial/marketing purposes, you ought to do it right or don't do it at all. Today's Internet surfers are very savvy and can spot an amateur attempt a mile away. You don't want to invest time and money in an amateur-looking website that only serves to do more harm than good. A good rule of thumb is the Hippocratic oath: First, do no harm.

There are essentially three options for proceeding:

1. Build it yourself.
2. Hire a cost-effective graphic designer to build a "brochure-ware" site.
3. Hire a professional firm.

For the build-it-yourself option: Generally speaking, I really do not recommend this approach, and it's not for self-serving reasons — it's truly a mistake. A poorly designed website can actually do more harm than good. People will see a lousy website with poor production values and project those thoughts and feelings onto the movie: The movie must be lousy, with poor production values.

When developing a website, most average Americans — i.e., those people not in the web design/development business — think of the visual graphic design. The graphical appearance is the website to them. Unfortunately, that's analogous to assuming that a doctor is simply an authority figure who signs off on medication prescriptions. It discounts years of training and specialization, and the doctor's ability to actually diagnose the correct cause of the symptoms, and determine the correct treatment plan. Similarly, most people think of web design as the creation of the visual elements, which really only begins to scratch the surface. This does not take into consideration extremely important issues such as:

Navigation and information architecture. There's an art to creating simple, clean, intuitive navigation and structuring content so that it's easy to find and makes sense. Most do-it-yourself projects suffer from a jumble of confusing links, hard-to-navigate menu structures, and confusing content arrangement.

Technology. Thinking about the graphics is one part of the puzzle but overlooks all of the back-end technology and programming that power the interactive features of your site. How will you get the programming done?

Business results. What does this website actually do? At the end of the day, will this website actually help you sell more tickets or get more rave reviews? Just banging out some graphics ignores the entire business side of the equation. "Build it and they will come" was great fiction for a movie but does not translate into website success.

And there's much more, but this should give a clear picture.

Q: I think I might do this DIY approach. What tools do I need?

ERIC ROBICHAUD: If you're still adamant about doing it yourself, here are a few tips. I'd suggest becoming familiar with an HTML editor such as Macromedia Dreamweaver. Personally, I recommend staying away from Microsoft's Front Page. This can be an issue of personal preference and much debate, but in my professional experience, Front Page has too many issues, and sites developed with it are not entirely portable and can become very problematic in the long run. Spend a few hundred dollars and stick with Dreamweaver.

You'll need graphics-editing software such as Photoshop to create the visual graphics. While several packages such as Corel-Draw and PaintShop Pro, etc. can handle the task, you might be better off to go with Photoshop — the "granddaddy" of image-editing software — for many reasons, including the fact that most templates [see below] will come with native Photoshop files, and interoperability with designers down the road — if you eventually hire someone and pass off your project — will be much easier.

If you're not a design whiz, search online for website template libraries. There are sites that offer predesigned templates for $30 to $60 that you can work from. This is "sizzle" with no "steak" — you're on your own for content, figuring out architecture, and any back-end programming. Plus, you'll be force-fitting yourself into a predefined template — and you'll look like every other templatized website out there. But, at least you'll look professional, and it's low cost.

Q: What else should be considered for a website?

ERIC ROBICHAUD: Don't put a Web "Hit Counter" on your home page to count visits. First, most Internet users are savvy enough to realize that 250,000 visits means you've visited your site 249,997 times, and three other people legitimately visited your site. All they have to do is hit "refresh" and watch the counter flip to see it's a sham. It's considered unprofessional and tacky by today's standards. Web developers and customers alike are much more sophisticated than that today. Unfortunately, many do-it-yourselfers haven't caught on yet. If you want real statistics on visits, use a product like WebTrends to report on your website visits behind the scenes. All Web servers can keep logs of their activity behind the scenes, and you can use WebTrends (or other similar log analyzers) to report on the data collected in the logs.

Ditto for a guestbook. The guestbook and hit counters were the first CGI [computer graphics interface] applets to appear, back in the mid-90s. But they're useless and considered tacky by today's standards.

Q: Okay, we won't put those online. But what should go online?

ERIC ROBICHAUD: Do include useful information such as movie schedules: Where can I find this movie? Where is it playing? Or where can I buy it on DVD? Think of content from the end user's standpoint. If I'm a random movie buff, why would I go to the site, and what would I look to find there? Then include content that answers those questions.

Once you factor in the cost of all of the software you'll need (Photoshop, Dreamweaver, the templates), you're probably better off moving into option 2 below anyway.

Option 2: Hire a freelancer or cost-effective graphic designer to build a "brochure-ware" site.

This option is similar to the do-it-yourself approach, except you're bringing on a professional graphic designer to do the work for you. You can get a basic brochure-ware site cobbled together for $3,000 to $10,000 depending upon how much content and complexity you desire to include, and whether or not you spice it up with Flash animations and any basic interactive programming elements. The content would be mostly static text covering the basic "who we are," "what we do," "about us," and "contact us" type of information.

If you really just do not have the budget to hire a professional, high-end firm, this is a reasonable compromise. At least the production work is being done efficiently by someone who knows what they're doing, and you'll get a reasonable level of professionalism in the end result — assuming you do a portfolio review and hire a reasonably talented person.

But keep your expectations in check. The average Web designer will be more of a graphics person and most likely won't have very deep back-end knowledge, so you won't get sophisticated back-end programming and applications — and even if he or she did have that experience, you won't be getting all of that for $3,000.

Typically, "small guys" are either designers or techies. They try to have some crossover capabilities, but at the end of the day they're one or the other. That's the compromise you'll have to live with — they can make it look sharp, but there won't be much actual interactive substance — programming code, applications, databases, etc. — or it'll be a functional site with some neat applications like real-time look up of theaters/showings, etc., but the graphics will be drab and the architecture/navigation and marketing side of things will suffer. Again, it's all a matter of compromise at this level. At the risk of alienating my computer science and engineering comrades, for your situation, I'd personally recommend erring on the side of the graphic designer and keeping the interactive functionality light.

Q: What if I should happen to win the lottery or get an NEA grant, and if old Uncle Scrooge kicks the bucket and leaves me his fortune — or at least enough money for professional Web design input. Where do I go from here?

ERIC ROBICHAUD: That's option 3: hiring a professional firm. Obviously this is the best of all worlds. You want to look for a firm with all of the core services under one roof: marketing communications, creative design, and technology/software solutions. Such a firm will help guide you toward implementing a solution that meets your business goals, communicates your message and value proposition clearly and effectively, looks professional and attractive, and includes reliable back-end technology solutions that work the way they're supposed to.

You will absolutely spend more than the first two options: You'll start at $10,000 and work upward from there. It wouldn't be unusual to spend $25,000 or more on a professional site. But the difference is that the right professional firm will move this from expenditure — the way most people think about this type of project — to investment! A firm that knows what it is doing, and has a marketing-communications discipline, can guide you toward creating a solution that properly generates profitable revenues. The website becomes an investment that yields an appropriate return, or ROI [return on investment].

This is where you must ask yourself: Would you rather spend $8,000 to have a website that hangs your slate out on the digital frontier, so to speak, and explains who you are and what you do, or spend $25,000 and have a website that generates $300,000 a year worth of new business?

My recommendation here: Establish a budget and be forthcoming with your firm about that budget. Sophisticated buyers realize that the only way to get the best bang for their buck is to create a true partnership with the creative team, lay out the budget, then squeeze the utmost amount of results-driving functionality into the project. The old negotiating tactics of holding back on budgets to drive the best price backfires here because this isn't a commodity sale. You're not bidding out the same pen to three vendors and looking for the best price. This is a complex, consultative project.

Q: *How do I know if I am choosing the right Web designer?*

ERIC ROBICHAUD: When reviewing firms [vendors], you'll want to review their portfolio, make sure they can deliver what you need and understand your business goals and can develop a plan for achieving them. That should be your criteria selection. Once you've chosen a vendor, then you sit with them, review the budget, and work with the vendor to create a plan of action and design a solution. Be part of the process; do not expect to "buy" a website the way you'd buy a car or another tangible product. You must be part of the process in designing the appropriate solution, then let the firm produce it.

Q: What about getting the website into search engines?

ERIC ROBICHAUD: Once your website is ready to go, you'll want to review it in terms of "search engine optimization." Your agency should be able to assist you with this. If you're doing it yourself, you'll want to read up on it. Essentially, you'll want to determine the types of keywords people will use to find you — or to look up movies in similar categories as yours, where you want to be found — when doing Web searches. Then you want to optimize your website content so that search engines will see you as being more "relevant" against those terms.

These days, search engines are pretty savvy to most people's attempts to "fake" their way to a higher ranking, and they look toward the actual content itself in determining relevancy. So that might mean slightly reworking your content. For example, if you want people to find you when they search on "movie Boston train" because your movie is about a subway in Boston, then you might want to rework sentences to include those keywords. For example:

Old sentence: "This movie provides an adrenaline rush as we follow our hero through the subway station!" New sentence: "Set in Boston, this movie provides an adrenaline rush as we follow our hero through the subway station, hopping from train to train."

This is a fictitious example, so let's assume the changes are still relevant to the description. As you can see, we inserted "Boston" and "train" into the sentence. You'll find that some of the text changes might sound a little lengthier or somewhat awkward — we wouldn't actually say this if we were talking with a friend — but they're still grammatically correct, and the casual reader wouldn't notice the difference. But the search engines will! They'll now find "movie", "train," and "Boston" together in one sentence.

Search engine optimization, or SEO, is one of the most important and fundamental things you can and should do with your site, before you launch. It's the most cost-effective, yielding the biggest return on investment. You can try it yourself, but I wouldn't recommend it. My overview here barely scratches the surface: Each search engine uses its own, different criteria for rankings, and often they directly contradict one another. What works for one search engine can hinder you at another. I like to say, "It's part science, part voodoo black art." It takes experience. Budgets for SEO can vary wildly depending upon the level of complexities involved, but you can typically get a basic SEO job done for $1,000 to $2,000 from your firm.

Aside from SEO, there's also SEM — "search engine marketing" — which refers to the general concept of marketing yourself through the search engines. Besides the natural, organic search results, a company can also buy sponsored listings, so that your results come up regardless of your rankings. In other words, you can buy your way into being shown in response to particular keywords. This entails a whole other strategy and area of marketing expertise. You can sign up with Overture (Yahoo!) and Google, and can get started with literally any budget (down to a few hundred dollars). But again, to do it right I'd recommend hiring a consultant that specializes in SEM and keyword ad placements. A typical consulting gig can cost $5,000 but the return on investment is well worth the price tag.

Q: How about putting up a trailer from the film on the website? How is this achieved?

ERIC ROBICHAUD: The three most common formats for streaming media are the Microsoft Windows streaming media format, MPEG, and Apple's QuickTime. I don't see the choice here as a major issue as all three are well supported. Personally, I tend to lean toward the Microsoft or MPEG formats because there's a larger installed base that will inherently support them "out of the box" — 98% of the Web browser market is running on a Windows platform, and they have the Microsoft Media formats installed by default, whereas QuickTime is an add-on. However, QuickTime is so popular and ubiquitous that most people have gotten a free QuickTime player installed along the way.

I would strongly recommend including a trailer on your website. Definitely. As for formats, I'd personally lean toward MPEG or the Microsoft format, but all in all this doesn't really show up on my radar screen as a major issue.

Q: What else can I do to make my site more attractive?

ERIC ROBICHAUD: I would strongly recommend commissioning "goodies" to be developed and made available for free at your website — items like screensavers, wallpaper images, and sound clips. Have them done professionally, and to a high quality. Again, the "do no harm" rule applies: You don't want to produce junk and turn people off. But you want to do everything you can to build buzz, foster brand loyalty, and get people living with and interactive with your movie/brand on a daily basis. Screensavers and wallpapers are cost-effective marketing tools with big ROI.

If your movie will become a brand with a cult following, or if your site is being used to promote a company that will be producing new movies, you'll want to collect email addresses of fans and email them regularly to keep their interest, continue the buzz, and foster loyalty. There's no point in collecting names and harassing people, though, if your movie is an isolated piece that won't have an ongoing mythology, sequels, etc.

7. Making contact

If everything is set, now it is time to make contact with the distributor.

First and foremost, make sure you know who you are contacting. Do not send a "Dear Sir or Madam" letter — invest in a telephone call and get the name of the person who is in charge of acquisitions at the distributor. Then make sure you have the proper mailing address. Do not rely on websites or telephone directories for addresses — companies have been known to relocate without updating their contact data.

In presenting your materials, make sure you enclose an introductory letter reminding your contact person of your previous telephone conversation regarding your film. If you want your film materials returned, make sure you enclose a self-addressed stamped envelope. If you are mailing your materials, make sure you have a delivery confirmation for the parcel; you may also wish to send it certified and insured, just to be safe. Overnight courier services are more expensive than the U.S. Postal Service, but they are faster and often easier to track when it comes to delivery.

But again, as with the press kit, make sure your cover letter is properly proofed before it is signed and sealed for delivery. Dennis Doros of Milestone has a major peeve when it comes to hearing from clueless filmmakers: "Unsolicited packages with letters filled with typos," he says.

8. How to respond if you get a contract offer

Okay, you have all of the elements in place and you've made contact with the distributor. And… the distributor expresses interest in the film. Now what?

Filmmaker Christopher Munch, who helmed such wonderful features as *Color of a Brisk and Leaping Day*, *The Sleepy Time Gal*, and *Harry and Max*, offers cogent advice on this issue.

"First and foremost, know the value of your film," says Munch. "Although you may have sunk years of your life and millions of dollars into a project, it has no intrinsic commercial value other than what a licensee will pay for it at a given moment. Talk to producers who have released similar films and learn what they earned from them. Have a realistic sense of the liquidation value of your project over its useful life were you to go out and license it yourself to TV and video, or, alternatively, self-release it to video and/or theaters. Know the business you're getting into. Don't rely on what you read in trade papers about multi–million–dollar advances paid for films at Sundance, which may give you unrealistic expectations and a very distorted idea of the marketplace. Read John Lee's *The Producer's Business Handbook* and William Bayer's hilarious classic *Breaking Through, Selling Out, Dropping Dead,* which, regrettably, seems every bit as relevant today as when it came out 35 years ago.

"If you find yourself negotiating with a distributor, make sure you know ahead of time how they make their money and, specifically, how much and the way in which they will make money from your film. You're then in a position to hammer out a deal that is realistic for both parties. Be prepared to compromise, but also be prepared to walk away from the deal you're negotiating at any point if it becomes unacceptable. Remember, you'll be tying up a lot of rights for a lot of years, so you'd better get the details of the contract right. Don't restrict your audit rights, because it's axiomatic that if your film is profitable, you'll have to audit. Just because a distributor is established doesn't mean they're reputable. Quite possibly the reason they've been able to stay afloat in a finicky and changing market is by having amassed a library of titles from which they receive ongoing income but for which they have not paid producers what they are owed.

"Talk to other filmmakers who've dealt with them. Meet the principals of the company, the people they employ, and their vendors. Are they a fair organization to work for? Do they pay their bills? Learn the exact corporate structure of the company and its parent and/or subsidiaries, so that you can research their business history. Even if you can't obtain exact information on their cash position, gather as much financial data as you can. If you have a sales agent or lawyer, they will be in a good position to advise you because — hopefully — they've been around the block many more times than you have."

However, Munch notes that just because you receive a contract does not necessarily mean the race is run. Inadequate or unsatisfactory contracts are just as bad (if not worse) than no contract. "If after testing the waters you decide that no distributor is going to pay you an acceptable advance, or otherwise structure a deal that ensures you'll make money down the road, you should then formulate a plan for self-distribution," he continues. "If you don't have access to an experienced film distribution lawyer, gather as much information as possible from other sources — i.e., advice from other producers, organizations like the AIVF and IFP, and any free legal clinics of which you can avail yourself. In the case of a first feature, the director, who's trying to establish a visible reputation in the marketplace, may be at cross-purposes with the producer/financier, who may want to liquidate his or her investment as expeditiously as possible. A director, for instance, might find the absence of an advance an acceptable trade-off to make in exchange for a certain P&A [print and advertising] commitment, in which case the director's career may benefit more than a producer's from the resulting advertising.

"In any event, if you venture into theatrical distribution, be prepared to lose money, and probably a lot more than an experienced distributor would lose under similar circumstances. Whether you do the bookings yourself or hire a distributor to do them for you on a 'service' basis, ask yourself ahead of time, 'Is this really going to be worth it? Would we be better off taking that P&A money and putting it into advertising and building a website from which to sell DVDs ourselves?' Examine self-distribution case histories like *What the Bleep Do We Know* and *Trembling Before G★D*, and learn from other filmmakers' success stories."

Munch raises great points regarding self-distribution, albeit a bit prematurely for the purposes of this chapter. We will address self-distribution later in this book.

Mike Watt, who directed the feature *The Resurrection Game* and produced the horror film *Severe Injuries*, also advises that caution and research are key to any negotiations with distributors.

"Beware of any company that wants to buy all rights for more than five or six years," he says. "Some companies want it for 20 or more. This should be a red flag to you. If your movie isn't moving for them for the first year, do you really think they'll continue to push it into stores for another 19? Companies should report to you every quarter — i.e., every three months — with how many units were sold, which stores are carrying your movie, etc. If you don't get a quarterly report — or if they're not offered at all — you may be in trouble."

Watt continues: "Know the difference between net profit and gross profit. Some companies will offer a 50-50 split of the net profits, which means you get paid after their expenses — duplication, replication, distribution, etc. — are covered. Some companies will do a 50-50 split of the gross, regardless of expenses covered, but want all rights in perpetuity. If it doesn't matter to you that you own your own movie or ever will again, then take the latter deal. If you want to regain control after a period of time, tough out the expenses-repayment period, but keep an eye on the reports. Remember the *Forrest Gump* debacle: That movie grossed hundreds of millions of dollars yet is still reportedly losing money! Red tape can go on for years in Hollywood, and it's not unknown in the indie circle either. Consider if other things are important to you: Will the distributors give you input into the package design? What percentage of foreign sales do you get (this is usually a separate deal)? Who writes the package copy? Who decides the tag line? Do you get a set amount of copies for free and the rest at a discount? Ask questions. There are dozens of companies out there; you don't have to go to the first one that answers the door when you knock."

9. How to deal with rejection

Okay, you have all of the elements in place and you've made contact with the distributor. And… you were rejected. It happens, and it is never pleasant. But how can you learn from this experience and build on it?

Matthew Seig offers sage advice here: "Why have you been rejected? If distributors don't respond to your film simply because it is not commercial enough you will have different options than if people are finding a fundamental flaw in your filmmaking. If you believe that there is an audience for your film and you are an adventurous, entrepreneurial type, and you probably are to have made a film in the first place, consider raising some more money and trying distribution on your own, or teaming up with one of those very small companies in a service deal arrangement. Do not assume because you made a unique, imaginative film that people didn't 'get' that next you should make a film that looks like every other film."

Dennis Schwartz, whose commentary on classic and contemporary films can be found in the online magazine *Ozus' World Movie Reviews,* is equally sympathetic and supportive of the rejected filmmaker. "Can there be more downside than at present?" he asks, rhetorically. "It's like the lyrics to Jim Morrison's song 'I've been down so long it looks like up to me.' It's a business and the filmmaker can make art, but to get a film seen the artist must understand how the business end works, which many a young frustrated filmmaker finds is the hardest thing to deal with. Nevertheless, if one believes in one's work, one must find a way of getting that work out without compromising it."

What advice would Schwartz give aspiring creative artists who want to get into the independent film business? "Become a corporate lawyer unless you are born to be an artist," he says. "It's a labor of love. If you have something to say and feel that the inside drive to be a creative filmmaker is what you should be doing no matter what, go for it and don't let anyone stop you. Modern technology has made it possible to make films at low costs, which might be the saving grace for many young filmmakers. The problem still remains getting that film released. My advice is keep at it; don't compromise; movies are the things of dreams, and it's a good thing to keep those dreams burning as long as you still have your imagination and the will to follow your inclinations."

But above all, do not view rejection in apocalyptic terms.

"Just keep trying," advises Rory L. Aronsky, a critic with *Film Threat.* "If you received any comments from the distributor, look them over and examine what was perceived as weak or anything else the distributor didn't find favorable about it. If there are no comments — and even when there are — just keep plugging away. Unfortunately, film distribution is nothing like the writing market where there are numerous publishers you can keep going to, before exhausting all options, so you just have to look for a distributor that is in the same market that you're seeking and then go from there. Don't feel dejected after that first rejection. You might not even make it at all, but keep trying until that end has officially been reached."

"And, above all, don't get discouraged," adds Mike Watt. "You poured your heart and soul into the movie, so your patience must be great. Keep a good attitude while pursuing distribution. Taste is all subjective; because one studio head didn't dig your movie doesn't mean that the movie isn't any good. Believe in your movie, believe in yourself, but get as much information ahead of time as possible."

INTERVIEW
BILGE EBIRI, FILM CRITIC/FILMMAKER

New York-based Bilge Ebiri has been visible on both sides of the cinematic fence. As a film critic, his reviews of contemporary movies appeared in such publications as *Time Out New York*, *New York* magazine, and the *New York Sun*. As the director of the critically acclaimed comedy feature *New Guy* (2004), Ebiri has shown a distinctive artistic vision with a tale of a jittery desk jockey's disastrous first day at a weird new job. Having supported independent films as a critic, and having sought support as an independent filmmaker, Ebiri is especially cognizant of today's indie film scene and the challenges of getting a movie seen.

Q: What does the phrase "independent film" mean to you?

BILGE EBIRI: At this point, it doesn't mean all that much, sadly. Once upon a time, say in the '80s and early '90s, it did mean something, obviously, with this veritable explosion of independent films being made by the likes of Jim Jarmusch and Spike Lee and others. But that's old news.

Right now, it doesn't even technically mean anything — "independent" used to mean that a film was made and often distributed outside of the studio system, but today the companies people think of as independent are often owned by the studios — Fox Searchlight, Paramount Classics, Miramax, etc., etc. And you can't really define it in terms of genre, or attitude. Because most films people think of as independent today hew to tried-and-tested formulas, the same way an action film might. There are many reasons for that — people think that you need to have a pet llama or a quirky adolescent as your lead in order to get into Sundance, or whatever.

Now, I don't mean this necessarily as a qualitative assessment. A lot of the films people think of today as independent are actually very good. *Sideways* is an excellent film. So is *Before Sunset*. And Miramax, for all its difficulties, has continued releasing excellent films. The problem is that it's not necessarily independent — of all the films nominated for Best Picture for 2004, *Sideways* was the only one that was entirely financed by a studio. And it was the one most people would have pointed to if you asked them to pick out the independent film among the nominees. Oh, the irony! So I guess today "independent" really means "low-budget."

Q: Some recent hit movies such as My Big Fat Greek Wedding *and* Lost in Translation *were talked about as independent films, even though all were made by Hollywood insiders with Hollywood money. Can a production genuinely be called an independent film even if there is relatively little independence from Hollywood in its creation?*

BILGE EBIRI: Like I said, "independent" doesn't really have a specific definition anymore, so sure. Call *Star Wars* an independent if you have to. Of course, *Star Wars* actually is an independent film according to the old definition, but that's another point.

The problem, though, is that you never know who has a connection and where they have it. Yes, Sofia Coppola is an heir to a Hollywood dynasty. But then again, there are filmmakers who have made much smaller films who also have very tight Hollywood connections. *Tadpole* was made several years ago for very little money, shot on video. But it was made by an established producer, it starred Sigourney Weaver and John Ritter, etc.

Q: What have been the most significant and memorable independent films, both features and documentaries, that you've seen in the past few years? And what makes these films stand out from the Hollywood fare?

BILGE EBIRI: I guess the one truly great American film I can confidently call independent that's been made over the last few years is *The Blair Witch Project*. Obviously that's a film that became a juggernaut and was released in a thousand theaters. I don't know if it really fits the whole "released under the radar" thing. As for documentaries, they're all indies in a way, but *Los Angeles Plays Itself* is a great example of a film that was made outside of the Hollywood system, distributed independently. They didn't even clear their footage. That takes balls.

Q: What does it take for an independent film to make the jump into mainstream consciousness?

BILBE EBIRI: Well, as we saw with *Blair Witch*, it helps to have a gimmick. *Open Water* had a similar gimmick — I wasn't a big fan, but it certainly grabbed some attention. I'm actually sort of an idealist — I believe that if you make a genuinely good movie, and manage to get it seen by enough of the right people, you can get it released, and strike a chord. Now, of course, some films work with mass audiences and some films don't. Genre works, obviously. A lot of the horror films that get released today are films made independently, even though they're often released by studios and such. It also helps to have a specific audience.

When I first saw *My Big Fat Greek Wedding*, I didn't really think it was funny at all, and I wasn't particularly impressed with the filmmaking in it. But there was a small group of older ladies there, and they were having a ball. Stepping out of the theater, I spoke to a fellow critic, and said, "You know, I don't think I'm really qualified to write about that film. It was clearly working with people, and had no effect on me. I can still criticize the filmmaking to a certain degree, but it's important to remember that the film was not really meant for me."

Q: Can smaller boutique distributors such as Zeitgeist, Wellspring, Palm Pictures, or Strand Releasing successfully compete against the Hollywood crowd in getting their films the level of attention and box office to make them commercially viable?

BILGE EBIRI: They can probably be more successful than the studios, in a certain way. I understand obviously that movie distribution is not all that profitable a business, but Hollywood's in a tailspin right now — they're spending too much money on movies and too much money selling them. It's getting increasingly harder for them to break even — when you're spending $50 million minimum on a film, that's absurd. The independent releasing method, which is a lot closer to what studios were doing with their films 30 years ago — opening them in certain cities and then expanding through word of mouth — is a lot healthier, I think.

And I think the stigma of independent films is gone, too. There are so many distributors — independent, pseudo-independent, major studio, etc. — that no viewer really pays any attention to who's releasing what now. If a friend or a respected critic tells them to go see something, they'll go see it. And the theaters are increasingly realizing that, too. A lot of the big multiplexes actually have some screens they devote to independent or pseudo-independent movies.

Q: What do you see as the potential downside — from an artistic and/or commercial viewpoint — of today's independent films?

BILGE EBIRI: I don't know. A smaller film offers some freedom. If you're making a film without having to deal with studio interference, obviously that's great. But then again, that means you have less money. And it really depends on the film: If you're going to make a science fiction epic, then it sucks to be an independent. If you're making a character-based drama, then it probably sucks to be doing it for a big studio that's going to need the film to clear $70 million in order to justify the expense.

Q: From your experience, do you feel that today's film festivals offer a viable launching point for independent films?

BILGE EBIRI: Most definitely. I think film festivals today offer the only real viable launching point for independent films. You need word of mouth, you need it to percolate, you need the first few reviews from the likes of *Variety*, the *New York Times*, the *Los Angeles Times*, etc. A big festival, like Sundance, or Tribeca, or the New York Film Festival, or Cannes, Berlin, Venice, etc., are the best stages for that.

photo courtesy Siete Macho Films

Kelly Miller uses a coffeepot as a defensive weapon in Bilge Ebiri's New Guy. "I think the stigma of independent films is gone, too," says Ebiri. "There are so many distributors — independent, pseudo-independent, major studio, etc. — that no viewer really pays any attention to who's releasing what now."

Q: What advice would you give aspiring creative artists who want to get into the independent film business?

BILGE EBIRI: The same advice people gave me — just do it. The technology exists out there for you to just start making films — shorts, docs, features, whatever. Save as much money as you can, and go. The only way to become a filmmaker is to make films. There's just no other way.

Q: How do you look upon films that are self-distributed by the filmmaker? Does that factor in to your consideration of the film?

BILGE EBIRI: I suppose it did once upon a time — I used to think of it the same way I used to think of self-published books. But over the years I've seen a lot of great films that were distributed by the filmmakers. There can be lots of reasons to do this, and not all of them quality-related. And of course, I have since released my own film myself, so I now have a whole new perspective on it.

Q: As a filmmaker, how did you go about getting New Guy *considered for theatrical acquisition? Specifically, which companies did you contact and how did you pitch them?*

BILGE EBIRI: Interestingly, they mostly approached me. Whenever I showed at a festival and got some good reviews, we would get a couple of queries. Big ones, small ones. Miramax asked to see it, Paramount Classics, Warner Independent, etc. I never really thought these big distributors would want to release the film — it's hard for them to spend money on something that has absolutely no recognizable faces in it — but I sent it regardless. But the best way to do it is to get an email address and query someone in acquisitions at a company.

Q: What were the responses you received back from the distributors?

BILGE EBIRI: For the smaller distributors, it's hard for them to do something with the film if there are no recognizable faces or a lot of festival awards or some big buzz or something. Because remember, these guys are only going to be able to take out a small ad — and they have to get something into that ad that will pique people's curiosity. In order to properly introduce a film like this, they'd have to spend more money, which is money they don't really have. And for the bigger distributors, they just have bigger fish to fry. It's too small a film, ultimately. And because it was shot on video, it would have required an additional $25,000 to $30,000 to strike 35mm prints. That's a lot of money for a small distributor to put into a film with no faces in it.

Q: What festivals did the film play in? And did you get any inquiries for distribution from these festivals?

BILGE EBIRI: The film premiered at Cinequest San Jose, then screened at Newport Beach, Istanbul, Raindance [London], the Central Standard festival in Minneapolis, the Magnolia Film Festival in Mississippi, and many others. I think when all was said and done we'd screened at 15 to 16 festivals or so.

Q: New Guy was booked at the Two Boots Pioneer Theater in New York by you, since it did not get theatrical pickup. Did the film's New York engagement stir any interest for acquisition from potential distributors?

BILGE EBIRI: Well, since New York is the main market for a lot of these guys, I knew that releasing the film in New York would basically close the door on theatrical distribution in the U.S. But as I said above, it has sparked interest from video distributors, and we're currently working on that. And getting interest for video was one of the reasons I released the film at the Pioneer.

Q: If you could to do this all over again, what would you do differently in regard to getting New Guy *a distribution deal?*

BILGE EBIRI: Well, I wasn't particularly smart about it at first. I would have been a lot more aggressive. I didn't approach any distributors initially; they approached me. But then I never called them back. When I didn't hear back from them, I just assumed they were no longer interested. But a lot of people have made it clear to me since that very often these people don't watch your film until you call them back and harass them a little bit — but very pleasantly, of course. I don't know if it would have resulted in a sale, but I would have been more aggressive, and I would have been better organized. I would have made myself a database of distributors, made a million dubs of the film, and then just sent it out to everyone, and then followed up. But of course, I had a job to worry about, and I had also blown most of my money making the film. For most filmmakers, this is the part where a producer would come in, but I didn't have that luxury.

[Postscript: *New Guy* was released on DVD by Vanguard Cinema in November 2005.]

❧

LISTEN TO WHAT THE MAN SAYS

Well, that was a lot of advice. Now how do you proceed from here? Simple:

1. Go back and reread the entire chapter, but this time create a running checklist of everything that was cited here. If you are missing *anything*, put a big red X next to that missing piece and make it your highest priority to be certain that void is filled. If you go out to the indie orbit with any of these pieces not in place, you will not succeed. And I am not saying that you run the risk of failing.... I am stating, in no willy-nilly language, that YOU WILL NOT SUCCEED!

2. I cannot stress enough how important it is to have high-quality photographs from your film available for promotional purposes. If you made a film without taking any publicity stills, shame on you! Nothing screams "amateur" more than making a film without proper publicity stills. Learn from that mistake when you shoot your next movie!

3. If you are hiring a vendor to assist you in any way (as a photographer, a Web designer, or even a lawyer), get references. And when you get references, make sure you ask many detailed and rude questions. You have a right to know about the depth and scope of the work the vendor can provide, the problems that may have come up, the financial value of the work, and the hiccups in communication that may have popped up along the way. If you have the time and inclination, do your own research on the vendor's work. All you need is access to Google and the patience to seek out online comments and coverage about the vendor.

4. If you hire a vendor, please pay your bills. This may sound elementary, but anyone who bounces checks or fails to

honor invoices will be branded as a deadbeat and that tag is impossible to shake. I knew one distributor who lost the chance to release several high-profile productions because he had a reputation of running away from his bills. Another distributor bounced a check on a Web designer, but that vendor turned around and posted the bounced check on the website for the distributor's film! Neither of those distributors remained in the business and, honestly, no one misses them (except the people who are still owed money, of course).

5. Check out the competition and be as catty as possible about their shortcomings. You can learn more from people's mistakes than from their successes. If you come across an independent production with a clumsy website, a sloppy press kit, and blurry publicity photos, take notes and go in the opposite direction. It is one thing to get inspiration from genius, but it is more relevant to get pointers from those who are oblivious to their cluelessness.

6. Take out a highlighter pen and mark off Christopher Munch's trenchant comment: "First and foremost, know the value of your film. Although you may have sunk years of your life and millions of dollars into a project, it has no intrinsic commercial value other than what a licensee will pay for it at a given moment." Munch is not being sour — he is on target. And if you can't figure out what he is saying, keep reading and then come back to the quote later.

IT'S NOT WHAT YOU KNOW, BUT…

It is wise to apply the oil of refined
politeness to the mechanisms of friendship.
— Colette

3

Did you ever hear the story of how a homosexual police officer helped to get an independent film about a Portuguese diva into theatrical release? No? Well, grab a cup of something and sit back, because this one deserves to be heard. I know, because I'm in the story (not as the homosexual police officer or the Portuguese diva — just pay attention and you'll learn something!).

Back in early 2000, I used my working hours doing what most people do in computer-driven offices: I was goofing off via the Internet. My time waster was the chat rooms of America Online, where I would encounter all sorts of strange, eclectic, and frequently demented individuals. At the time, my favorite chat buddy was someone who identified himself as "Cord." If I was to believe what Cord said, he was a gay motorcycle patrol officer with the New Haven (Connecticut) Police Department.

Now Cord wasn't your typical gay motorcycle patrol officer with the New Haven Police Department. He was a fairly erudite conversationalist who took great pains at displaying his intellect, urbanity, and appreciation of the finer things in life. Or, in layman's terms, he was a snobbish show-off. But his conversation was diverting enough and Cord had a way of bringing up the most unlikely aspects of history, culture, culinary arts, travel, and political science. Believe me, I didn't mind putting my work-related responsibilities on hold to play audience to his ramblings and raconteur spins.

One afternoon, however, my work interfered with Cord's conversation. Knowing that I was involved in the film industry, Cord inquired if I knew where he could locate any films starring the Portuguese singer Amalia Rodrigues. My initial reaction, which I kept to myself, was: Who's Amalia Rodrigues? But since Cord was the type who openly gloated when he one-upped someone in the pursuit of intellectual superiority, I bluffed and told him I would need to research that further. The answer wasn't entirely dishonest, and Cord seemed satisfied with my promise to report back with a solid answer.

But the question bothered me: Who was Amalia Rodrigues? And how is it that a gay motorcycle patrol officer with the New Haven Police Department can know something that I didn't? Okay, I was displeased that my ignorance was showing. To level our playing field, I dove into research on the subject.

I learned that Amalia Rodrigues was one of Portugal's most beloved performers in the twentieth century. She specialized in a style of music called *fado*, an emotional folksong styling unique to Portuguese culture. Now I knew who she was, but I was no closer to discovering whether any films she appeared in were available in the United States. I suspected they were not, given that very few Portuguese movies were ever released in American theaters.

To my surprise, I discovered that a documentary on the life and music of Amalia Rodrigues was recently completed, called *The Art of Amalia*. Even more surprising was that I knew the filmmaker: Bruno de Almeida, who had completed another feature called *On the Run*, which I was supposed to do the PR for later that year. I was unaware of Bruno's film on Amalia Rodrigues from my earlier conversations with him, and reading about the film on his website only served to increase my curiosity.

I contacted Bruno and, as luck would have it, he had just completed the film and was able to provide me with a video screener. I found the film to be highly rewarding and utterly fascinating. His mix of rare footage and recordings plus a detailed late-life interview with Amalia Rodrigues made *The Art of Amalia* one of the most fascinating documentaries I had seen.

Furthermore, I had just begun writing for *Film Threat* and I opted to do an interview with Bruno about *The Art of Amalia*. This turned out to be the first coverage he received on the film; it was also his first interview for an American media outlet.

Even luckier (at least for Bruno) was another gig I was enjoying: as programmer for the Light+Screen Film Festival in New York. That was a weekly film series that presented oddball classic movies and edgy new independent films for crowds of discerning cineastes. I felt *The Art of Amalia* would appeal to the Light+Screen audience and I arranged with Bruno to give the film its first public screening.

As one of the guests for that screening, I invited Robin Lim, the president of Avatar Films. Robin had recently launched Avatar as a boutique distribution company and he was on the lookout for new movies to acquire and release. I was working with Robin as the public relations consultant for his releases and he was open to having me suggest possible titles for his acquisition consideration. I thought *The Art of Amalia* might be a good fit for his cinematic canon, so I made it clear to Robin that he needed to see this film with an audience to gauge their reaction.

The audience for that screening was standing room only — the venue was packed, in large part, because I sent out a press release to the local Portuguese-language media announcing the special one-time screening of this film about Portugal's biggest singing star. The screening was also announced in the local mainstream media, and it seemed there were more than a few Amalia Rodrigues fans who came out for the movie.

During the screening, I introduced Robin and Bruno and casually suggested that they talk about working together. Robin was clearly impressed with the turnout for the film and Bruno was impressed with Robin's conversation. By the end of the evening, *The Art of Amalia* had received a standing ovation from the screening audience and Avatar Films had agreed to pick up the film for distribution. Within six months of that evening, *The Art of Amalia* opened in New York and enjoyed a commercially successful engagement.

And to think... had it not been for that gay motorcycle patrol officer from the New Haven Police Department who asked an off-kilter question in an America Online chat room, none of this would ever have occurred!

Oh, in case you are wondering what became of Cord, that's a strange postscript. He never got to see the film at its first exhibition — he declined my invitation to attend the Light+Screen presentation. Shortly after that time, I lost touch with him. But I did receive an email from someone claiming to be Cord's brother, and this missive stated that Cord went to Colombia on a special drug investigation and was kidnapped by the rebels who supposedly control that nation's drug traffic. Why I was being told this was unclear, since my relationship with Cord was strictly chat room–based (we never had any offline contact). Also, it wasn't hard to notice that Cord's brother had a writing style that was virtually identical to the show-off cop who started this whole tale. I found the "brother" in a chat room and spoke with him via instant message — and, yes, the style of talk was the same. I made a brief inquiry with a reporter who covered the police beat in New Haven and I was informed that no one from the local constabulary was missing in Colombia — but one cop was supposedly AWOL and turned up in New Jersey having suffered a nervous breakdown. Whether this was Cord is something I don't know. About four years later, through a fluke, I came upon this guy again in (where else?) another online chat room. This time he claimed to be a writer in Washington, D.C., who ran a journalism syndicate — and he added he was a former motorcycle cop who liked Amalia Rodrigues. But he did not claim to be Cord from New Haven.

Of course, the normal route for getting a film picked up for release is not found via online chat rooms occupied by odd characters claiming to be gay policemen in Connecticut. And, admittedly, the bulk of that story involves my work as a journalist, publicist, and programmer — the mysterious Cord just planted the seed and stepped out of the picture, albeit with a lot more flourish and theatricality than most people could offer. Yet ultimately, the peculiar route that brought *The Art of Amalia* into theatrical release shows there is life and wisdom in that old, old adage: It's not what you know, it's who you know.

One of the key problems facing independent filmmakers is the sense of professional isolation. It is easy to find oneself working in a vacuum; this is especially the case for filmmakers who are not based in Hollywood or New York, where there is no shortage of film professionals to offer advice, wisdom, observations, or contact with those who can bring films to power players.

INTERVIEW
ERIC BYLER, FILMMAKER

For Eric Byler, the journey of *Charlotte Sometimes* (2002) could have been a tough road. His low-budget feature (made for under $500,000) featured an Asian American ensemble in a quirky romantic drama — not exactly the stuff of box office gold, even in the allegedly enlightened world of indie cinema. But Byler was fortunate to have been assisted through his contacts with the right people: the Visionbox Media team, who aided him throughout the production. Byler won several awards on the festival circuit and was nominated for the Independent Spirit Award; the film was also theatrically released through Small Box Pictures and received critical acclaim.

Q: Is it true that Charlotte Sometimes *came about from a rather precarious financial situation?*

ERIC BYLER: I made the film in a loose production services agreement with Visionbox Media, who lent me office space and advice but invested no funds during production. In sum, they said if you and your family are willing to pay the $20,000 to shoot it, we'll help you see to it the money is well spent. And they did. For a deferred fee, they allowed me to edit *Charlotte Sometimes* on one of their FCP systems. My secret agenda was to interest them in helping me finish the film, as I knew they had funding and expertise that could benefit the film greatly. I enticed them into my "editing closet" to watch scenes here and there. Slowly, they began to see the artistic merit. When post supervisor Chris Miller joined the company, he advocated Visionbox paying for sound editing and color timing in exchange for more deferred fees. Visionbox agreed and I readily accepted the offer. Later, after the film's success with critics, awards, and nominations, Visionbox bankrolled and oversaw theatrical distribution as well.

I was literally editing in the closet. During 2001, Visionbox was focusing their time and resources on projects they had invested money in — films they thought were more commercial and more likely to earn them a name in the industry. One of the films featured a young woman in a bikini living on the beach and videotaping other people having sex. Anyway, to be fair, once *Charlotte* fell into favor at Visionbox, I was given a room to edit in instead of a closet, and later given $750 for a weekend of reshoots, on which I served as DP and director, and had only a makeup artist and a sound mixer in my crew. The camera we used that weekend was rented for $100 from the writer/director of the bikini voyeur movie, who was a very nice person I saw often while both films were in post. I think the awards and nominations took most of them by surprise. When they realized that *Charlotte* was also a commercial project, and one that could help them earn a name in the industry, they decided to distribute the film theatrically as well to increase its exposure and to improve DVD sales.

Q: When you were preparing a festival strategy for Charlotte Sometimes, *which festivals did you specifically go after? And on the flip side, were there festivals that you specifically chose not to pursue?*

ERIC BYLER: I was eager to exhibit at Asian American film festivals, but the plan at Visionbox was to skip those fests. I saw the wisdom in it, but I felt a sense of loyalty to the APA arts community who had nurtured me almost from the day I graduated from college, and I ended up paying the entry fees myself. As it happened, each of the first three Asian American festivals I entered declined.

Visionbox decided to premiere at South by Southwest as a work in progress — the sound mix was very rough, and it had not yet been blown up to 35 mm. The sound mixer, Brad North, and I stayed up 36 hours straight to get the movie in good enough shape to show. I flew to Austin with a Beta tape in my duffel bag. Cast members Jacqueline Kim, Michael Idemoto, and Matt Westmore joined me in Austin (we all flew at our own expense). Jacqueline and I made flyers at Kinko's late one night when we realized everyone else had not just flyers, but other gizmos to hand out including beer goggles and jockstraps with movie titles on them. It was a crash course in film festival competition for audiences. With little to offer other than a piece of paper with the screening times on it, we ended up talking to a lot of people face to face at bars, restaurants, and screenings. A lot of them showed up to see the movie and we ended up winning an audience award. The experience at South by Southwest emboldened me to spend the only money I earned that year — the screen adaptation fee for my current feature, *American Knees* — to blow the movie up to 35mm.

In June we premiered at the Florida Film Fest with a completed sound mix on a fabulous-looking 35mm print. We won a jury prize and I was enthralled to call the Visionbox people to let them know. Distributors came to screenings a few days later at the Los Angeles Film Festival, where word of mouth was strong and we were fresh from winning prizes at our first two fests. They also came to screenings at the Hamptons International in November, where we were fresh from Roger Ebert's review written during the Hawaii International Film Festival. They also came to a CAPE [Coalition of Asian Pacifics in Entertainment] screening in NYC in December shortly after the Spirit Award nominations were announced, but this was a disaster because of projection problems. The only offers we received were not satisfactory. When 2002 ended, it seemed as if the film would not be distributed theatrically. But we did have a deal with the Sundance Channel, and some good offers for DVD/video distribution. As I mentioned above, Visionbox then decided to distribute the film itself.

Q: Charlotte Sometimes *played in festivals specializing in Asian American cinema. How can niche festivals focusing on a single theme — Asian American films, Jewish films, gay films, etc. — benefit an independent filmmaker and his work?*

ERIC BYLER: As it turned out, two of the Asian American fests that turned *Charlotte Sometimes* down in 2002 were used as platforms for a theatrical release in 2003. It turned out to be a nice accidental strategy — go with mainstream festivals to start with, and if you're lucky enough to get distribution, play the Asian American festivals just prior to theatrical release. I don't know if it helped, but considering that we had so little money to support the release, the festivals helped us with things like publicity and my travel costs, and created word of mouth in an important target group for the film.

Q: *How did* Charlotte Sometimes *get picked up by Small Planet Pictures for release? Did you know the distributor, or did they see the film at a festival, or was a third party involved in connecting the film and the distributor?*

ERIC BYLER: After Roger Ebert's first review — he wrote two, both available on the film's website — was published and the Independent Spirit Award nominations were announced in the last two months of 2002, Visionbox decided to release *Charlotte Sometimes* theatrically. They had already made a deal with the Sundance Channel, and had a short window of time to get the film out before it would be running on cable. They hired Small Planet to do the booking and basically the two groups teamed up on advertising strategy.

Q: *Can I ask what distributors you contacted prior to signing with Small Planet Pictures? And if so, why did they opt not to pick up the film?*

ERIC BYLER: I can't remember the names of them. There were a lot that contacted us after Ebert's review and during the Spirit Award hubbub. Prior to that, they had to be dragged into screenings kicking and screaming. Reasons for not distributing a film are always the same, I think. For us, it had to do with there not being any precedent for an art film focusing on Asian Americans.

Q: What was the depth and scope of the Charlotte Sometimes *theatrical release? And were you satisfied with the theatrical release strategy or do you feel it could've been wider and/or stronger?*

ERIC BYLER: Visionbox and Small Planet were able to book the film in 24 of the largest cities in the U.S. before the Sundance Channel started airing it, I think, in July. There were only five prints, so they had to stagger the openings. I was flown in to attend and promote the premieres in Chicago, San Francisco, Berkeley, San Jose, Los Angeles, New York, and Honolulu. Chicago and the Bay Area were timed specifically to follow immediately after film festivals in those cities, or nearby in the case of Roger's film festival in Champlain/Urbana. The first city was Chicago in May of 2003. When I arrived in Chicago after Roger's festival, I found out that the publicist Visionbox had hired was a 19-year-old woman who had been working in the basement of the Watertower theaters for three weeks. I complained to Visionbox/Small Planet until they hired the best publicist in town. The first-ever Charlotte Sometimes advertisement was printed in the Chicago Tribune, Chicago Reader, and the Chicago Sun-Times. It was created at Small Planet Pictures on MS Word and looked as if it took half an hour of hurried attention. The best publicist in Chicago was appalled. I was embarrassed. But the reviews were strong and the film had a nice opening weekend despite the fact that most Chicago residents had previously thought the Watertower theaters had closed down — they had, but had recently reopened as an art-house theater. Meanwhile, the advertisements were redone the next weekend — we could only afford ads on Saturday and Sunday. I never really liked any of the ads, which featured a very low-res still taken from the film negative of Eugenia Yuan waving a black camisole with a "come hither" look on her face. I couldn't decide which was worse — having no advertisements at all, or very small advertisements that looked like massage parlor ads rather than ads for an art-house movie. I felt the low-res, cheap-sex approach misled filmgoers into thinking *Charlotte Sometimes* was an Asian cheesecake flick, Roger Ebert quotes notwithstanding.

In other cities, we were also relegated to theaters that had resorted to "art house" titles because the new multiplexes had stolen all their business. The reviews, thankfully, were our saving grace. We got a fresh tomato in every major newspaper of every city we visited except the *San Diego Tribune* [referring to *rottentomatoes.com*].

Q: What practical and professional advice can you give to any aspiring filmmaker who just completed a feature film but has no idea how to bring it into release?

ERIC BYLER: Once you've made the film, it's kind of out of your hands. There's only so much you can do with jockstraps that have your film's name on them. I would just say make the film you want to make in your heart, and hopefully an honestly approached, personal film will appeal to distributors as much as they appeal to festival-goers and indie film lovers like me. I would recommend against trying to emulate studio films, or Indiewood films, because with less money and less-experienced cast and crewmembers, you'll end up making the same thing they make, only not as good. Better to make a personal film. In the end, you'll be proud of it, and it will mean more to you, whether distributors find it marketable or not.

Eric Byler's success is serendipitous in that he was able to get his film into release with the assistance of the right people. More often than not, independent filmmakers find themselves curling their fingers for that proverbial knock on the door — or curling their toes with the hope of getting a proverbial foot in the door. And, unfortunately, the majority of these filmmakers wind up with little to show for their efforts but bruised fingers and battered feet.

Syracuse, New York-based filmmaker Ryan Dacko has been there and done that. In trying to get interest in his feature film *And I Lived*, he originally planned to offer the movie along with a book that detailed the history of his production.

"The book acts as an inspirational guide to making an independent feature film," Dacko explains. "It tells of all the trials and errors that were made as well as the successes and triumphs also experienced by the cast and crew. The DVD of *And I Lived* was created on the same computer we edited the film on and was given the 'special edition' treatment, complete with director's commentary

photo courtesy Visionbox Pictures

Michael Ideomoto and Jacqueline Kim in Eric Byler's acclaimed Charlotte Sometimes. *"Once you've made the film, it's kind of out of your hands," says Byler.*

track, storyboards and production stills, even a hidden blooper reel. I self-financed a limited publication of the book, titled *I Guess the World Could Always Use Another Ed Wood*, also featuring the 'DVD Film School: First Edition'."

Admittedly, that is an interesting idea. It also helped that both the film and the book were quite good. So far, Dacko scores points for creativity.

"So with the book and DVD finished, I packaged them together and sent them out to various companies," he continues. "It was all negative feedback at first, with the usual 'We don't accept unsolicited materials' type of response. The next step was to look for a literary agency to represent the book and DVD. Since the movie wasn't being accepted into any of the current film festivals, I didn't feel it had enough legs to stand on its own, so it would need the book to act as a companion to the film. I sent out letters upon letters and emails upon emails, I think around a hundred or so. They were your basic query letters, describing in brief the details of the work. Out of that 100, I received 18 replies back from various agencies. And out of those 18 replies, four were positive and requested to look at the material. So far, I've heard back from two of the four who decided, in their opinions, that the material wouldn't sell on the market, but encourage me to keep trying other agencies."

Needless to say, Dacko's encouragement eventually began to fray. "At that point I was looking for anyone to listen. In the meantime, I sold promotional copies of the book on eBay and the responses were all extremely positive. That really helped boost my confidence to take the book to the next level. I thought, 'Maybe they will listen to me if I walk it right into the offices around Los Angeles.'"

One Greyhound bus trip later, Dacko was in Los Angeles. "I went to Los Angeles with a box full of promotional packages made up of a book, an *And I Lived* DVD, and the screenplay to the next film," he continues. "My friend Jason, who lives in downtown Los Angeles, and I drove around town to various studio offices and agencies that I had selected as ones that would likely listen or take a look at the package. I remember I was a nervous wreck, because there is nothing I fear more than getting rejected: Even though it has happened quite a few times in my young career, each one still sucks the life out of me. So we spent a day driving around L.A. and I would jump from the car and walk each package into each different address. We had about 15 selected. I wanted to get the packages to anyone in the major studios who might want to take interest in some potential independent film investments, but at the same time get the material to those whom I was a big fan of their work. So if worst came to worst, there was at least a chance that someone who inspired the creation of And I Lived would get a chance to view the film. The biggest name was Frank Darabont, writer/director of *The Shawshank Redemption* and *The Green Mile*. I was able to deliver a package personally to his offices at Darkwoods Productions. It was a kick to see the sitting room with an enormous *Shawshank* poster stretched across the wall. I was able to drop a package off to his assistant or producing partner, and then we moved on to the next office."

Sadly, the admiration between Dacko and Darabont was not mutual. "Later, we were informed via email that Mr. Darabont and Darkwoods Productions do not accept unsolicited material — if I only had a nickel for every time we ran into that one — and that we need to be referred to them by an agent," he adds. "In the meantime, the materials we delivered would have to be destroyed. They were the only ones who responded — who knows what happened to the other packages? I like to think the material wasn't destroyed and that Mr. Darabont was able to see a film that was greatly inspired by his work and the fact he is a filmmaker who began in lower-budget horror films [screenwriter for *The Blob, Nightmare on Elm Street 3: Dream Warriors*] and moved on to making A-list blockbusters [and garnering two Oscar nominations]. I hope to get a chance to thank him someday, only not as a package courier."

Still, Dacko has not completely lost hope. "So now, I am back into agent search mode — it seems that one is needed to get your movies to any of the big guys in Hollywood or your written work into the publishing world," he says. "In the meantime, it is full speed ahead on the next true independent film, 100% outside of the mainstream studio system. I am still remaining positive because you never know — Frank Darabont might just someday call."

Persistence in the face of constant rejection and Micawber-worthy optimism that something good is going to happen soon are crucial for independent filmmakers who lack the connections to be seen and heard. This is not to say the motion picture industry is overpopulated with people who take uncommon pleasure in heaping cruelty on struggling neophytes. It is not a question of being treated with deliberate scorn, but rather it is a situation where indifference reigns over those who are not plugged in.

Filmmaker Thomas Edward Seymour, part of the three-man Hale Manor Collective (the creators of the indie features *Thrill Kill Jack in Hale Manor, Everything Moves Alone*, and *The Land of College Prophets*), never feels that unresponsive or discouraging distributors are treating him badly. "I would say I'm not treated at all," he says. "I feel like most of the time they never get back to you. It's not like you're 10th on the list or 20th on the list — you're just not on the list. They don't have time for you."

Seymour notes that in all due fairness the distributors' lot should be kept in mind, since they are under constant bombardment from a multitude of aspiring Tarantinos. "If I was a secretary and every ten minutes someone called trying to get the director of acquisitions, I could see how that would be a nightmare," he says with a laugh.

As luck would have it, the first of the Hale Manor Collective productions (*Thrill Kill Jack in Hale Manor*) went through 30 rejections before a small company called HV Video agreed to release the movie to the home entertainment market. Ironically, the evasions and silences that Seymour met while shopping the film continued after the distributor agreed to release it.

photo courtesy Hale Manor Productions

Philip Guerette and Thomas Edward Seymour, who starred in and co-directed (with Mike Aransky) the comedy Everything Moves Alone. *"If I was a secretary and every ten minutes someone called trying to get the director of acquisitions, I could see how that would be a nightmare," says Seymour.*

"We started talking to them, but at some point their phone got disconnected," he recalls. "We could no longer get in touch with them. I think their website went down and stores stopped carrying their titles. And that was the last we heard of them. We had 30 rejections, but that one hurt because that was an acceptance and the company went under."

What independent filmmakers can learn from Dacko's and Seymour's respective experiences is this important lesson: If you want to get ahead in the indie film world, you need friends. Not just a happy, let's-have-lunch friend, but a serious professional who knows the right people, speaks the right language, and understands what is required to get a film on a screen or into a DVD retail outlet. Here are some important people who are critical for the support and marketing of a new film.

❧

THE PRODUCER'S REP

Call it a producer's rep or a sales rep, it is the same difference. The producer's rep is the individual who can (for a fee, naturally) help to connect a filmmaker with a distributor or (in some cases) the programmers for an upper-tier festival. This can be arranged either by having the rep coordinate screenings for acquisitions executives or by having them pass along video or DVD screeners directly to the acquisitions officers.

Most reps are not famous, and rightfully so — if everyone knew who they were, everyone would be after them. The most notable exception is the colorful Jeff Dowd, a.k.a. "the Dude," whose project list has included such now-classic titles as *Desperately Seeking Susan* and *Hoosiers*. The Coen brothers were repped by Dowd when they created *Blood Simple* and the cinematic siblings returned the favor by inventing the larger-than-life character of the Dude in *The Big Lebowski* in his honor.

Yet reps can sometimes have their own agenda, which may do more harm than good. I once did the PR for the Gen Art Film Festival in New York and a rep (who will remain anonymous here) was the power behind five of the seven films that were in that event (quickie background: Gen Art only offers a slate of seven features, one for each night of the weeklong fest). However, this rep refused to allow his five films to be reviewed by the New York media in conjunction with the festival. This severely crimped the publicity for the films in general and the festival as a whole, since the local media was not going to give coverage to an event unless they had some idea what was being screened. The rep's decision was disastrous on several levels: The festival's press coverage was less than anticipated and his five films came away from their New York premieres without any media or industry buzz whatsoever. A couple of them turned up in theaters many months later, one didn't show up in theatrical release until two years after the festival, and one never had a theatrical or home video release.

Among distributors and established filmmakers, the effectiveness of reps is open to debate. Academy Award-nominated filmmaker Kirby Dick also supports the notion of working with a rep, albeit at a specific time in the film's progress. "If a film has its premiere in a major U.S. or European festival where there are distributors picking up films, such as Cannes, Sundance, Berlin, Los Angeles Film Festival, Tribeca, SXSW, etc., I would definitely recommend working with a producer's rep," he says.

Another Academy Award-nominated filmmaker, Bill Plympton, agrees. "Yes, it is always preferable to get a good sales rep or producer's rep," he says. "That way, the distributors know that the film has some cachet."

Peter M. Hargrove, president of the boutique distributor Hargrove Entertainment, notes the nature of the industry gives the reps an edge that outsiders lack. "The mini-major art distributor acquisitions staffs are all in cliquish relationships," he says. "It is a known fact that they will only look at films that their friends send their way. This is why so many bad films are getting released."

James Eowan, the former senior vice president of operations and public relations for Seventh Art Releasing, acknowledges that reps have their advantages and disadvantages. "There are definitely occasions when producer's reps can be effective," says Eowan. "However, because producer's reps are in the business of getting advances in most cases and most films are at a level where advances could easily kill the deal, a producer's rep can end up passing on distribution opportunities where the film could have made money over time. On more than one occasion, we have been passed over because we weren't willing to give a hard advance on the film, but instead were willing to put up a small theatrical and a P&A budget. I have seen films disappear into the abyss after getting representation and then finding no takers. We have had filmmakers come back to us in many instances after the producer's rep moved on to other projects. This is not to say that producer's reps cannot be effective. They can. A filmmaker should realistically gauge the value of his or her film in the marketplace. The value of a film is not based simply on the quality of filmmaking. The value is based on many contributing factors, primarily the possibility of interest from an audience. Is there an audience base for this film? How big is it? Are there angles that would make the film appealing to new audiences, press and marketing opportunities? Ask around and see what other similar films are getting and then move forward."

Yet Eowan notes the changing nature of the film world may negate the power and influence that reps once possessed. "Five years ago, the producer's rep was almost a necessity for all filmmakers because the distributors were not as easily accessible and, I believe, filmmakers were less savvy," he says. "With the growth of the independent film world and documentaries in particular, filmmakers have become more knowledgeable and distributors have become more readily accessible."

And filmmaker Keith Gordon weighs in with this comment: "There's a lot of controversy in the indie world about this question. I've had some friends say that producer's reps really helped them. I've had more say they just felt ripped off, and ignored once the rep had the film on their list, or after the film didn't just take off on its own at a festival."

THE PUBLICIST

If your idea of a publicist is the smarmy, skanky character embodied by Tony Curtis in the 1957 classic *Sweet Smell of Success*, turn off the TV and join the real world. Today's publicist is a vital team member in the marketing success of any entertainment endeavor. This is particularly the case for independent films, which more often than not lack the financial backing and star power to attract immediate high-profile attention.

"The only way to break the name barrier, in my opinion, is to hire a publicist," says Steve Kaplan, president of the DVD distribution company Alpha Video. "Make sure your film is exposed as much as possible *everywhere* — like a new band starting out."

Some filmmakers might feel they can easily do their own publicity. However, this is probably the worst possible idea imaginable. Unless the filmmaker has peerless connections with the media and knows how the media operates, getting press coverage will be an exercise in futility: all sweat and no results.

"When push comes to shove, it all comes down to administration and access," says Nate Towne, CEO of the public relations/marketing agency Xanadu Communications. "The main reason to hire a publicist is that generating positive publicity is often laborious and time-consuming. The best publicists come with their own media utility belt, meaning they already have the press connections you'd likely work weeks, months — or years! — to cultivate. If you're raring to get into the *New York Times*, you'd better have an amazing story or know a publicist with good connections — otherwise you might have a long wait. Therefore, the successful — read: busy — filmmaker might find a publicist desirable if they have the money but simply do not have the time to wage an effective publicity campaign. Once a filmmaker becomes established, of course, having a good publicist is a necessity to keep the positive press coverage, or buzz, flowing."

Public relations is a very specialized field and there are a finite number of individuals and agencies handling motion picture promotions. Some publicists work exclusively with independent filmmakers and distributors, and these specialists clearly understand the terrain better than entertainment generalists.

"The best way to locate a publicist is to first understand your publicity needs," says Towne. "Ask your filmmaking peers if they use publicists and if so, contact their sources as it's likely their publicists will be looking for more work or will be connected with other relevant publicists who are looking for new clients. It's always best to work with a publicist in your field who already has proven success or positive professional relationships with your peers. If you fail to generate any leads, look up your local division of the Public Relations Society of America (*www.prsa.org*) and see if they have any publicists looking for work in your region. If all else fails, check online job search engines such as Craig's List or *Monster.com* — sometimes publicists looking to expand client rosters will list their services online in hopes of connecting with suitable employers."

When looking for a publicist, be certain to inquire about the depth and scope of services provided. Individual publicists who run one-person operations are often better to work with than midsized or larger agencies, where the assignment may be given to those who are either new to the field or are low on the corporate totem pole due to unsatisfactory job performance.

"Publicists should be dealt with directly and not be allowed to lay off your film on junior publicists or interns," explains Peter M. Hargrove.

Some publicists are strictly in the mind frame of generating media coverage and nothing else. While there is nothing wrong in getting one's name in print, it does not help the quest for distribution if the press coverage is inconsequential or without any leveraging power. Hargrove, in his two decades in the entertainment industry, has seen a surplus number of that breed: "Most publicists are a complete waste of time and are hand–holders, not marketing specialists."

One filmmaker who hired a publicist who was a marketing specialist was Nick Day, co-director of the documentary *Short Cut to Nirvana: Kumbh Mela*. While Day self-distributed his film theatrically, he was able to sign a DVD deal with Zeitgeist Films, a celebrated indie distributor. And how did that happy event come about?

"Through our guardian angel, Sasha Berman!" he exclaims. "After all our efforts self-distributing theatrically, we're very happy to find a home with such a well-respected distributor as Zeitgeist for our DVD release. Our publicist Sasha Berman made the initial introduction; we started a discussion and quickly found common ground."

Now who is Sasha Berman? Funny you should ask...

INTERVIEW
SASHA BERMAN, FILM PUBLICIST/MARKETING SPECIALIST

Sasha Berman has been operating her own public relations company, Shotwell Media, since 1997. As a film publicist, Sasha handles foreign-language, independent, and documentary film releases in New York and Los Angeles. Prior to working for herself, Sasha was the director of marketing and publicity at New Yorker Films, and the executive director of the Coolidge Corner Theatre in Boston. She is widely regarded as being among the finest publicists in the film industry today.

Q: For those who have either no idea or the wrong idea of the profession, what exactly does a film publicist do?

SASHA BERMAN: A film publicist is the liaison between the film and the press, and thus the audience. It is the film publicist's job to generate awareness and visibility for the film, as well as for the filmmaker and the actors in the film.

Q: Does it make sense for a film without a distribution deal to have a publicist?

SASHA BERMAN: I get many phone calls from filmmakers who think that they need a publicist before the film is ready for a theatrical release. I tend to disagree with that. For independent films, if there is a theatrical release on the horizon, it is important to save publicity for the theatrical release. Sometimes feature stories get "wasted" for a one-time screening, and filmmakers imagine that the newspaper will reprint that story when the film comes out — but that does not usually happen. I feel that it is best to save all press for the theatrical release, when people actually have a chance to see the film.

Q: How can a publicist help a film without a distributor on the festival circuit?

SASHA BERMAN: A knowledgeable publicist has connections not just with the press, but also with other people in the industry. Some publicists on the film circuit can suggest the right distributor to take a look at the film, and that can help secure the distribution.

Q: As a publicist, how do you determine which films you represent? And will you do PR for a film that is not currently in release and does not have a distributor?

SASHA BERMAN: I have relationships with some distributors whose taste I trust, and I know that if they are releasing a film, then I will be happy to work on that film. I specialize in foreign-language films, as well as indie films and documentaries. If a filmmaker approaches me with a film that I find interesting, I will take it on, even if it does not have distribution. I also consult for films without distribution, and I help them with their theatrical release strategy, and after the theatrical is done, I help the filmmakers find a DVD distributor. *Short Cut to Nirvana: Kumbh Mela* is one of the films that I worked on in PR and consulting capacities.

Q: For a typical film PR project, what materials would you need from the filmmaker to help raise awareness for the film?

SASHA BERMAN: A good press kit, photos, trailers, one-sheets — all of these materials are important for a theatrical release. On the set, photos are very important to have, so filmmakers should remember to have a photographer on the shoot.

Q: Is it possible for a smaller film, one that is either self-released or is being distributed by a boutique distributor, to get killer coverage in the major national media? If it is, what does it take to get the national media interested?

SASHA BERMAN: It helps if the film opens in more than one market. Since I do PR for New York and for Los Angeles, I find it easier to get national coverage when the film opens day-in-date in both markets. It is not easy to get TV coverage for "smaller" films, but if there is a political angle, or if there is a recognizable face in the film — that helps.

Q: You wore two hats, as publicist and distributor, for Greg Pak's acclaimed feature Robot Stories. *What inspired you to try your hand at distribution?*

SASHA BERMAN: Having worked in distribution, I knew what it takes to release a film theatrically, and I was ready to try that on my own. When I met Greg Pak, he and I got along so well, and I liked his film so much, that it made sense for us to do this together.

Q: Robot Stories *was a small film from a filmmaker who at the time was not very well known. What was your PR strategy for this production? And also, what was the distribution strategy for the film?*

SASHA BERMAN: *Robot Stories* was unique in that it appealed to an Asian American audience, to sci-fi enthusiasts, and to the general art crowd. We opened the film in New York at the Cinema Village and had a hugely successful week. Partially, the film's success in New York was due to all the great press that the film received, and partially it was due to all the grass roots marketing that was done on that film. When your budget is limited — as was the case with *Robot Stories* — grass roots becomes incredibly important. Since we knew who our target audience was, we were able to go after them very effectively.

photo courtesy Shotwell Media

Greg Pak in a scene from his feature Robot Stories. "We opened the film in New York at the Cinema Village and had a hugely successful week," says publicist / distributor Sasha Berman. "Partially, the film's success in New York was due to all the great press that the film received, and partially it was due to all the grassroots marketing that was done on that film."

Q: What professional advice can you give to a filmmaker who receives an uncommonly brutal review? Should the filmmaker respond, in any way, to the critic?

SASHA BERMAN: As hard as it might be, the filmmaker has to believe that the review represents just one person's opinion. It must be very painful to see your film torn to pieces by a critic, but try to walk away from it. When you are brave enough to create something personal, you are putting yourself in a vulnerable position, and that takes guts.

Q: From your work in film PR, what has been your greatest success and your greatest challenge?

SASHA BERMAN: My greatest challenge has been to learn not to take the rejection personally. Because I believe so strongly in the film that I am representing, and because a magazine or a newspaper is not able or not willing to give this film as much coverage as I feel it deserves and needs, I still try as hard as I can to get as much as possible. But if the answer is a no, it is not a personal rejection, nor is it necessarily a rejection of the film — it is just the nature of the business.

What inspires me to continue working in this business is the quality of films and incredible filmmakers and actors that I am lucky enough to meet and to work with.

My greatest success, in terms of a film's recognition, has to be *Nowhere in Africa* — when that film won the Oscar for the Best Foreign-Language Film, I felt very proud to be a part of its success in the United States.

A personal aside: Sasha Berman's good fortune in working on the PR campaigns for great films reminds me of my work in film publicity, where I often found myself being presented with films that were at the other end of the quality spectrum. One rep for a particular cinematic atrocity asked if I could mount a winning PR campaign for his wreck of a movie. My response: "I'm a publicist, not an alchemist!"

❧

THE MEDIA

The media can be a friend to an up-and-coming filmmaker, provided that writers and editors and producers are treated as friends. The one main benefit of being a filmmaker with a DIY approach to public relations is being able to have direct contact with members of the media. Nate Towne notes this might even be a blessing in disguise: "If you are just starting out and money is scarce, you're likely better off being your own publicist. You'll likely learn more about your industry as a whole, including the media outlets involved, and you'll also be building one-on-one relationships with journalists who cover your particular specialty."

There is a wide variety of factors that determine media coverage. Even veteran filmmakers who are well known in their genre find that coverage for each new offering is not guaranteed. Berkeley, California-based Antero Alli has almost given up on trying to make sense of this unpredictability.

"Some years, I cannot get any coverage in my own home-town while a thousand miles away three papers are writing stories about my upcoming shows," he comments. "Another year, it's just the reverse! Media can be such a fickle beast. Who can say what success is attributed to or how? Is it the mood of a particular critic the night they sit down to pen their review? Or a sudden tightening in the national security agenda that escalates the fear quotient in people to rush toward escapist entertainment? Since all my work is counter-mainstream in its values, aesthetics, and themes, my kind of success also runs against the grain of any mainstream idea of success. My kind of success as an underground filmmaker is remaining true to my vision and seeing that vision reach others. To me success is totally subjective and amounts to making the movie I want to make and sharing that vision with kindred souls or those adventurous enough to venture away from the hub and to the outer fringes of culture and human consciousness."

But remember this: If your film is not set for theatrical release, there is a good chance the mainstream print and broadcast media will not cover it. Don't take it personally. These media outlets have a finite amount of coverage slots and their priority has to go to films that are in release or that are coming to theaters in the very near future.

However, some genre-specific media (especially documentaries, horror, and sci-fi) will give coverage to films not in release. Some online media will also provide reviews, most notably *Film Threat*, *eFilmCritic.com*, and *Movie-Gurus*.

Media relating to independent filmmaking is also an excellent target for press coverage. *MovieMaker* magazine, *Filmmaker, The Independent*, and *Micro-Film* are well-regarded publications that serve this orbit. Broadcasting has traditionally been unreceptive to smaller films in limited or zero release, but the relatively new field of podcasting has been welcoming. New Jersey–based filmmaker Chris Cavallari created his own weekly program on low-budget independent filmmaking called *The Martini Shot* in early 2005 (but no longer online). Cavallari came to podcasting in a rather roundabout way.

"I had heard about podcasting from a friend back in January 2005, and I was intrigued by this new medium," he recalls. "I had wanted to do a video blog for some time but wasn't comfortable with being in front of the camera. I'm a behind-the-scenes kind of guy. Podcasting offered the solution. I had all the equipment necessary to do a basic podcast, so I gave it a shot. I knew I wanted to talk about something related to one of my hobbies, whether mountain biking, photography, or filmmaking. I decided film-making would be a great topic to talk about, and I had plenty to say. It also gave me an excuse to watch more movies, write more scripts, make more movies, and learn more about the craft. Almost all the podcasts I saw in the directories were movie review shows; there wasn't really a good resource in the podcasting world that gave people information on how to really make a movie using low-budget, indie-style techniques."

Cavallari hoped *The Martini Shot* would inspire and educate his filmmaker audience. "I would like this show to light the way for those people who have the will, the desire, and the tenacity to make their own movie but who don't necessarily know where to begin," he says. "Making a movie, no matter how small, is very difficult, time-consuming work, and it takes a certain kind of person to do it. I want the people who have the tenacity and the ambition to make a good movie to know that the resources they need to get started are right at their fingertips. Everything is very accessible these days, with digital video becoming a vi-able filmmaking tool. There will be a lot of garbage out there because of this, so I want listeners to be able to learn from their mistakes and refine their style until it becomes great. I also want my listeners to be able to learn from the professionals. My goal is to get professional filmmakers from around the world to offer their tips, tricks, and insights on the filmmaking business. These guys are almost always very open and engaging, and they offer a wealth of knowledge that has always inspired me in my career. The people I've met inspire me to persevere in an otherwise grueling and highly competitive business."

Podcasting is not strictly an indie domain — Hollywood found it during 2005, and even the notorious Paris Hilton in-vaded the technology to promote her Tinseltown effort *House of Wax*. But Cavallari believes podcasting will not only survive Paris Hilton's intrusion, but help to build buzz and excitement among the indie community.

"I think there are many *possibilities* with podcasting," he says. "Like the Web for the folks who made *The Blair Witch Project*, podcasting offers a new kind of viral marketing. Sneak peeks, behind-the-scenes on-set "soundseeing" tours, interviews with cast and crew, or audio plogs (production blogs) are all possibilities. In fact, on my show I have a production journal segment where I document my progress on a short movie I'm making. If it's entertaining enough, people will listen, and as any marketing exec will tell you, if it strikes a reaction, people will talk. As of right now, the medium is wide open for creative people to come in and exploit it — whether that's a good or a bad thing, I don't know. Shows like *The Martini Shot* encourage filmmakers to be guests, or send emails, or call the comment line, to plug their flick. I want those good films to be seen, so I open the format up to just about anyone who has something to show. I don't just let them plug and hang up; they have to come on and talk about the movie. We want to know everything about it: how it was made, for how much, what camera, where'd you get the lights, how you would finagle the food from the deli down the street... everything! It can, however, be difficult for a filmmaker to create their own podcast for the purpose of promoting a film. I'm not saying they shouldn't, but podcasting is a time-consuming and somewhat complicated pursuit. If the proper resources are allotted to it, the podcast for a movie can be another great marketing tool, a way to reach more people. The problem is, you have to come up with new, innovative, and most importantly interesting programming for it. Otherwise, it's a waste of time, and people — especially podcast purists — will be very turned off by it. For example, the Paris Hilton podcast for *House of Wax* got trashed by every podcaster and listener I know. What she said had nothing to do with the movie."

Now let's remember what was said earlier — you know, about treating the media as a friend? But what happens when the media doesn't act like a friend? How can you respond to a bad review, unsatisfactory coverage, or no coverage whatsoever? There are a number of ways this can be approached. "If I'm a new filmmaker and I receive a terrible review, naturally I'm going to be upset," says James Kendrick, editor for the *QNetwork Film Desk*. "Who really wants to receive a terrible review? As far as contacting the critic, I think that's fine, as long as the filmmaker is interested in engaging in genuine dialogue, not just shooting back to 'get even.' Critics aren't necessarily always right — not that you heard that from me — but neither are filmmakers, and I think both are in the position to learn from each other. If a filmmaker is going to contact a critic, especially if the filmmaker is a neophyte, he or she needs to be open to the idea that he or she might actually learn something from the critic. He or she should certainly feel secure in defending his or her work, especially if he or she genuinely thinks the critic is off base, but it should be done in the spirit of dialogue, not verbal attacks, especially when done over email, where people sometimes gain in courage far and beyond what they lack in discipline."

Nate Towne offers this view from his publicist's perspective: "One of the pitfalls in being an artist is the fact that others, no matter how hard you try, will not appreciate your work. Negative reviews from critics and journalists, especially those you've worked so hard to obtain, can be incredibly painful and soul-withering. However, as an artist, one must be prepared for some constructive criticism — often delivered in acerbic savagery for entertainment purposes. The best advice is to read every painful word, do your best to glean the nuggets of wisdom for said advice, and to retain a clipping of the review for your files. (Always keep a copy of good and bad reviews; however, resist putting the negative reviews into your press kit if at all possible.) As painful as it may be to hear, the best response to a critic is to thank them for their time and ask them if you can approach them with future story or film pitches. It's possible they've said some hateful things about your work, but press is press — this is what you're after. Politely respond to their attentions, feed off the experience by using the information to make your next work better, and you'll likely win the respect — if not the favor — of the journalist going forward. If this is not possible, remind yourself you are an artist, while they merely reflect on others' art, so ultimately, you win."

Kent Turner, editor for *Film-Forward.com*, has this opinion: "Unless there are errors or wild misinterpretations within the review, I don't think it's necessary for the filmmaker to respond to the reviewer, whether the critique was a pan or a rave. Why try to convince or change the mind of the reviewer? It's a matter of opinion. By responding, a director probably will come across as being defensive, angry, and/or desperate. I think the best bet is to take the slams as well as the praises with equanimity, whether you're a director, writer, actor, etc."

And Ed Gonzalez, editor at *Slant* magazine, provides this advice: "Having been on the receiving end of an incredibly nasty and personal attack from a director whose first feature was a surprise hit several years ago, it's probably safe to say that it's much harder for an aspiring or first-time director to cope with poor press coverage. I'm sure many of them feel as if they only have one shot at breaking into the film industry and a barrage of negative criticism for their first project validates their worst fear: that they may not be cut out for this line of work. While I don't think there's any one way of responding to this kind of criticism — in the end, it's probably best to keep mum — I imagine it's probably a good idea to learn from the experience and use it to grow as an artist. Then again, if the film is a commercial success in spite of the critical lambasting, what's going to stop a film-maker from repeating the same mistakes? God knows Michael Bay would make films differently if audiences didn't consistently validate their crapitude!"

Perhaps the best advice for filmmakers to follow in regard to bad reviews is to remember the fact that no film will please everyone. Antero Alli recognized this and shrugged it off after the now-defunct *Amazing World of Cult Movies* dismissed his 1995 feature *The Drivetime* as "a silly mess" and called Alli a "ninny."

"Though I often remind myself that any review is only one person's opinion, harsh reviews always hurt," says Alli. "What are you going to do? Stop reading all your reviews? That's just more self-stabbing victim bullshit. Why not pick up some objectivity and identify the bias of the reviewer just to see where they are coming from. Just for fun. When I do this, it's understandable why the *Amazing World of Cult Movies* calls me a 'ninny' and my movie a 'silly mess.' That's very funny. If I were as cynical and jaded as them, I'd probably say the same thing. To confound things, *The Drivetime* was also given glowing reviews by *Wired* magazine, the *Pacific Film Archive* and the *NW Film Forum*, and these guys didn't even call me names. Of course, their bias and outlook are, for the better part, already more aligned with my own. And I like that. If they had trashed my movie, I'd probably feel more hurt than by the cynic who called me a ninny. For me, the best reviews are instructive and these are very, very rare. Most film critics have seen too many movies and suffer imagination loss, in addition to having weakened their critical judgment for constructive praise. That's a mouthful. The worst reviews must be the most indifferent reviews and, knock on wood, I've not seen one for my work yet."

photo courtesy SRS Cinema LLC

The recently deceased return to the Big Easy in Zombie! vs. Mardi Gras. *Co-director Mike Lyddon's approach to fielding negative reviews is borderline insouciant: "Ah, we deal with morons every day, and this is no exception."*

Mike Lyddon takes an even more insouciant approach. The co-director of the 1999 feature *Zombie! vs. Mardi Gras*, Lyddon saw Lawrence Van Gelder of the *New York Times* barbecue his film as "sluggish and starved for style and originality." And that was among the more positive reviews! Several critics actually named *Zombie! vs. Mardi Gras* the worst film ever made.

Lyddon's response: "Ah, we deal with morons every day, and this is no exception."

PROFESSIONAL RESOURCES

Filmmaking is, ultimately, a collaborative effort involving a small community of artists and technicians. Many independent filmmakers can find invaluable information, connections, and support (professional, emotional, and perhaps even financial) by taking advantage of the many motion picture industry resources available to them.

A full listing of such resources can take up a book unto itself, so for the sake of editorial consideration we'll just focus on the best places to be heard and to listen.

The Internet spans geographical boundaries, thus making it the natural place to begin. The best online resource for anyone in the indie film world is *Rotten Tomatoes* (*www.rottentomatoes.com*). Don't let the strange name fool you — the harvest of knowledge and communications you can reap from its online forums is peerless.

All of the nation's major film journalists are part of the *Rotten Tomatoes* database. Going back to the previous section regarding the media, this would be the best place to find out which critics would be most supportive of an up-and-coming filmmaker.

"The success of independent films tends to be review-driven," explains Senh Duong, the *Rotten Tomatoes* founder and director of design and production. "Because independent filmmakers and their distributors usually don't have much of a marketing budget, a lot of it is based on word of mouth. The starting point for that is usually getting their films reviewed by critics from local and national papers, online sites, TV, and/or radio. From that, they can potentially reach millions of moviegoers relatively cheaply, and if the reviews are good, word of mouth will spread from there. *Rotten Tomatoes* is a great place to, sort of, get to know the critics. We have thousands of critics listed in our database. They are categorized by source, media type — print, online, broadcast — region, and film association/group. Because critics, in general, watch hundreds of films a year, it's probably a good idea to read their reviews and see what makes a quality film in their eyes. Critics also tend to attract various marketing groups, so they could be a great resource to learn how other independent studios/filmmakers market their films. *Rotten Tomatoes* also has a Critics Discussion forum, so it's a good place to take part in discussions with film critics who may possibly be reviewing an aspiring filmmaker's film someday. In addition to all of the critics-related features, there are other features on *Rotten Tomatoes* that can help aspiring filmmakers gain a greater

```
    #600   12-27-2012 3:06PM
 Item(s) checked out to p10101275.

ARCODE: 31232001050501
ITLE: Positively fifth street [sound re
UE DATE: 01-17-13

ARCODE: 31232004286318
ITLE: Independent film distribution : h
UE DATE: 01-17-13

ARCODE: 31232003260140
ITLE: The Stanley Kubrick archives
UE DATE: 01-17-13

ARCODE: 31232001464702
ITLE: Killer poker hold'em handbook : a
UE DATE: 01-17-13


       Skokie Public Library
   Renew by phone: 847-673-2675
```

knowledge of the industry. They can read up on the latest news and happenings from Hollywood on our recently launched news section; check out what films are popular with the general public on the box office page; watch the latest trailers; look up info — synopses, credits, production notes, movie stills — for particular movies; and discuss films with other aspiring filmmakers in the forums. Sometimes, a film professional like Jeff Vintar, screenwriter of *I, Robot*, would hop onto his forum on *Rotten Tomatoes* and discuss the film and the process of making the film with the users. Through blogging, groups, and social-networking features, aspiring filmmakers can create a journal, keep in touch with other aspiring filmmakers, and create or join a filmmaking-specific group."

The distribution company Film Movement is involved in the Virtual Producer's Lab on *Rotten Tomatoes*. Stephen Wang, vice president and publisher of *Rotten Tomatoes* (which is part of IGN Entertainment), notes the popularity of this particular online resource: "The Virtual Producer's Lab is our forum for aspiring independent filmmakers. Initially, the forum was set up in participation with Larry Meistrich (producer of *Slingblade* and *You Can Count on Me*) at Film Movement in an effort to connect these filmmakers with experienced producers who have a long and successful history in the independent film movement. *Rotten Tomatoes* was initially a sponsor of Larry's original Shooting Gallery series and we wanted to support his continued efforts to highlight previously undistributed independent works. As a consequence, *Rotten Tomatoes* set up a forum in September 2002 where these filmmakers could interact with one another as well as with Larry and other filmmakers that were a part of Film Movement. Since that time, the forum has grown into its own self-organized community of filmmakers with over 1,600 members contributing to the dialogue. They provide both artistic and nuts-and-bolts production tips to one another as well as share their independent works. At the current time, the VPL members are self-organizing an online film festival with several dozen self-produced works. They also semi-regularly hold online screenwriting competitions as a method of receiving constructive input on their works. In total, I believe the Virtual Producer's Lab has achieved the initial goal of providing a viable online community for aspiring filmmakers to receive help from one another."

Wang notes that *Rotten Tomatoes'* popularity continues to grow, attracting film professionals and movie lovers alike. "*Rotten Tomatoes* is host to the most active community of movie fans online in our forums," he says. "In the forums, we have around 200,000 members who contribute vigorous discussion in many separate organic communities. One thing we learned early on when we established the forums was that our forum members tended to 'self-tribalize' into their own organic small groups. These groups would form on their own based on interest and movie tastes and provide tribes of several dozen members each. Interestingly enough, many of these tribes crossed regions or even languages and countries, providing true virtual communities that would not have existed without the benefit of the forums. In fact, many of these tribes would even go as far as to have semiofficial 'clan names' and rosters to differentiate themselves from other clans."

The Internet is rich with many online forum discussion groups, blogs, and communities relating to film production issues. Many, like *Rotten Tomatoes*, do not require paid registration. Forums can be located within online magazines such as *Film Threat* (*www.filmthreat.com*) and *IndieWire* (*www.indiewire.com*) and within generalized websites relating to specific communities, such as *The D-Word* for documentary filmmakers (*www.d-word.com*), *B-Movie.com* for low-budget filmmakers specializing in horror flicks, and *StudentFilms.com* for those still in the academic portion of their lives. Several independent filmmakers also have their own forums within their websites, most notably Peter John Ross (*www.sonnyboo.com*) and Greg Pak (who runs forums on his *GregPak.com* website and also edits *FilmHelp.com* and *AsianAmericanFilm.com*). Michael Wiese Productions, the publisher of this book, also has an online community for filmmakers at *www.mwp.com/forums/*.

Be aware, however, that many online forums bring out both the worst and the best in people. The best in people includes important tips, observations, and commentary relating to the film world. The worst, however, runs the sorry gamut from rude remarks and name-calling to sad attempts by perpetual malcontents to pick fights with everyone around them. It is easy to lose one's temper with the latter group of people, but too many people become impatient too early and drop out of forum discussions right after joining them. Be patient, stay focused, and do not allow yourself to get baited into nasty forum fights — or as they say in many forums, do not feed the trolls.

The film world is not lacking in professional associations and trade organizations. Some of these offer their own publications, others have festivals and seminars, and all have an online presence. Among the most prominent in the industry today are the American Film Institute (*www.afi.com*), the Association of Independent Feature Film Producers (*www.aiffp.org*), the Association of Independent Video and Filmmakers (*www.aivf.org*), the Directors Guild of America (*www.directorsguild.org*), the Filmmakers Alliance (*www.filmmakersalliance.com*), the Independent Feature Project (*www.ifp.org*), the National Alliance for Media Arts and Culture (*www.namac.org*), the Producers Guild of America (*www.producersguild.org*), the Screenwriters Guild of America (*www.sga.org*) and the Writers Guild of America (*www.wga.org*).

Furthermore, there are organizations relating to specific demographic groups, such as the American Indian Film Institute (*www.aifi.org*) and CineWomen New York (*www.cinewomenny.com*). Even historic film archives provide a much-needed sense of community for specific demographic groups who have been traditionally overlooked or excluded from mainstream cinema.

"As a repository of black film history and culture, the Black Film Center/Archive is a valuable resource primarily for scholars, but also for filmmakers who are interested in knowing more about their predecessors and their contributions to the filmic arts," says Audrey T. McCluskey, director of the Black Film Center/Archive at Indiana University. "Early examples of black detective films and the beginnings of the race uplift films can be explored and researched at our facility. We welcome one and all!"

Many state and municipal film offices provide seminars and special educational gatherings for local filmmakers. Film societies and regional film festivals often host year-round special screenings and discussions. These can provide a fine opportunity to preview works in progress or to get audience screenings of works prior to their submission to major festivals or distributors. This is not only in major markets, but smaller regional settings as well. For example, Delaware-area filmmakers can take advantage of the Rehoboth Beach Film Society's many activities beyond its annual festival.

"The Rehoboth Beach Film Society sponsors several year-round film initiatives," says Sue Early, managing director of Delaware's Rehoboth Beach Independent Film Festival. "Monthly screenings of independent films are held on the fourth Thursday of the months September–June. The Film Society co-sponsors the Independent Focus Series with the Movies at Midway. RBFS recommends an independent film to be featured as part of the theater's regular film lineup and then assists with promoting the screenings through various advertising strategies. RBFS members are eligible for a discounted admission on the first day's screenings for each film."

Microcinemas can be a wonderful resource for connecting with audiences eager to seek out alternative film experiences. "There are a lot of small theaters, bars, clubs, and schools that would love to show an independent film," says Oscar-nominated filmmaker Bill Plympton. "It helps if the filmmaker accompanies the film. You won't get rich, but you'll spread the word and make a few bucks."

Many microcinemas host touring film programs. Typical of this resource is *minicine?* (yes, it is spelled in bold print and italics!), a Shreveport, Louisiana–based operation run by an architect and cinephile named David Nelson. With local and touring offerings ranging from The Super Super 8 Film Festival to archivist Bill Taylor's hilarious collection of vintage antigay "educational" films entitled "Lock Up Your Sons & Daughters" to multimedia presentations by artists including Luis Recoder, *minicine?* has offered a startling mix of alternative cinematic considerations to Shreveport audiences (who, truth be told, rarely get anything in the way of alternative cinematic considerations). The *minicine?* folks have found themselves and their films in such locations as galleries, coffee shops, and vacant buildings. Well-known filmmakers such as Craig Baldwin (*Sonic Outlaws*) have paid a visit to this microcinema.

"We are all about creating an environment for artist-audience interaction," says David Nelson. "Shreveport is too small and isolated to have an indie film scene, but there are a handful of people here who are into the essence of handmade film, experimental film, self-made narrative film. These are the volunteers who operate our venue or are key supporters."

And who has Nelson attracted? "Our audience is primarily artists, musicians, filmmakers, lots of arts people. Shows average 40 but have been up to 1,000, depending. While we host mostly touring DIY filmmakers for public shows, often we have 'after hours' when the more-interested audience members retire to a separate space to break out what they have been working on to share with the visiting filmmakers. The visiting filmmakers often pull out work not part of their public screening."

THE LAWYER

In the event you are able to receive a contract from a distributor, do not sign anything until the contract is thoroughly reviewed by a lawyer specializing in entertainment-related law. Tommy Lee Thomas cites legal counsel as being a crucial element for any indie endeavor. "Get a good lawyer," he says. "Without a good attorney, you will most certainly get taken to the cleaners."

But where can a filmmaker without a lawyer find one? Jordan Hiller, who wears two hats as a film journalist/editor (for the online magazine *Bang It Out*) and as an attorney (for the New York firm Tell, Cheser & Breitbart) offers this trenchant advice:

"A filmmaker seeking to have a contract reviewed, whether from a distributor or any other party while making a film, needs a lawyer proficient in contracts," says Hiller. "As is common knowledge, there are many kinds of contracts and a filmmaker wouldn't want to take his business to a lawyer specializing in marital or corporate contracts. Thankfully, there is an entire field of law called entertainment law. Entertainment lawyers deal with these types of contracts every day and would be able to look out for their client and assure no advantage would be taken by the distributor. There are many firms that hold themselves out to be entertainment-law firms and most large firms have entertainment-law divisions. It is perhaps better for a first-time or less-affluent filmmaker to find a smaller firm specializing in entertainment law so they will not need to pay top dollar for the same service. As far as choosing a firm or lawyer, the best way to choose a firm is the best way to choose a plumber or a dentist — referrals. Talk to friends and colleagues who have been through the ordeal and see which lawyer or firm has the best local reputation for taking care of small, independent filmmakers. The other ways to find entertainment-law firms in your area are by simple search engine searches on the Web, or try the site *Martindale.com* and use its lawyer locator, and search by 'area and practice.' From there, choose your state and city and you're on your way."

THE SOMEONE WHO KNOWS SOMEONE WHO...

Of course, there are situations where one might find a way into commercial release thanks to the good fortune of knowing someone, or knowing someone who knows someone. Producer/ actor Tommy Lee Thomas made his first sale of his 2000 action thriller *Proverbial Justice* to foreign markets thanks to a pal who packed plenty of muscle, in more ways than one. "I made an agreement with Westar Entertainment, which was owned and operated by a friend of mine, Franco Columbu, the two-time Mr. Olympia and one of Arnold Schwarzenegger's best friends," he recalls. "Franco set up Westar Entertainment to be an honest distributor that handles not only his own films, such as *Ancient Warriors*, but also films like mine that might not have otherwise been given any opportunity in the marketplace."

Likewise, Judy Irving was able to see her 2005 documentary *The Wild Parrots of Telegraph Hill* into theatrical release based on well-connected word-of-mouth praise and advice. "Mike Getz, who runs a movie theater in Nevada City, heard about the film from his friend Gary Snyder — Snyder, a Pulitzer Prize–winning poet, had written a blurb for Mike's memoir. Mike suggested seven likely distributors, including Shadow Distribution. I sent all seven info about the film after it had been in the San Francisco Film Festival and had gotten some good reviews. Several responded, two made offers, and after consulting with filmmakers and relying again on intuition, I went with Ken Eisen at Shadow."

For James Fotopoulos, an invitation to a party ultimately led to Facets Video releasing three of his features on DVD. "I was at an after party for a screening a friend of mine was having," he says. "While I was there the man that was the video coordinator of the Facets label approached me and asked me to send those titles to him. I did and two days later he called and said they wanted to release the films on their label."

BUT THEN AGAIN…

However, this is not to say that an unsolicited inquiry will go unnoticed. Greg Ross at Go-Kart Films has no problems in receiving submissions out of the blue.

"We are open to unsolicited inquiries," says Ross, adding with deadpan humor: "Basically, we watch everything — we have no lives."

photo courtesy Shadow Distribution

The eponymous stars of Judy Irving's documentary The Wild Parrots of Telegraph Hill. *"Mike Getz, who runs a movie theater in Nevada City, heard about the film from his friend Gary Snyder — a Pulitzer Prize–winning poet who had written a blurb for Mike's memoir," recalls Irving "Mike suggested seven likely distributors, including Shadow Distribution. I sent all seven info about the film after it had been in the San Francisco Film Festival and had gotten some good reviews. Several responded, two made offers, and after consulting with filmmakers and relying again on intuition, I went with Ken Eisen at Shadow."*

ALBERT LAI, PARTNER AND COO, MATSON FILMS

Breaking into the film distribution business is no mean feat, especially if the distributor is a smaller company lacking the deep pockets of a Disney or Dreamworks. But with a lot of imagination and spirit, a distributor can strike gold — especially if the gold mining takes place on the Internet.

For its first release, Matson Films brought the British biopic *It's All Gone Pete Tong* to the American market. The film is a comic mockumentary focusing on Frankie Wilde, a faux-legendary coke-fueled DJ on the European club scene who keeps at his craft despite going deaf. World-famous DJs including Pete Tong, Carl Cox, Lol Hammond, and Paul van Dyk appear in the film as well.

To connect the film with its potential American audience, start-up distributor Matson Films put a heavy emphasis on Internet marketing. It seems like every film has some degree of Internet presence, but few have pursued the Internet with such tenacity as the U.S. release of *It's All Gone Pete Tong*. For aspiring distributors or filmmakers seeking to self-distribute their work, the Matson experience is more than required reading.

Q: It's All Gone Pete Tong *was the first film for Matson Films, and how did it come about?*

ALBERT LAI: We saw the film after it screened at the 2004 Toronto Film Festival, where it received the City Award. After screening it again in New York City, we realized the potential of the film — which eventually received Best Picture and Best Actor at the U.S. Comedy Arts Festival and the Grand Jury and Audience Award at the Gen Art Film Festival — and also the challenges of marketing and distributing the film.

In a nutshell, the film is a U.K. production by Canadian director Michael Dowse set in Ibiza about a DJ who loses his hearing. It's easy to try to classify the film as a mockumentary or a film about the disabled or a foreign film or a music film, but really we thought of it as a simple story of a man who rediscovers who he really is and what he truly values, with a romantic twist thrown in for good measure. The music and the deafness are used to enrich the fabric of the storytelling. With that in mind, we approached the producers with a marketing strategy that focused on expanding the story beyond the 90 minutes of the film. We wanted to shoot new content, use unused footage, and treat the marketing activities as a storytelling endeavor, whether it was traditional (e.g., TV spots, radio spots, print) or nontraditional (e.g., Internet, wild posting, postcards, promotional parties).

However, this strategy required the producers, director, and key cast members to agree to participate and to support us. It was only after our discussions with these individuals that we realized all of us had the same belief in how to bring this film to audiences, especially the need to tailor the marketing for U.S. audiences. About three weeks after we had first viewed the film, the deal was signed on a menu at Pravda in New York's SoHo neighborhood.

Q: *Many filmmakers still talk about* The Blair Witch Project *as the groundbreaking Internet-based marketing campaign. But that was back in 1999. How come there have not been other Internet-based film marketing campaigns of equivalent imagination — let alone results — since* Blair Witch?

ALBERT LAI: *The Blair Witch Project* came at a very unique time. The Internet boom was occurring and many people were just beginning to use the Internet not just for email but also for social and leisure activities. The film itself would not have been as interesting without the possibility that it was rooted in some element of truth. The Internet became an effective medium for propagating misinformation about the film in order to build a groundswell of interest. The challenge since then is that the industry tends to use tried-and-true models and has to deal with exhibitors and producers who also have fairly standard approaches for marketing and distribution. It's fairly rare to find a situation where all parties involved are willing to take a financial and marketing risk to use the Internet as a core mechanism for marketing.

We looked at all the Internet-based sites for our favorite films over the past five years and realized that they are practically all the same design, layout, and set of features. Most of these marketing campaigns use the Internet for a very defined set of informative needs: synopsis, trailer, cast, crew, and theater locations. Independent films tend to try more-unique approaches, but it remains difficult to convince people to spend dollars for extensive Internet marketing, beyond banner advertisements, when people more easily understand and accept the traditional media channels — television, radio, and print. From a logistics point of view, television, radio, and print are guaranteed channels of communication.

You can assume that a person in Kent, Ohio, will view the same 30-second spot as the person in Queens, New York, though one might be watching it on a 42-inch plasma while the other is watching it on a 27-inch tube. With the Internet, there are worries about operating systems, browsers, connection speeds, monitor sizes, audio capabilities, etc. that can render an experience completely different from one viewer to the next, and that's a major risk.

Q: What was the specific strategy designed to spread the word on It's All Gone Pete Tong *across the Internet? And how did you come up with this particular strategy?*

ALBERT LAI: From day one we realized that the context of the film, a DJ who lives and works in Ibiza, was a fairly foreign concept to people in the U.S. Even though dance music grew out of the U.S. — New York, Chicago, San Francisco — dance and rave really exploded in the U.K., Europe, and elsewhere. We needed to educate the audience so that they could, at least on a base level, relate to Frankie Wilde, since he is such an unlikable character.

Given the film covers a short period of Frankie's life, we felt it was necessary to provide context not just for Frankie, but for Max Haggar, his agent, Jack Stoddart and the record label, his Austrian bandmates Ladderhause, etc. We flew in the director and a number of the key cast members and filmed new content over a period of four days in New York City. This wasn't PR material; this was original content to help tell the story of Frankie Wilde beyond the film. No one we worked with had ever heard of doing this. We thought it would only give the viewer a better appreciation for the film before and after watching it in the theater. All this content was digitized and used in the websites that centered on the film and characters. We closely integrated the Internet campaign with promotional events and parties we had in New York, Los Angeles, and San Francisco. We had different posters and postcards that connected with each character. From an Internet perspective, we had people watch the film, and if they were excited, they helped us "spread the good word" on Internet sites.

We approached the Night Agency in New York (*www.night-agency.com*) to help ignite this push of reaching out to dozens upon dozens of Internet sites and feed the grassroots movement and build awareness and curiosity about the characters and the film. Before Matson Films, a partner and I at Transmission Films used P2P networks as a distribution mechanism and we are still proponents of using P2P as a means to legally disseminate material. Instead of fearing P2P and piracy, we encouraged people to share materials from the film and actively shared clips, Frankie Wilde's music, and even had *InternetDJ* show the first seven minutes of the film online.

Q: *There are a seemingly endless number of film review sites on the Internet. From a marketer's viewpoint, which ones are the most important to hit?*

ALBERT LAI: From a high-level perspective, it's unwise to ignore any film review sites. It's often seen negatively to "hold back" a film, whether it's from online or traditional reviewers. Positive reviews provide publicity and marketing opportunities, obviously, but even negative reviews help us understand what about the film resonates with viewers and whether the marketing should be repositioned. The difficult aspect is traditional advertising. Most people still identify with the traditional media brands: the *New York Times*, the *L.A. Times*, *Entertainment Weekly*, *USA Today*, the *Chicago Sun-Times*. While the indie community looks to *Ain't It Cool News* and *Film Threat* as the top review sites, the challenge for the distributor is how to present that information to the general public that doesn't read online reviews.

Q: Can a filmmaker do effective Internet marketing by himself or herself? Or is it beneficial to bring in a professional marketer to create and coordinate the Internet push?

ALBERT LAI: It's a challenge to do Internet marketing by yourself. The most effective technique is to think about the overall marketing strategy and decide how Internet marketing can be an effective means to communicate the message. I'm sure there are instances where the Internet may not be appropriate. We worked with a number of key partners, including the Night Agency and RTMooreDesign, but the most critical factors were support from the producers, director, and talent and integrating the Internet marketing into our other marketing activities.

Q: How has your Internet marketing for It's All Gone Pete Tong *affected the film's box office and industry buzz?*

ALBERT LAI: Our release in New York in April 2005 was very strong and we released it nationwide on May 13, 2005. The Internet has been crucial to generating buzz about the film to both industry and viewers. The most critical factor about the Internet campaign is that it can be modified relatively quickly, and near real-time statistics about usage can be obtained to help us understand awareness and what messages are working. Of course, the Internet as a repository for viewers' reactions is the ultimate test of the film. For better or for worse, the Internet marketing results in dialogue about the film, and as they say, there is no such thing as bad press.

❧

LISTEN TO WHAT THE MAN SAYS

Fine. Now how does all of this apply to you? Well, let's consider what we learned....

1. The film world is a collaborative effort. As filmmaking involves the combined talents of many people working for a single goal, the selling of a film to a distributor is also a joint project. If you think you can do it all by your lonesome self, then you are being foolish.

2. Whatever you do, never bad-mouth anyone who declines to assist you. No one respects a person who maligns others, and talking trash about industry experts will not enhance your artistic or commercial viability. Keep the nasty comments to yourself — in public, be polite and professional.

3. The story about the gay cop who was accidentally responsible for the chain of events that resulted in the release of *The Art of Amalia* might be the funniest story in this chapter, but Ryan Dacko's story of his attempt to gain a foothold in Hollywood is actually the most relevant. Go back and read it again. Dacko wisely learned from the mistake he made and expressed no malice to those who were not receptive to his faux pas. You can learn from Dacko's example and his aftermath professional behavior. If you are going to work with someone like a producer's rep and a publicist, work *with* them. This means the following: If they require specific materials (press kits, stills, screeners), have them available. If you are needed to make the rounds for meetings, screenings, or conference calls, be there. From personal example, I once publicized a small indie film with a New York opening. I needed the filmmaker to be available for interviews, but the filmmaker decided he'd rather be skiing in Colorado than answering press questions in New York. Not surprisingly, his film received a much,

much lower level of media coverage than it would have enjoyed if he'd bothered to cooperate with the PR effort.

4. The PR push is a Sisyphus-worthy task for many indie films because the filmmaker is usually an unknown and there are rarely any name talents in the cast or crew. But this can be overcome by having in-depth strategy sessions with the publicist to identify imaginative story lines that the media would be interested in pursuing.

5. Do *not*, under any circumstance, get into a pissing contest with journalists. You will never win. At the very least, you will be ignored. At worst, you will earn their wrath and it can color the tone of coverage you may receive. And do not try to get bad reviews withdrawn. I once gave a negative review to a documentary and the filmmaker's wife (who claimed to be the producer of the movie) made false and borderline-libelous claims that I had a personal vendetta against her husband. This silly woman even went so far as to attempt to have my review taken off the *Rotten Tomatoes* database, which was totally without precedent. Needless to say, my review (which was actually one of many, many bad reviews) remained in print and in the *Rotten Tomatoes* database. And the angry woman only succeeded in making herself and her husband look like idiots.

THE HARD AND BITTER TRUTH ABOUT FESTIVALS

There is always order in the distant view. No matter how strange the happening, it can never project from the frame, from the order which this distant view possesses.
— Kobo Abe

In an article that appeared in the *New York Times* on January 16, 2005, Adam Leipzig (the president of National Geographic Feature Films) cited there were "at least 2,500 film festivals around the world." Leipzig also noted that one of the most prestigious of the 2,500 festivals, the Sundance Film Festival, harvested inquiries from 2,613 feature films for its 2005 edition. That's a 29% rise from the 2,023 submitted to Sundance in 2004. But out of the 2,613 features bidding for screen time in Utah, only 120 films (fewer than 5% of the total submissions) made it to the Sundance screens.

These numbers are clearly depressing on a variety of levels. Not only is there a glut of movies in circulation today, there is also a glut of festivals. But when it comes to the biggest film festival in America, Sundance, the chances of getting out of the slush pile and into the program is more than a little tough.

And still, festivals continue to attract aspiring filmmakers. Even the smallest and most obscure festivals have no problems finding filmmakers to share their wares. But can the festival circuit genuinely help new filmmakers get that proverbial foot in the door? The answer is a solid and unqualified... maybe.

THE VIEW FROM YESTERDAY

First, let's get a brief idea of where this situation came from. The first film festival was the brainchild of an unlikely source: Benito

Mussolini, the Italian dictator who was more famous for his bad politics than good taste. *Il Duce*, however, was smart enough to cull the favors of those with more talent than he possessed, and in 1938 he inaugurated the Venice Film Festival. From the very beginning, there was controversy: The first film ever honored at Venice was Leni Riefenstahl's *Olympia*, a three-and-half-hour documentary celebrating the 1936 Berlin Olympics. Many people felt that a tilt toward Mussolini's pals in Germany, and grumbling of a fixed vote to swing the honors to the German epic, left a sour residue among the participants at the event.

The French, not surprisingly, felt they could do better and decided to launch their own film festival at Cannes the following year. Alas, the day of the festival's premiere was September 1, 1939. The Germans, who clearly had other agendas to pursue outside the film world, took their cameras and their guns to the Polish border that day. Cannes was canned (trivia alert: The first film that was supposed to be screened was the RKO version of *The Hunchback of Notre Dame*) and Europe fell into a rather messy war.

The festivals returned after the war, with Cannes and Venice competing for attention. Again, the situation was political rather than cinematic: France wanted to use the festival to re-establish itself as the capital of European filmmaking (postwar France was drowning in American imports), while the Italians wanted to regain national pride after the humiliation of the war.

The notion that a festival could actually launch a film and a career didn't take root until the 1951 Venice festival, when Akira Kurosawa's *Rashomon* was shown. Ironically, the film was not meant to be seen in Venice: The Japanese delegation to the festival was deadlocked on which film to submit and picked Kurosawa's effort as a compromise. *Rashomon* created a sensation, launching Kurosawa as the first world-recognized Japanese filmmaker and (in a major way) helping to reintegrate postwar Japan into the family of nations. The Venice buzz was so powerful that *Rashomon* was picked up for U.S. release by RKO Pictures, making it the first time a Hollywood studio acquired a film at a festival (not to mention making it the very first non-English production released in America by a studio).

The following year, Cannes had its own moment of discovery when Orson Welles snagged top honors for his self-financed Moroccan-based film version of *Othello*. Having been in self-exile from Hollywood since the debacle of the 1948 version of *Macbeth*, Welles used the Cannes festival to reestablish himself as a force of artistic power, and Cannes actually breathed new life into Welles' struggling career.

Americans did not initially need to have their own festivals. After all, Hollywood dominated the world movie business and independent filmmaking was too marginalized to have any genuine impact via a festival presentation. The first U.S. festival was in San Francisco in 1957. Other festivals followed, most notably the New York Film Festival in 1962, but mostly these festivals were designed to bring global cinema to America rather than encourage American independent filmmakers.

Sundance began in 1978 as the United States Film Festival. Robert Redford's Sundance Institute took over operations in 1984, switching the festival's name and expanding the selection of unreleased independent films in its lineup. The Redford star power gave Sundance more attention than it previously possessed and, as previously discussed, the 1989 presentation of *sex, lies, and videotape* made Sundance the top American festival.

Over the years, Sundance would be the site of many highly publicized, high-dollar acquisitions: *The Brothers McMullen*, *The Blair Witch Project*, *Open Water*, and *Napoleon Dynamite* got their distribution deals at Sundance. But over time, Sundance began to attract more films than it could ever show. Furthermore, the festival began to incorporate higher-tier films with big-name stars that already had distribution deals in place. Filmmakers with dreams of getting noticed at Sundance found themselves facing a rude reality with films such as *The Butterfly Effect* starring Ashton Kutcher guaranteed a spot at Sundance.

Some filmmakers decided to one-up Sundance by creating parallel festivals that took place around the Sundance location in Park City, Utah. Slamdance, started in 1995, was the first and quickly became the biggest of the bunch: Within five years it fielded 2,050 features for consideration. Slamdunk, No Dance, and Tromadance followed, but they have yet to reach Slamdance's level of popularity (let alone Sundance's).

Meanwhile, during this time other festivals began to either start up or to give a new push to gain cred with the film scene. Among the most notable have been the Telluride Film Festival, which began somewhat quietly in 1974 but which picked up steam in the 1990s with the world premieres of such influential films as Robert Rodriguez's *El Mariachi* and Michael Moore's *Roger and Me*; and *South by Southwest* (*SXSW*), which launched in 1994 and quickly became a major force by attracting both the finest in contemporary independent films and the most prominent filmmakers themselves for appearances in panel discussions.

THE VIEW FROM TODAY

But these gems are just the major attractions in the annual festival circuit. Indeed, the quantity of festivals is staggering. Almost every major city has its own festival, and in one case a city with no cinemas even has a festival named for it (the Atlantic City Film Festival, which is actually held in neighboring towns). There are also endless niche festivals covering a variety of film genres and demographics: gay and lesbian films, African American films, Jewish films, Asian American films, Hispanic films, science fiction, comedy, "B" movies, underground movies, documentaries, animation, etc.

Smaller festivals, on the whole, have been more generous in giving screen time to films without distributors. Typical of this mind frame is Sue Early, managing director of Delaware's Rehoboth Beach Independent Film Festival, who is especially accommodating to these works. "We welcome the opportunity to review film submissions of unaffiliated filmmakers and our festival's history demonstrates a well-balanced offering of films from unaffiliated new filmmakers, films from unaffiliated filmmakers whose previous work we have screened, and films under distribution," she says. "Our door is open to review all submissions, so submit your work."

And the new festivals keep coming. One of the latest is the Deep Focus Film Festival, which had its debut in March 2005 in Columbus, Ohio. Not unlike many festivals, this one was created to fill a niche — in this case, a geographic niche.

"With the preponderance of new films opening each week, it's not possible for the average moviegoer to see every worthwhile film or for the theaters to book all of them," explains Mark Pfeiffer, a writer and video producer who was part of the programming committee for the first Deep Focus Film Festival. "Some films may not even be made available because they performed poorly in New York and Los Angeles, so the distributors don't believe there is any use expanding them to smaller cities. The purpose of the Deep Focus Film Festival is to give a higher profile to movies that might not have opened in Columbus or merit extra attention even if they will appear on area screens in the upcoming months. Unlike their blockbuster brothers, small films are often competing for limited screens, so they too face make-or-break situations on their opening weekends. It isn't unusual for well-received indies to vanish after seven days if their Friday and Saturday box office receipts aren't up to snuff. This tiny window shuts out a lot of people who might like to see these films but don't keep close tabs on what is opening when and how long — or not — the films will stay."

In the case of this new festival, the films did not come looking for a slot on the program. "I am unaware of any distributors initiating contact, which isn't surprising since this is the inaugural festival," continues Pfeiffer. "We weren't specifically looking for films with distribution, but with this being our first festival — and one without a submission process — having a distributor certainly helped. At least 100 titles were suggested as films we might be interested in programming. Festival director Melissa Starker attended part of the Toronto International Film Festival in 2004, so she had a few specific titles in mind, some of which we acquired and some we didn't. I had a list of films that I wanted to see but didn't know if I'd get the chance to see them, so getting involved as a festival programmer was a dream come true."

Pfeiffer adds, "Probably 20 to 30 films received serious consideration — screeners were watched or serious talks were initiated with the distributors or filmmakers — for the final list. It's a small sample, but with the short period of time between confirming that the festival was a go and needing to secure the lineup, that was the best we could do."

The Deep Focus Film Festival did not kick off with an immediate publicity bang in the manner of New York's Tribeca Film Festival, nor did it offer the buyer's market frenzy of Sundance. Yet Pfeiffer states festivals such as Deep Focus still offer value to aspiring filmmakers.

"Festivals not expressly set up as marketplaces have value for independent filmmakers because they provide ways for undistributed work to be seen," he explains. "Whether through audience awards at these fests or positive reviews in press coverage, building good word of mouth is paramount for these filmmakers."

INTERVIEW
RYAN DACKO, FILMMAKER/AUTHOR

Inspiration can come in the most unlikely places. For Ryan Dacko, the inspiration to create the screenplay of his feature film debut *And I Live* came in a location that few people ever consider for bringing out their creative nature: Antarctica.

No, Dacko did not graduate from the Captain Scott School of Filmmaking. Instead, his South Pole odyssey came while he was on active duty in the U.S. Coast Guard in 2000. While circumnavigating the lower part of the planet on the USCG *Polar Star*, Dacko used his free time to draft the screenplay of *And I Lived*, a gritty yet bittersweet tale of two high school lovers whose relationship is threatened by peer pressure rooted in a fervent class warfare that ruthlessly separated the haves and have-nots.

After completing his military duty, Dacko returned to his hometown of Syracuse, New York, to focus on the creation of *And I Lived*. Bringing the story off the page and into the screening room took a few years, but it was worth the effort. Shot on locations across Syracuse and Rochester, *And I Lived* used an impressive array of local talent both behind and in front of the camera to relate Dacko's mature and insightful vision of young love attempting to find stability in a hostile environment.

Dacko wrote about his unusual entry into filmmaking in the entertaining memoir *I Guess the World Could Always Use Another Ed Wood*, and that book included a lengthy subsection called "The DVD Film School," which detailed how aspiring filmmakers can take advantage of home entertainment to learn filmmaking skills. Dacko never attended film school, and he is a strong believer that film school is not only a problem unto itself, but also has a negative effect on the festival circuit.

Q: Okay, what is your concern about film schools and aspiring filmmakers?

RYAN DACKO: The absolute downside to today's independent film scene is its dependency on film schools and the emphasis on a "need" for a film school education.

I know, I'm going to get some frowns with that, but it's true — you do not need film school to make a movie. Robert Rodriguez first openly said it in his book, *Rebel Without a Crew*, and I will go to my grave repeating it. Still, the basic public perception is that if you want to "get into filmmaking" or "become a filmmaker" you need to learn how to be one first. Therefore, you must go to film school and learn how. I believe this film school deception is one of the major killers of the true independent film scene.

Q: Can you be more specific?

RYAN DACKO: If you stand back and look, you would be shocked at how the mainstream media and film school system go hand in hand. With page after page of glossy advertisements in the monthly movie magazines, thousands of young filmmakers are steered toward the doors of the closest overpriced film school. Young potential filmmakers are sucked in by tractor-beam tag lines such as: "If you're serious about your dream, we'll take your dream seriously" (from the ad for Full Sail Film School) or

"Ready to become inspired? You belong here" (from the ad for the Arts Institute Film School).

Do any of them advertise the cost of their programs? Of course not — that would steer half of their business away. But when you do the research you will find the New York Film Academy has one-year programs for every dream, ranging from directing for film, acting for film, screenwriting for film and TV, to producing for film and TV. The cost: $12,500 a semester, or $25,000 for the entire one-year course. And if you add in the New York City room and board for the entire year, you could be pushing $40,000. That's enough for a movie budget right there!

Now what if I were to tell you that Steven Spielberg, Alfred Hitchcock, Orson Welles, Peter Jackson, James Cameron, and John Frankenheimer all never attended film school but went on to become some of the most extremely successful filmmakers in the industry? Would you still think you need a film school education?

Q: I don't know what I would think. Where did you learn filmmaking?

RYAN DACKO: I taught myself the filmmaking process through books and DVD commentaries. All the successful film-makers have left you textbook information and lectures on how they made their films in the form of running audio commentary on various DVDs. I put all the information in "The DVD Film School," where you learn how to make a movie from the actual professionals who make them, and it can be followed by watching 45 different DVDs — about $20 for a one-month Netflix movie pass.

Q: Really?

RYAN DACKO: It is all true. Most of the great filmmakers — especially the ones they use as examples in film schools — never even set foot in a film school class. It is a fact — whatever information and instruction you need in learning how to write a screenplay or make a movie can be found in your local book and video store. The only question that is left is what to do with that $40,000 you would have spent on film school — or $38,980 after you subtract your one-month Netflix membership. Why, you make a movie with it and as every professional filmmaker will tell you, the most you ever learn in filmmaking is on the set of your first feature film.

In my experience, it took years of sacrifice to see my first film to the finish. I had risked friendships and alienated some who were really close to me. Thank God for the support of my family, some of whom thought I was flushing my life down the drain the whole time, but still they supported me in the three-year process it took to make the film. It is bad enough I had to go into debt with the first film due to budget shortcomings, but I can honestly tell you, I could never have done it if I had started out already $40,000 in debt from a film school education. And that's small: What if I went to a two- or four-year film school program?

Q: That would be quite the financial mountain to scale, no?

RYAN DACKO: I believe a huge amount of debt will kill your movie production faster than a jammed camera or a disgruntled actress. When you have debt hanging over your head, you are then limited to the choices and moves you can make if the production gets into a jam. This is why so many who graduate with a film school degree or diploma never even attempt to get their first feature film made. They have to go to work to keep up with the loan payments and never find the time to pick up a camera.

It is a terrible waste — because if there were no film schools, I wonder how many great filmmakers would have emerged over the years or great independent films would be in our DVD players. Instead, they all went to the price of a film school education. Remember, Robert Rodriguez made *El Mariachi* for $7,000. That means he could have made four more films before he reached the amount of a one-year film school education at the New York Film Academy.

Q: But don't you believe film schools can provide something worthwhile in return for such high tuition?

RYAN DACKO: If you strip away all the fancy slogans and glossy magazine advertisements, the only aspect of the film school education that everyone always uses to justify its existence is "the connections." It just boils down to politics — and you thought it was all about your dream in making a movie, right? So they tell you that you make some great connections and use them to get a foothold in your career and if you graduate from film school and successfully make a feature film, you can have your film professor call in a favor and have it shown at the local film festival.

This is what is so damaging, and I have witnessed this firsthand, when I directed a feature film only to see it get denied from film festivals because it had no political backing. I had no film school experience, and no film professor backing me up. What a kick into reality that was! Up until then, I thought film festivals judged you on your filmmaking merit, not on what film school you attended or who is vouching for you. I even was recommended by some, after I made a feature film, to "go to film school, sit through the courses, and then enter your film into a festival after you graduate." How backward is that?

Q: Sounds backward to me. But what does that say about the festival process?

RYAN DACKO: The end result is that independent film genre has been politicized and pulled away from the art of telling a story — turned into a "who do you know" ballgame. That is so sad, because on average, the major independent film festivals receive thousands of film submissions a year, and only a few of them ever get picked to be shown at the festival. Not necessarily are the most intelligent or well-crafted ones picked, but who has the better connections. I can only imagine how many talented filmmakers gave up after seeing their films get denied festival after festival because they used the budget money to go shoot a film instead of sit and listen to someone tell them how a film is made. They probably walked away thinking they didn't have any talent when it was the complete opposite.

Q: Can this situation be changed?

RYAN DACKO: Not until the independent film world breaks its relationship with film schools and film school professors will we see a surge in an art form that is currently being held back by ever-increasing tuition costs that are never needed in the first place.

Q: Let's go back to festivals. From your experience, do you feel that today's film festivals offer a viable launching point for independent films?

RYAN DACKO: No, and if you combine my previous comments on the film school/film festival connection and factor in the major studios big-budget "independent" films, you will find that most film festivals are no longer a viable launching point for independent films. A true independent film is usually hit from two sides in major festivals: The upper slots in the festival — more prestigious spots, opening night, etc. — are taken up by the movies that have had million-dollar advertising campaigns and major studio backing, while the smaller spots are taken by those who have a film school edge or connection, or maybe won an award or two in a previous festival. And since many other smaller film festivals want the prestige of showing movies that won awards at the bigger festivals, many movies are invited and accepted into small festival lineups on the grounds that they have been successful at other film festivals. So a cycle starts and carries itself throughout the year. What is left behind? You guessed it, the true independent films.

Hey, some may call me paranoid, but there is a reason why you don't see innovation in the world of independent film nowadays in the same way you saw it back in the late '80s and early '90s. Since filmmakers such as Soderbergh, Rodriguez, and Sofia Coppola can still be tagged with the "independent filmmaker" title, there is little to no room for the next Soder-bergh, Rodriguez, Coppola, etc. It's becoming like the Supreme Court, where you have to wait for one to die or retire before another can take their place at the bench.

Over the years, starting with the early '90s, the Hollywood studios found that there was money to be made in underground independent cinema. Like MTV siphoning the energy off the raw, unprocessed power of a Nirvana or Soundgarden, the studios found the same momentum in the guerrilla filmmaking of a *Clerks* or *El Mariachi*. There was a big fan base for the one-man, one-camera filmmaking approach — like a rebellion or uprising against the studios' big-budget hold on the cinema of the 1980s. Thousands immediately stood up and said, "You know what? I can make a movie that is just as entertaining as those million-dollar flicks — and I don't have to be from Los Angeles to do it." Naturally, film festivals became overwhelmingly popular as an alternative to the big-budget cinema — a rebirth of the American dream — where a man who was a convenience store clerk could become a successful star by making a movie on his own.

This attention and audience base gave way to the studios. Most definitively was when Walt Disney Studios acquired a then-independent Miramax back in 1993. This gave Miramax millions of dollars to make movies and build subsidiary companies — such as Dimension Films — all while operating under the visage of "independent filmmaking." The other major studios followed suit and merged with smaller studios to carry on the great independent film makeover, and the scene has never been the same again.

Q: And how does this affect the festival circuit?

RYAN DACKO: Most affected at this time were the film festivals, which turned into staging grounds for big-budget "independent" studio films. And since then, everything that has been successful in the independent film world — from actors to filmmakers — has been acquired by these major "independent" studios. I feel that you have an absolute suppression of underground cinema going at this time, and it is dying to break out and be recognized. That is where the underground film festivals will rise and succeed.

A long time ago, maybe ten years or so, a few filmmakers down in New York City grew sick and tired of seeing their movies get denied film festival after film festival, so they rebelled and created their own festival, calling it the Slamdance Film Festival. It was a great idea at first, but that in itself became so popular and overblown, it resembles everything about the film festivals that inspired its creation. At the time, what made the Slamdance Film Festival so popular was that it was a lone ray of light for the indie filmmaker who didn't have the money for connections. But like everything else, corporate sponsors and studio executives came knocking, and its once-valued independence turned into commercial property.

Q: This is getting a bit depressing. Is there a solution here?

RYAN DACKO: Not to worry, because technology has helped us to overcome that hurdle. We are now at an age where the solution is to organize and hold your own film/video festival. With the quality digital projectors found on the market — consistently lowering in price — one can hold a film festival in any theater that is willing to set one up. This makes it possible for a movie shot with a $10,000 budget to be able to be screened without spending another $10,000 to make a film print of the final cut in order to project it in the theater. You can simply screen your film by transferring it to DVD and digitally projecting the image in a theater.

What I believe will happen is that you will see filmmakers take this opportunity to break away from the film school/film festival hold on the industry and show their movies in their own film festivals. This will pave the way for smaller distribution companies to get involved and see what has been overlooked for all these years — true independent films.

Q: What advice would you give aspiring creative artists who want to get into the independent film business?

RYAN DACKO: The first bit was touched on in your question — to realize that it is a business, first and foremost. I know some will disagree because filmmaking is an art form — that I will not deny — but unlike painting a picture, you are going to need thousands of dollars to make this type of art. That money will come from investors who will eventually want their money back and also a return. This is why you have to start out in a business mind-set, like you are creating a product to sell to a market, and you will sell this product to make the money back that has been invested in its creation.

Does this mean you can't be artistic? No, of course not. However, the most successful filmmakers are the ones who are able to find a balance in the business and artistic side of motion pictures. To not lose perspective on both is the first step to creating a quality product. This means they are able to make a film that tells a story with creativity, and in return it is also able to be sold on the open market.

The next bit of advice is to plan on life after film festivals. This is one bit of advice I had to learn the hard way because we never planned on trying to shop the film to distributors — we were only concerned with getting the film finished and into film festivals where we could meet other production companies and look to make the next movie. Since I had written five screenplays while in the military, my plan was to use the first film as a calling card and get a foot in the door with it in order to secure financing for the next production. In our extreme focus on the production side of the film, we bypassed paperwork that would have helped in securing the movie for an official release by a distribution company.

For example, we had soundtrack music from bands that lived all around the world. From Germany to Mexico, I was able to meet these bands in my military travels and discuss with them plans for the movie and the possibility of using their music for the movie's soundtrack. Only film festival rights were granted and most of the time it was done verbally or in a handshake. After all, they were independent artists as well, who could use some extra exposure, and I know we could definitely use their music in the film. Now, one hurdle in getting *And I Lived* cleared for distribution is to get the rights to use the music. We are only able to play in film festivals so far. If I were to do it all over again, I would have researched the proper forms years ago and brought them with me to obtain the necessary signatures.

Remember, you never know what will become of your film, so always plan for life after film festivals and get your paperwork in order while you move throughout the production — you will be thankful you did the extra time and legwork in the long run.

And the final bit of advice is… DO NOT GO TO FILM SCHOOL. Please, there isn't an aspect of filmmaking you can't learn from a DVD or book that will be repeated to you in thousands of dollars of film school education. I wrote "The DVD Film School" specifically to make sure no one ever has to go to film school again. Write me if you need a copy (*www.ascension3.com*). With the money you save, go out and make one great independent feature film. The experience you will gain in making that film will be more than any film school can ever teach you. I am serious about this one, and if you need a second opinion, go read *Rebel Without a Crew* by Robert Rodriguez — that's the book that put me on a whole new direction, which led to our own movie set. It will do the same for you.

ARE FESTIVALS WORTH THE BOTHER?

Ryan Dacko would not totally write off the festival circuit: In March 2005, he entered *And I Lived* in the B-Movie Film Festival, held near his residence in Syracuse. The film won two awards at the festival and was nominated for three other awards, including Best Director for Dacko, and the buzz from the fest enabled him to get the film shown in other festivals and to get a distribution deal for his next feature, the vampire thriller *Dead Heaven*, which is currently in preproduction.

As a first-time filmmaker Dacko enjoyed success at a smaller festival, while at the same time a two-time Academy Award–nominated filmmaker had problems getting into festivals. *Waging a Living*, a 2005 documentary on the state of the working poor in America, did not get into many festivals, even though it was helmed by the celebrated filmmaker Roger Weisberg. *Waging a Living* was lined up for presentation on PBS and even had a New York premiere. Weisberg states the film's subject matter was too glum and serious for festival consideration.

"The have-nots and their daily struggles are not sexy," he says. "Mass audiences are drawn to glamour, violence, sex, and youth culture. Everybody seems to have their own mundane struggles with making ends meet. So, devoting an entire film to these struggles may not seem too compelling on the surface. However, there is growing income inequality and shrinking upward mobility in America, and I'm convinced that a well-told story that puts a human face on these disturbing trends can and should find an audience."

Although *Waging a Living* played at Cinequest, the Newport Beach Film Festival, and the Santa Cruz Film Festival plus many smaller festivals, it did not make the cut at the higher-prestige events — which is curious, given Weisberg's eminence in documentary filmmaking and his peerless background.

"The film, which was submitted to Sundance at the rough-cut stage, was not accepted," he says. "I regret that it was not invited to Hot Docs, Full Frame, San Francisco, Tribeca, or South by Southwest."

So what can this say about the festival experience? To be frank, the verdict on the festival circuit is still mixed. Many people in the film world embrace it, others deride it, and a few honestly aren't certain. Donald J. Levit, senior critic with *ReelTalk Reviews*, falls into the last category.

"I don't follow the festival circuit — nor, alas, get offered bankrolled trips to their exotic locales overseas or even here—and I couldn't name but a couple of them, anyway," he says. "But with maturity and success, they look like paparazzi/glitterati affairs from afar. Every place seems to have developed its own, often supposedly specialized, festival, e.g., gay, fantastique, feminist, gross-out, fringe, ethnic, so on, and I've screened any number of quite ordinary films, and worse, trailing like wines and beers their Golden Bears, Wolves, Elks, Palms, Shells, Coconuts, and whatnot. Still and all, it is one way to get people to see your 'selection,' if you have the staying power to enter enough lotteries."

Kent Turner, editor at *Film-Forward.com*, feels that today's film festivals offer a viable launching point for independent films — provided the films are up to the task. "Films at a festival are like actors auditioning," he says. "A film has to stand apart to be noticed. It's no wonder that *Open Water*, which took an unconventionally depressing approach to a high-concept story, stood out in 2004. Unfortunately, many films are too easily pigeonholed as small art films, such as *Assisted Living*. That's where critics play an important part, by focusing attention on noteworthy films."

Ed Gonzalez, editor for *Slant* magazine, notes that some festival organizers are more progressive in choosing these non-cookie-cutter films than most distributors. "Most festival programmers are more dedicated to enriching the film community than your average distribution company, which decides how many people are really going to see a film," he says. "I understand most boutique distributors can't afford to take risks, but this hesitation seems to be having an adverse effect on the way films are made all around the world. Distributors buy films they think audiences want to see. This means that really good films by first-time directors often fall through the cracks if they're not edgy or snarky or polemical. It really does seem that the attention distributors pay to a film is directly proportional to the attention audiences are willing to give it. Audiences are impatient nowadays, but I do think distributors underestimate the average theatergoer. I'm convinced that Turning Gate would have done very well if a distributor had taken a risk on it. Both audiences and distributors could stand to give and take a little more, but that's the business of buying, selling, and consuming films. I don't think it's something that's ever going to change."

But other industry observers wonder about the festival circuit's viability, not only for helping filmmakers but also for bringing films to the audiences that could drive them to success.

"My understanding is that many films get stuck in the film festival circuit," says Eric Monder, a critic with *Film Journal International*, a monthly motion picture trade journal. "They're never launched anywhere. Perhaps there are viable outlets, but I believe the Internet and DVD will be more and more of an answer for some of these films. Even in the festivals, many films are not shown because they don't make the cut… What happens to them? And I know a friend, Kevin Willmot, who made a film, *CSA: The Confederate States of America*, that took years to get distribution after being rejected by many festivals for being too controversial! Of course, once Spike Lee signed on as executive producer, the film generated great buzz and looks like it will be a hit."

One aspect of festivals that many people overlook is, ironically, among the most important: Who is in the audience?

"It is very difficult for Joe Consumer to attend a film festival," says Kamal Larsuel of *3BlackChicks.com*. "The cost of purchasing a festival pass, the airfare, the hotel and food — plus the amount of films being shown. There are usually only two or three breakout films. What about the numerous others that are shown?"

Indeed, what about them? Who is seeing these films, anyway? In some cases, not the right people.

"In my experience, film festivals basically play to relatively small audiences of film lovers and party people," comments Eric Phelps, former development director for the Atlanta International Film Festival. "By 'party people,' I mean folks who want to be in the 'film world scene' but don't necessarily know anything about film. They are a good vehicle for getting work in various locations throughout the world in front of audiences… but 95% of what gets shown at festivals does not make it to video or to a larger audience."

It is easy to get caught up in the aura of film festivals without having a clue if your film is reaching the right audience. Too often, many people are dismissive of smaller festivals as not being helpful for filmmakers to get noticed. Christopher Null, editor of *FilmCritic.com*, bluntly states, "Smaller festivals — of which there are now hundreds — are functionally worthless for getting noticed."

The juvenile inmate Megan ponders her future in Liz Garbus' documentary Girlhood. "I have had great success with a film after premiering at Sundance, but also have had great experiences showing the film at smaller festivals," says Garbus. "For example, Girlhood won the jury prize at the Atlanta Film Festival, and found its distributor — Wellspring — because their acquisitions exec was on the jury!"

But there is always an exception. The aforementioned success of Ryan Dacko at the B-Movie Film Festival (an event celebrating low-budget cinema) helped jumpstart his plans for a second film. Even more noteworthy was the good fortune that blessed Liz Garbus, the Academy Award–nominated filmmaker (*The Farm: Angola USA*) who was ready to have her 2003 feature-length documentary *Girlhood* (which did not have theatrical distribution) play in a few festivals before going straight to television after a single New York engagement that she booked on her own.

"In terms of festivals, of course, given the above, the festival circuit has been hugely valuable to me," says Garbus. "I have had great success with a film after premiering at Sundance, but also have had great experiences showing the film at smaller festivals. For example, *Girlhood* won the jury prize at the Atlanta Film Festival, and found its distributor, Wellspring, because their acquisitions exec was on the jury!"

Filmmaker Eric Byler found success for his 2002 feature *Charlotte Sometimes* at a festival that many people consider as being off the beaten festival path — but that happened to attract the participation of someone in the position to assist a young unknown filmmaker. The place was the Hawaii International Film Festival and the powerful person was none other than Roger Ebert.

"None of us had met him before," recalls Byler. "I saw Roger at the press conference on the first day of the festival and asked Jacqui [Jacqueline Kim, the star of the film] to go invite him because I was too nervous. She was brave and introduced herself, then introduced me, and some other cast and crew. He seemed to like us all but said he'd need to check his schedule to make sure he could attend. That night, at the opening night party, we all approached him and either implicitly or blatantly asked him if he'd checked his schedule yet. He mentioned that he had and that he was going to attend the first of our two screenings. We all yelled out hooray and he ducked his head, embarrassed, and said something like, please be discreet, there are a hundred other filmmakers at this party who asked me the same question today.

"The screening went very well, and we had a really fun Q&A. Honolulu is my hometown, so there were a lot of friends in the audience. Roger asked two or three questions and our dialogue became the foundation for a more in-depth discussion recorded on video at Roger's film festival [Roger Ebert's Overlooked Film Festival] the following April. Roger graciously agreed to allow us to include his *Tonight Show*–style interview with me, Michael Ideomoto [another star of the film], Jacqueline Kim, and John Manulis, CEO of Visionbox, which helped produce the film, on our DVD bonus features. Afterward, Roger asked if he could take us out to dinner. I said that I had made plans with a dozen friends and family members, so Roger came along with us. It was a great little party. We took over a place at Aloha Tower, or maybe it was Restaurant Row. I got to see grown-up versions of the kids I went to high school with sit down and talk film history with Roger Ebert, with proud family members and other lifelong friends in attendance."

Of course, that same year Ebert attended another festival and helped raise attention for another indie film — albeit with very different results.

"Vincent Gallo's *The Brown Bunny* would have been completely ignored had it not earned the attention of Roger Ebert at Cannes!" notes Christopher Null of *FilmCritic.com*.

INTERVIEW
CHRISTIAN DE REZENDES, FILMMAKER

One of the most talented up-and-coming filmmakers is Christian de Rezendes. He began his career in films while still in high school. His first documentary, *Branches '93*, focused on his graduating class of 1993 from North Smithfield High School in northern Rhode Island. It received a Certificate of Merit from the Chicago International Film Festival in 1996. Christian's professional filmmaking debut was *Alzira's Story* (2000), a critically acclaimed documentary on the life of his grandmother, her immigration from Portugal in 1929, and her decades of work to sponsor her family in a better life in America. Later in 2001, Christian directed the improvisational dramedy *Getting Out of Rhode Island*. The entire film was a party-gone-wrong story shot Dogme style in real time with 44 actors in a single location.

While his films have met with critical praise, festival programmers have been somewhat more uncertain of how to approach his work.

Q: What festivals did your films play in? What awards did you win at these festivals?

CHRISTIAN DE REZENDES: *Getting Out of Rhode Island* played at a few festivals — most notably the Black Point Film Festival in Lake Geneva, Wisconsin, where it won Best Feature and Best Director in 2003. *Alzira's Story* played at many festivals as well — Bare Bones International Film Festival in Muskogee, Oklahoma, and at Worldfest-Houston, where it was honored with the Silver Award in its category.

Q: Which festivals did you apply for and get rejected from? Did you receive explanations why you did not get accepted?

CHRISTIAN DE REZENDES: What *haven't* I applied to and got rejected from? It's usually a form rejection letter. *With Getting Out of Rhode Island*, it was strange, because we came very close to being included a couple of times. One instance was at No Dance

— at least that's what they told me. People found the film too rough around the edges, too raw, maybe too amateur-looking — but its look was "part of the joke," and I think some people didn't understand that. Another festival sent me a strange rejection letter that read something like, "We had a lot of competitive films this year, few of which made it into our finalist round. Your film made it to that finalist stage. However, unfortunately, we cannot show it." I was like, "Jesus… why don't you stab me and twist the knife a bit?? I didn't really feel it go in."

A Portuguese American family portrait, circa 1925, from Christian de Rezendes' Alzira's Story. "What haven't I applied to and got rejected from?" asks de Rezendes.

Not to be bitter about nothing in the end, but give a reason if you're going to go that far. Don't give me that crap. Over time, I've learned this festival has many issues, so I simply consider them ignorant and out of touch with their public — mostly for reasons outside of this particular incident.

Festivals are also more interested in what's going to make their audiences happy instead of pushing the medium and raising the creative bar, which is what film festivals were originally created for. Like independent film itself, festivals became "popular" — and like our news, they'll probably all be run by corporations someday. The word "independent" is tossed around just as loosely as "genius." While their vision may be independent, they have the money, resources, and stars to sell their films. Meanwhile, the true independents who did it themselves with next to nothing are being shafted for directors who have access to these resources and get their films *seen*. There is nothing wrong with what they do. Some of the work is wonderful, but I cannot call their films independent when so much has become so "dependent."

Q: How did you go about choosing the festivals that ultimately accepted your films? Specifically, what criteria went into selecting them?

CHRISTIAN DE REZENDES: My choices often depended on whether or not they might seem open to my type of film. Those that would be interested in a one-hour doc about a Portuguese grandmother [*Alzira's Story*] would not necessarily go for a raw Dogme-inspired party feature with lots of anger and bad language [*Getting Out of Rhode Island*], or vice versa. Nowadays, if I submit to a festival, I do as much research on it as possible before entering — to get a feel for whether or not they'd take my work seriously, or more to the point, if it stands a chance. *Getting Out of Rhode Island* would have been thrown out at Sundance, so I chose not to enter it. Other industry people — filmmakers, critics, distributors — suggested festivals to me. Some I entered, some I didn't, but most rejected it. Just because someone you may know that loves your film has a great connection to a festival director, that does not guarantee anything. Your friend may have the best intentions, but that can only go so far. After all, it's your dough that's going toward those entry fees, so spend it wisely. Fifty dollars can always buy you seven new mini-DV tapes for your next shoot. This is not to say that I don't respect and appreciate risk. I do — intensely. I wouldn't have directed *Getting Out of Rhode Island* if I hadn't. However, having served as a festival programmer — for an organization that I will not name — I choose to be a realist. Oddly enough, I feel that my new documentary currently in completion, called *41*, may have a strong chance, so I would probably take more risks in entering it.

Q: Did your festival experience result in to any leads for theatrical screenings or distribution deals?

CHRISTIAN DE REZENDES: Yes, connections are connections. Network the hell out of your film! I do my own press — getting my films out there for reviews and articles. Through those, I have gained attention and invitations to screen at theaters. When festivals did not respond, I booked local theater venues in Rhode Island and Massachusetts to screen *GORI*. I did not rely on festivals to get my film out there.

My previous festival programming experience led me to the writer of this book, who was working for them at the time. That is my Film Threat connection. He has reviewed my work — honestly, good and bad — and that is what has gained *Getting Out of Rhode Island* its attention: He gave five stars. Months later, *Film Threat* editor Chris Gore let the world know his plan to expand its distribution base, and I made contact with him.

Q: What has been the release history of Alzira's Story*? And who handled the release of it?*

CHRISTIAN DE REZENDES: For the past few years, I had distributed the film through an online company where the film-makers were responsible for co-promotion of their own products. For at least three years, the film was available through these means, and eventually a DVD format was added. I created and authorized the discs and updated the covers when it came time for a new look. Unfortunately, this Web-based business did very little to push sales, so I recently pulled the film from their site.

Currently, a new company called Cineclix, out of Vancouver, is distributing it. They sell it as a download-to-own option and are in the process of creating the DVD. We are in the beginning stages of our agreement, but so far so good.

Prior to all of this, it was difficult to get people interested in that film, because no one seemed to know how to market it or think it was all that interesting. Reception of this one-hour film has mostly been strong, warm, and emotional. Perhaps its home-grown look automatically made people feel it was an amateur at work. In the end, however, it was good enough for Rhode Island PBS Channel 36 to show in January of 2004. The response from the Portuguese community, through calls and letters, was very sweet indeed.

Q: Was releasing a documentary like Alzira's Story *easier or harder than a feature like* Getting Out of Rhode Island*?*

CHRISTIAN DE REZENDES: The two films are apples and oranges — in concept, story, style, and genre. So it's very hard to compare. One thing I will say is that there's far more interest in a new, edgy, and invigorating feature film than a one-hour documentary about a Portuguese immigrant grandmother. I think that goes without saying in this industry. Two very different audiences responded to both projects, and often the audience from one film knew nothing about the other. Either *Getting Out of Rhode Island* was a bastard child that came after something sentimental and sweet, or *Getting Out of Rhode Island* was a something new from a guy they'd never heard of. In the end, *Alzira's Story* was the harder film to sell, because of the marketability of its content alone.

Q: Did early press coverage for your films help leverage interest from the festival programmers?

CHRISTIAN DE REZENDES: In the case of *Getting Out of Rhode Island*, the interest came mostly from distributors. Thanks to the strong review on *Film Threat*, many indie distribution companies asked for screeners of the film. All turned it down, but some gave very constructive feedback with positive comments — and realistic reasons as to why they could not distribute it. No names, no celebrities, no knowing of where its audience was. Eventually, Chris Gore decided to expand *Film Threat* into DVD distribution, so we jumped on the opportunity and we were embraced with open arms. Okay, it wasn't that romantic, but they have been great!

   Alzira's Story drew more interest locally from the Portuguese community and in pockets throughout the U.S. A couple of distributors approached me online. One was obnoxious, rude, and unprofessional. Another was Cineclix, which the film is signed with now.

Q: What professional advice would you give aspiring filmmakers considering their first steps into the festival world?

CHRISTIAN DE REZENDES: Make your own films. Do not compromise your vision. Treat your crew and actors fairly.

Learn to grow with them. Feed them too. Embrace the obstacles that come to you. Don't try to control them. Work with them — and in some cases, around them — realistically. Know your budget and stretch your creative limits as best you can within your limits.

Read about these festivals. Know what films they accept and who/what they have honored in the past. Prepare to submit repeatedly and lose your money. Selling your film at a festival will take a year or two. Finishing your film does not end the work. You must get out there and push, push, push.

Then, when you finally get into a festival, stop — and have a beer. You deserve it!

Well, don't have too many beers because you'll need to be sober to get the most out of the festival experience. Working a festival to draw attention to your film and yourself is a full-time job. What many filmmakers fail to realize is they can become the central attraction of the festival by lending a hand in the PR department.

"The best way to win publicity for the festival is to play publicist for the festival while promoting your own work — i.e., demonstrate to the organizers your own ability to generate press around your work and the festival," explains Nate Towne, CEO of the public relations/marketing agency Xanadu Communications. "The more involved you become with the film festival's publicity department, the more likely it is they'll push your film harder than others. That's not to say they'll give you top billing, however; their main goal is to sell festival tickets, not help an up-and-coming filmmaker with publicity."

Still, Towne notes one can get a surplus of attention by knowing who to contact and how to work with them. "Upon acceptance to the festival, contact the publicists and introduce yourself as a filmmaker appearing in the festival, and explain that you're working on your own to promote your film's appearance in the festival," he says. "Ask them to provide a festival press kit if possible, so you can include it in any materials you send out to the press yourself, whether you plan to or not.

"It's important to ask for a copy of their materials to demonstrate your interest, publicity savvy, and get a better understanding of how the publicists are promoting the festival. If you're able to speak with the publicists in detail, discuss your film, its potential audience, and how you're planning on promoting its festival appearance to the public. At this point, ask the publicists if there is any way you can arrange to have your film featured in the festival's publicity push — the best way to do this is to offer yourself as a source for potential interviews with journalists should the opportunity arise. Publicists depend on having reliable sources they can offer to the press for interviews and such, so making yourself available is an excellent way to ingratiate yourself with the festival publicists while furthering your own cause — publicizing your film. A matter of importance: If this tactic works and the publicists arrange media interviews, be on time and on your best behavior. Not only are you representing yourself, you're now representing the festival — so choose your words carefully and don't bite the hand that feeds you. After all, that's every good publicist's unspoken motto."

Speaking of the media, at least one festival programmer recommends smaller festivals in smaller markets as a way of harvesting larger media coverage.

"You get incredible press coverage at smaller festivals, especially if you have a world premiere," says Doug Hawes-Davis, programmer for the Big Sky Documentary Film Festival in Missoula, Montana. "This is a nice thing to take to your next event." Being an active part of the festival itself is crucial. "When accepted into a film festival, you should always be proactive with your film," advises Josh Koury, a filmmaker who launched the Brooklyn Underground Film Festival in 2001. "It's the film festival's job to promote the film, but the more a filmmaker helps with the film's promotion, the better it is for both parties. Make sure you request Official Selection laurels from the festival for promotional purposes. Post it on your website, send out emails, contact local publications to let them know the film will be screening. These are all important ways of getting the word out about your film and your screening. If your film makes the final program, it's for a reason: The festival believes in your work and they want to be on your website as much as you do theirs. It's a simple cross-promotion that ultimately helps create buzz for both parties."

Koury adds that if the festival accepted your film, then make sure you are present at the event. "It's also very important to try to visit a festival your film is playing," he says. "Usually it's a wonderful chance to meet other like-minded filmmakers, meet the festival staff, industry professionals, etc. Be very friendly, go to see other filmmakers' work, meet the staff, and stay in touch. We love this at the Brooklyn Underground; we're building a real global community. We believe in our filmmakers and stay in touch with them; we help them promote their work in the future, push their films to other festivals and screenings. It's important to take advantage of the actual event as an opportunity to make new connections."

One of the filmmakers who made a prominent presence at the 2005 Brooklyn Underground Film Festival was Matt Zoller Seitz, the movie critic for the *New York Press* weekly newspaper who turned auteur with his feature film debut *Home* — which was actually shot in Seitz' Brooklyn residence.

"*Home* is a great NYC narrative," says Koury. "Matt's said this himself in a few interviews. The film is of course made for a general audience, but as a New Yorker there are so many details that you can appreciate from living in the city. There's nothing quite like a Brooklyn premiere of a great New York film, and the audience reacted exactly as we expected. Matt's film had one of the strongest audience reactions from the crowd. He is a perfect example of someone who took advantage of the opportunities the festival presented. He could only attend the first two days of the festival, as he was off to another screening after, but in that short time he had a real presence at the festival and met many of the other filmmakers. He attended many of the screenings and his positive attitude made a great difference to the event. We love filmmakers like this. There were a lot of similar cases this year, which is part of why we do the festival; it's very exciting for us to see filmmakers get a lot out of the event."

Being welcomed at the Brooklyn Underground Film Festival clearly impressed Seitz, who had more than his fair share of rejection when bringing *Home* to the circuit. "We had the same festival plan as everybody else, which is submit to any festival that seems important and/or interesting and hope somebody accepts us and that we don't run out of application money before the end of the year,"

photo courtesy Brooklyn Schoolyard Productions

Nicol Zanzarella in a scene from Matt Zoller Seitz' Home. "We had the same festival plan as everybody else, which is submit to any festival that seems important and/ or interesting and hope somebody accepts us and that we don't run out of application money before the end of the year," say Seitz.

says Seitz. "We got rejected by every major U.S. festival during the first part of the year, except Cinequest, which jumped on us within weeks of getting the screener. That was kind of amazing considering that throughout this whole process, in the back of my mind, I thought about this movie as a private, personal thing that wouldn't make sense to anybody but me and the actors and crew who worked on it, and that would probably take years to be discovered and widely seen. We also got invited to the Trenton Film Festival, the Dallas Video Festival and the Independent Film Festival of Boston, where we're playing a day after *Lonesome Jim* by Steve Buscemi, whose first movie, *Trees Lounge*, was a huge influence on *Home*. Hopefully there will be other festivals. I don't think it's a coincidence that we've had our best luck with festivals that are young and hungry."

Seitz did not have to worry about putting on his sales hat while at the festivals. "We didn't get into any festivals where there's a lot of buying action, and in retrospect, that was not a huge surprise," he says. "Mine is a movie with no sex, no violence, no genre elements, and no movie stars, shot in an apartment by a guy who's never directed a feature before, and it's basically a zoo with people, mostly unconcerned with exposition and three-act structure. You don't even learn most of the characters' last names or what they do or where they're from. You just watch them behave, and while some profound changes happen, they happen internally and privately, so that if you're not really into the movie you won't catch it. There's a two-minute monologue in the middle, in Spanish with subtitles, that's edited as if it's a magical incantation, and a long scene in the middle where a prison psychiatrist stands in the backyard interpreting people's dreams. I just put that stuff in there because it seemed to fit; I could never defend any of it rationally, and if people are baffled I just shrug because it's what I wanted. Plus, the movie deliberately does not allow you to get too close to the characters, which is considered acceptable in European movies but not American ones. Another filmmaker who didn't like the movie talked about that, particularly in regard to Nicol's character, whom he adored. He said, 'At the end of the movie, I felt like I knew her heart but I didn't really *know* her,' and I thought, 'Well, I wish you hadn't described that as a liability, because it's exactly the effect I was after.'"

In regard to selling, a few festivals have their own sales markets that run simultaneously with the main festival activities. The most famous is the Cannes Market, held alongside the starry Cannes Film Festival. New York-based filmmaker David Giardina made the trip to Cannes in 2005 to sell his independently produced thriller *Taffy Was Born*.

"Being at the Cannes Film Festival was literally a trip and half," says Giardina. "Cannes has such a famous name and truthfully the idea of having a screening there was a bit daunting. Going in, I knew that *Taffy Was Born* was a teensy tiny little movie compared to the other films there — can we say *Star Wars*? — so I didn't imagine we'd get any kind of attention. We were lucky enough to have a reporter from the *Hartford Courant* [the major Connecticut daily newspaper] there to do a piece on it the night of the screening, which surprised me, but otherwise it's a big-name town as far as the festival goes. Cannes did not start off this way back in the late 1940s. The festival was originally an answer to the trite commercial productions being made, a place to show more original and offbeat fare. But since then it is all about the big stars, big directors. I understand that and I'm glad I got a chance to go and experience it. Cannes is a lovely spot to begin with."

photo courtesy Synchronicity Pictures

Filmmaker David Giardina lines up a shot on the set of his thriller Taffy Was Born. *"Being at the Cannes Film Festival was literally a trip and half," says Giardina.*

What did Giardina do at Cannes to drum up interest for the film? "I was brought to Cannes by a distribution marketing company called ITN," he continues. "They took a handful of films there to be screened at the market. While there they do their best to interest potential distributors and programmers to buy the films in their catalogue, of which *Taffy* was one. Like any other industrial market, there are booths set up in the Palais, which is a sprawling convention center. ITN had one of these booths and they spent their days showing industry people samples of different movies they had. I noticed, not surprisingly, that the movies that were getting all of the industrial attention were the 'blood and guts and exploding cars with buxom bikini babes with fangs' variety. *Taffy* was the black sheep, as it were, so I don't think ITN knew how to promote it. I did my bit to go to the Palais each day and hand out promotional material to buyers, etc. However, this is not my forte and being that I'm not a 'name,' in a big-name environment it was a challenge."

The challenge ultimately proved too great. "The screening of *Taffy* in Cannes was very frustrating," admits Giardina. "There were about 20 other films screening the night of our screening, so potential buyers would stroll into our screening room, sit for a few minutes, and then stroll off to another screening room. Being that *Taffy Was Born* is the kind of movie that must be watched from beginning to end, I was appalled. I mean, how can they feel they've gotten a good enough idea of what the movie is about just from a few minutes? It was explained to me later by an experienced Cannes-goer that this is how they do it there. They are, essentially, shopping. Also, the screening room itself was not acoustically sound. We could hear some of the other films being screened nearby very clearly. You'd think at Cannes this might be considered *tres mechant*, but apparently not. So far I have not gotten any distribution hits from this festival screening. Again, going in I wasn't expecting this to happen. I just wanted to go and experience this famous event."

THE NEW FESTIVAL PARADIGM

Love them, hate them, or stand in confusion before them, festivals are a necessity of the indie film world. "For most independents, film festivals are the only distribution they will ever have," says Matthew Seig, independent producer and executive director of the Rivertown Film Society in Rockland County, New York, and the former programmer for the Two Boots Pioneer Theater, a leading New York indie cinema venue. "Film festivals now constitute a market of their own. There may not be a direct economic benefit with festival distribution — although every now and then it is proposed that festivals should be paying for programming — but making the most of the festival circuit can advance a career and help a film get a video or cable release, if not theatrical distribution. The phenomenon that film festivals, microcinemas, and other nontheatrical venues — with the latter two basically functioning as all-year festivals but without the parties — are the major part if not the entire life cycle of many independent films should be better appreciated by filmmakers. These kinds if venues are essential for exposing audiences to new filmmaking styles and for helping new audiences appreciate film as an art form. Films that don't look like what kids grow up watching on television or at the mall can be an acquired taste. Audiences for the ever-growing number of independent films need to be nurtured and expanded." Some creative people have taken it upon themselves to expand the reach of independent cinema beyond the traditional festival structure. Alternative festivals have been popping up over the past few years. These have inevitably been held in unconventional locations and have been programmed by filmmakers who want to bring new ideas to film presentation.

One of the most notable examples of this trend can be found in New Jersey, courtesy of filmmaker Kipley Wentz. "The Hoboken Digital Film Society was actually born out of frustration on my part," he says, "first and foremost, the frustration of receiving so many rejection letters from festivals. You work so hard to finish your film and then if it just sits there on the shelf; all that work is in vain. So initially, the idea was to show my own work and that of my friends. Furthermore, as I went to more film festivals, I began seeing a lot of great films that, for whatever reason, are never going to be distributed. Maybe they don't have any stars, or the production quality is rough. But there are a lot of really great films out there that just aren't being seen. So I wanted to do what I could to get those movies out there — both by providing a venue for a screening, and also posting interviews with the filmmakers online. I know how hard it can be to generate any interest in your film, and I saw that I could perhaps help by exposing new films to the audiences and visitors to the site.

"To get Ho-Dig up and running has mostly required tenacity. I put the website together myself, and beyond that it's just a matter of getting the word out. I accept submissions through the website, but I'm also constantly tracking down films and asking my trusted friends for suggestions. I send out a lot of emails and generally filmmakers are receptive to the offer of a screening of their film. It takes time, but it's something I love doing. I screen the movies at a local independent bookstore called Symposia. They're a very community-based organization and already had a projector and a pop-up screen that they use for presentations and such. It just seemed like the perfect place to do it — it's casual, it's frequented by people looking for something other than your usual corporate fare, and the bookstore was looking for ways to attract more people."

Getting the people to come was Wentz' first challenge. "Initially, the crowds were small," he continues. "I don't charge admission, but that alone wasn't attracting people. So, because of my experience catering for my own shoots, I just started cooking dinner for the crowd. It's relatively inexpensive and again, it's something I enjoy. So that, plus good movies, has helped build the crowd.

"The main thing has been consistency: keeping the website updated, putting up posters around town, finding good films, and creating a fun, party-like atmosphere. These things have to be done consistently so people know what they're going to get."

So who comes out for these screenings? "We've had a wide range of ages and backgrounds, but mostly the audience is single people in their 20s and 30s," says Wentz. "Depending on the film, we may attract an older audience or a specific type of person. For example, I screened an evening of dance films recently and, naturally, the audience was mostly dancers. We do attract some filmmakers, but it has been my intention to reach out to people beyond 'the industry.' I wanted to keep it fun and casual and avoid the feeling that the screenings are big schmooze fests. Personally, I'm not a big schmoozy type of guy and I think that's reflected in the Ho-Dig vibe. I just wanted something hype-free, something genuinely relaxed and fun. Audience size depends largely on the film or films we're showing that night and how aggressively we promote it. Because I do it every week, it can't always be a huge blowout, but for the bigger events we'll have 35-40 people show up. That's the point at which we run out of chairs — it's a small venue! Generally we have around 25 people show up. Recently I was dismayed when we were having a really horrible storm on a Saturday night. I figured no one in their right mind would venture out on such a night, but I made a pot of chicken soup and we actually had a nice crowd. It turned out to be one of my favorite screenings yet."

As with Josh Koury's earlier advice, Wentz notes it is important for the filmmaker to promote the film. "It always helps when the director or a cast member shows up for Q&A," he says. "That's a great selling point that helps us promote the films. First and foremost, it's a screening event that you can tell people about. Even if they can't make it to the screening, you have a reason to contact people and talk about your film. And there's something happening with your film; it's not just a random pitch to some distributor or something. You can contact them with positive news: 'My film is screening this weekend at the Hoboken Digital Film Society, I hope you can make it.' Hopefully, it creates a sense of energy around the film. Also, I post interviews with the filmmakers on the website. People read the interviews, there are photos and links to the film's home page.... It's just one more bit of information about the film and the people involved. If someone Googles your film, they'll see something other than just the official home page. It's my opinion that the more information you have out there about your film, the better. Ultimately, whether 'Official Selection of the Hoboken Digital Film Society' means anything or not, you cannot go wrong by putting your film out there. Aside from simply sharing your work with the world, you have no idea what seeds are being scattered."

Wentz has been amazed by the depth and scope and volume of available independent films for consideration. "I think what's interesting to me is that independent film is becoming more like theater," he adds. "A small group of people can get together and for a couple thousand dollars can produce their own movie. They don't need to raise millions of dollars and are not beholden to giant corporations with stockholders. There are no creepy investors lurking around, no accountants and lawyers stalking the set. So, you get a lot of personal films, a lot of experimental films, and personally I think that's a great thing. Digital technology has democratized filmmaking — it's like the invention of the printing press. As far as where the independent film scene is headed, I really don't know. It seemed that for a while the point of making an independent film was to get it screened at Sundance, get 'discovered,' and then go make studio movies. I don't know if that's the case so much anymore. Sometimes I get the feeling that some of that 1990s 'get rich and famous' exuberance has faded. I think filmmakers and actors have now seen enough films go nowhere that we're a bit more realistic in our expectations."

Wentz also notes that the ease of setting up this micro-cinema-style setting will enable its popularity to continue. "I've been reading about some cool microcinemas for a few years now, really creative events where they'll screen movies outdoors projected onto walls, rocks, barges — anywhere!" he says. "Really all it takes is a DVD player, a projector, some speakers, and a blank white wall or sheet strung up. Given the ease with which a microcinema can be set up and moved around, they seem to be popping up all over the place. Coffee shops, bars, community centers — anywhere that people gather you can set up your own little cinema. I think what's so exciting about the whole micro-cinema movement is that each one is unique. Sometimes when I travel I can't tell the difference between one place and another. It's all becoming one big strip mall out there: all the same stores, the same restaurants, the same movie theaters playing the same movies. But if you happen upon a microcinema, at this point it's likely to be a group of people who are passionate about films, are looking for something different, and are there because they love it, not because they're making big bucks. It's a scene largely devoid of cynicism and greed, and it's very exciting to be playing a part in that. I love that there's a group of people who would rather come sit on a crappy folding chair and watch a movie they've never heard of than go to the local cinema just a few blocks away."

An alternative to the microcinema approach has been the concept of a touring festival. Filmmaker Kevin Fitzgerald created the Hip-Hop Film Festival as a way to spread the word on African American independent cinema.

"In 2001, I raised the idea that we should start a hip-hop film festival," he recalls. "First we called it the Hip-Hop Film Fest. We formed a filmmaker-run co-op touring film festival to provide a platform to present our films to the public. Up till that time other festivals kind of dissed us because we were hip-hop, even though we had great films and were selling out screenings left and right. So it was kind of a survival empowerment thing. Now we call it the Hip-Hop Film Festival and the rest is history."

Taking the festival on the road has worked for Fitzgerald's mission of reaching wider audiences. "The benefit is that a lot of different kinds of people see your film and you get exposure to markets that are kind of niche, but you can actually target your audiences much better," he says. "We are in touch with press and get the picks in the local weekly. And we personally invite buyers from all the video and record stores, do radio ticket giveaways. It's like running your own distribution company from a grass-roots level. It's kind of cool. But without sponsors you end up doing *a lot of work* and spending a lot of your *own* money in the process. It helps to have friends that work at Kinko's. But it was a great way to learn the film business and how to book theaters, etc."

Fitzgerald estimates his audience for the festival is "mostly from 20s to 30s. A lot of people who buy music and DVDs. A lot of urban consumers who have a certain artistic community spirit. I think everyone really gets what are trying to do and it's like they are part of a movement."

Technology is taking festivals to even further extremes. A company called Robotube Games LLC, a mobile and online game-development studio located in New Haven, Connecticut, has created the Robotube Film Festival, where short films can be viewed on a cell phone.

"This is an opportunity for new and seasoned filmmakers to let their films be seen by more than just the traditional festival crowd," says Jason Cirillo, partner and creative director at Robotube Games. "Our venue is the now billion-plus cell phones worldwide. Our audience is a global, open-market audience. There is no subscription fee for viewers and no service provider limitations. Anyone with a Web- and multimedia-enabled phone can watch. Who knows who will see your film? A prime minister? A goatherd? A college student in Sri Lanka? A Hollywood studio exec? Our aim at Robotube is to provide filmmakers with a new way of passing out their 'calling card' and providing cell phone users with free, mobile entertainment! At its best, Robotube Film Festival will provide you with the most diverse audience and the most connected network in the industry. We want to build a database of independent short filmmakers: directors, producers, writers, art directors, cinematographers, actors, and give them a place to connect and a place for people who need them to find them. All selected filmmakers will have the opportunity to hyperlink film info and their personal info to the Robotube site. We are not looking to buy content: All content remains the property of the filmmaker. What we are looking for are people with new ideas who are not afraid to explore."

But even if a film does not get into a festival, that doesn't mean you cannot use the festival to your advantage. An amusing case in point involved the trio of filmmakers known as the Hale Manor Collective, whose 2001 feature *Everything Moves Alone* was reviewed and rejected by the Telluride festival programmers.

"In their rejection letter they said *Everything Moves Alone* is 'an original and admirable work that deserves to be seen by many,'" says Thomas Edward Seymour, one of the Hale Manor artists. "So we took their rejection letter quote and put it all over our material. And we put the guy's name and the Telluride festival on the quote."

Seymour notes that he never actually states the quote came from a rejection letter rather than a festival program, nor is he eager to reveal the source of the statement. "And every now and then, people see that and say: 'Ahhhhh, Telluride!'" he says with a laugh.

INTERVIEW
MARK DOYLE AND BRUNO DERLIN, FESTIVAL PROGRAMMERS, VISIONFEST

If any location has too many festivals, it is New York. With the New York Film Festival, the Tribeca Film Festival, New Directors/ New Films, the Human Rights Watch Film Festival, and too many niche festivals to list here, the city seems like a never-ending festival.

In this mix is Visionfest, created by Mark Doyle and Bruno Derlin to give a home and a screen to smaller independent features that often seem ignored by the bigger events. In many ways, the festival's name is most appropriate: Doyle and Derlin allow visions from unheralded filmmakers to find their way to New York audiences.

Q: When did Visionfest begin? And what was the idea behind its creation?

MARK DOYLE: Visionfest began in the early months of 2001. My company partner, Bruno Derlin, and I were publishing a magazine called *Guerrilla Filmmaker* and we were getting tons of emails from our readers asking us how and where they could possibly see some of the films we were covering. We had already had some experience in the festival world. He had worked as a programmer at the Brooklyn International Film Festival and I had programmed the Film Fleadh in New York for a few years. So, I spoke up and suggested we do a film festival too. I was actually just kidding and wanted to do it only if we could secure very early sponsorships, but Bruno was incessantly determined and convinced me to immediately place a "call for entries" ad in our own magazine.

BRUNO DERLIN: After I arm-wrestled Mark Doyle into placing a "call for entries" ad in *Guerrilla Filmmaker*, I quickly began to brainstorm for thematic angles that might justify the existence of yet another festival in New York. What was missing? As I searched for that missing link, it occurred to me that showcasing many of the films we covered on the pages of our magazine would be the best and most appropriate starting point.

Q: How does Visionfest stand out from the city's many other festivals?

MARK DOYLE: A lot of the New York festivals cater to foreign films. We don't. Visionfest keeps it simple. We also only screen around 50 movies. That enables us to have a close relationship with each and every filmmaker. I think it's pretty embarrassing when a press person asks a question like, "Who can we expect to see shine at your festival?" and you cannot come up with a single name. I have seen that happen.

BRUNO DERLIN: Our magazine did extensive coverage on U.S.-made product. We were always looking for that next new wave of American indie auteurs and so it really made the most sense to label our festival — which was then known as the Guerrilla Film & Video Festival — as a forum for domestic films. We realized that it was much easier for foreign films to find showcasing forums in the U.S. than it was for American films. That's how we stumbled into our complete "mission." We just tried to fill a void that existed in the national festival circuit.

Q: What is your opinion on the overall state of the festival circuit? Specifically, do you feel that independent filmmakers can find fame and fortune on the festival circuit — or is that just movie hype?

MARK DOYLE: It's not just hype. It really does come down to how good your film is. You may believe you have a decent movie on your hands, but distributors are looking to make money, so the product has to be way better than decent, particularly if there are no recognizable names in it. Celebrity names will get your film noticed, and often even distributed, but I think that good writing and acting are still the primary attributes buyers are looking for. Take *Open Water*, for example. No one recognizable is in the film, but the film has an intriguing story and the acting is quite sharp. I feel that story and acting must come first. That's your best chance at having a runaway hit.

BRUNO DERLIN: The film festival circuit is a tricky gamble, as it costs the filmmakers money, time, and relentless dedication — all the perfect ingredients for a huge blow to the ego whenever a film is rejected by a festival. I think it comes down to one's understanding of his/her own film. What's the genre? Is there a specific target audience? And keep in mind there always should be. I've heard filmmakers who claim that their films are for everyone as they "capture a reality that appeals to all audiences." Well, guess what? While reality is for everyone and it's free, films are for audiences, and since those audiences are asked to shell out several bucks to suspend their own reality and dive into that new reality, which is presented by the filmmaker, it's always best to know the master plan. Filmmakers should take the time and responsibility of researching the festival circuit and knowing what festivals are more apt to embrace their films. That type of research may indeed avoid harsh rejections and possibly target the filmmaker in a more specific direction toward fame and fortune.

Q: *What are your criteria in judging films for Visionfest?*

MARK DOYLE: We have two stages of screenings for judges. One, our "previews committee," which consists of ten or more individuals from different walks of life, views each submission received for pre-selection, which helps us in the early planning stages, when out of 500-plus films, we need to select approximately 10% for final programming. The second stage involves our "Independent Vision" judging, which is comprised of film industry representatives who are asked to watch only a select number of entries — all of which have already been accepted to the festival — and provide us with ballots that contain their votes and opinions. These are used to determine award eligibility.

BRUNO DERLIN: As co-directors and co-programmers of Visionfest, Mark and I ultimately make the final decisions, especially when two or more preselected entries receive the same number of votes. We understand that while our choices are obviously influenced by a somewhat subjective, underlying scope, we do also consider countless factors in coming down to our final choices. Sometimes, we'll need to find a balance in subject matter; other times, blatant shortcomings from a technical standpoint — always taking budgetary constraints into consideration — may make the difference. Ultimately, however, we do watch every single entry, even when our pre-selection committee unanimously votes a submission out to the "rejection" bins. As for the awards we hand out, we spend days deliberating with our "Independent Vision" judges and always make sure that before we assign an award to a film or its filmmaker, we have all come down to our decisions "beyond all reasonable doubt," and are proud to have those winning entries represent the best of the best in what we already believe to be very solid programming.

Q: What have been some of the best-known films to play at Visionfest?

MARK DOYLE: As far as known films, we have had several since our inception. We've had films that have been classified as great films throughout the fest circuit, but may not be widely recognized by the mainstream public. And that is not a fault one can attribute to the various festival organizers. Take a film like Nyle Cavazos Garcia's *Clean*, for example. That film won more Visionfest awards in 2004 than any other film since our very first year. It continues to win awards at virtually every festival it enters. We were first to premiere it in the U.S., and we truly feel it is one great film that not many have ever heard of. Sadly, it's not even listed on *IndieWire's* "best films without distribution" chart. Far too many films get festival accolades galore but for whatever reason seem to go unnoticed by buyers and distributors, which ultimately translates to having no mainstream appeal. We keep a very close relationship with our filmmakers. I still speak with filmmakers from the 2001 or 2002 fests on a regular basis. It really is up to the festival directors and programmers to have open communication with each other. That's why the Film Festival Summit held every year in New York is important. It gives festival programmers and directors a chance to get together and talk about what is happening in the world of film festivals. In my opinion it should happen more than once a year.

BRUNO DERLIN: We've been really lucky to have some very important titles at our festival during the past five years. In our first edition, our top-prize fest winner was the feature comedy, *Passing Stones*, by Roger Majkowski, which has had numerous screenings on IFC's DV Theater series and has won several awards at many prestigious film festivals worldwide. Lisa France's *Anne B. Real* had its NYC premiere at Visionfest in 2003 and six months later it was nominated for two IFP Independent Spirit Awards. Among other notable titles are: *One-Eyed King*, which featured Armand Assante, Chazz Palminteri, William Baldwin, and Bruno Kirby, just to name a few recognizable names; Sundance Special Jury Prize winner *Fits & Starts*, which premiered at Visionfest and eventually got writers Vince DiMeglio and Tim Rasmussen several writing gigs at major Hollywood studios; and *Able Edwards*, the first all green-screen low-budget digital feature, executive produced by Steven Soderbergh.

Q: What advice can you give to aspiring filmmakers seeking to navigate the festival circuit?

MARK DOYLE: Research is free. Do your homework. It's really the cheapest part of the filmmaking journey and the one you can often spend the most time on. Try to get the background on the festival you are submitting to. Find out what films they have screened in the past. Read about how the festival interacts with the filmmakers.

BRUNO DERLIN: I think Mark has summed that one up quite eloquently and with all its truth. All I'd like to add is that one should not be discouraged by a rejection letter, as often one festival's rejected film may wind up to be another festival's biggest award recipient. Keep the faith.

❧

LISTEN TO WHAT THE MAN SAYS

Wow, there seems to be a lot of contradictory opinions about the festival circuit. So who is right and who is wrong? At the risk of playing favorites (and creating ill will in the process), let me just say that I have some sage advice to share on the subject:

1. Get involved with a local film festival as a volunteer. By doing this, you'll have an insider's view of how a festival operates, what goes into its planning and promotion, and how programmers are able to determine what gets shown. You might even make some dandy connections among the festival staff.

2. Do extensive research on the festival websites to determine the type of films that get screened. This will save you a ton of money and bother when the time comes to submit films for consideration. If it appears that the festival's previous incarnations were stacked with studio products or international offerings, there is a fairly good chance that your small and unaffiliated film is not going to be on their next slate. And you should check out Chris Gore's book *The Ultimate Film Festival Survival Guide*. It is now in its third edition, published by Lone Eagle Press, and it is the definitive source on information regarding the festival orbit.

3. Check to see if the festival has seminars or panel discussions that are held in conjunction with the screenings. Seminars and panel discussions often bring out well-regarded talent who can offer advice or connections — or might even want to pick up your film. Remember Liz Garbus bringing *Girlhood* to the festival in Atlanta and coming away with a Wellspring distribution deal thanks to the serendipitous presence of a Wellspring executive in one of the festival's seminars.

4. If your film is accepted at a festival, ask the festival organizers if it is possible to sell DVDs of your film after the screening. If people like the film and the production does not currently have distribution, this is the only way for people to literally take the film home with them. It can also earn you a fast collection of cash.

5. Before you go to a festival, print up some business cards with your full contact data. Why? If someone wants to stay in touch, the professional way to establish contact is to exchange business cards. And if someone gives you a business card at a festival, send over a thank-you note (either by snail mail or email) after the event to express thanks for making your acquaintance. It's a classy touch that will be remembered.

6. Ultimately, when it comes to the pursuit of the festival circuit, the best advice comes not from a film text but from *Ecclesiastes 3:1* — "To everything there is a season, a time for every purpose under the sun." No, this is not an invitation to turn, turn, turn. What it means is this: There is a time to pursue the festival circuit and a time to get your film off the circuit. I have to concur with Eric Monder: "My understanding is that many films get stuck in the film festival circuit. They're never launched anywhere." If your film is only playing in festivals, something's not working. Be honest with the situation and fix it.

SO YOU THINK YOU CAN DO A BETTER JOB THAN MIRAMAX?

Everything you can imagine is real.
— Pablo Picasso

5

INTERVIEW
ARTHUR DONG, FILMMAKER

Filmmaker Arthur Dong should have no problems getting attention from distributors. In the course of his career, he has racked up an Academy Award nomination and five Emmy nominations and he has won three Sundance Film Festival awards, a George Foster Peabody Award and a Guggenheim Fellowship.

Indeed, Dong's acclaimed 1994 documentary *Coming Out Under Fire*, which detailed the struggle of gay and lesbian service personnel in the American military during World War II, received a substantial theatrical release from Zeitgeist Films, a prestige boutique distributor.

But in 1997, Dong turned away offers from distributors to release his documentary *Licensed to Kill*. Instead, Dong took this riveting study of murderers convicted of homophobic hate crimes and successfully released it himself. In 2002, he repeated the self-distribution success with *Family Fundamentals*, a portrait of politically conservative families who discover one of their own is gay.

Dong continues to book these still-relevant films through the website of his production company, Deep Focus Productions. It would appear his decision to self-distribute paid off.

Q: With Licensed to Kill, *you turned down three potential distributors at Sundance to self-release the film. Why did you opt to do that? And did you also turn down distribution offers to release* Family Fundamentals?

ARTHUR DONG: At that time, I was inspired by successes with several social issue documentaries that were self-distributed in theaters, particularly *Maya Lin: A Strong Clear Vision*, *Last Call at Maud's*, and *Sex Is*. I already had experience with distributing my film *Forbidden City, U.S.A.* in two markets back in 1989, when self-distribution in theaters was almost unheard of. And my 1994 film, *Coming Out Under Fire*, which was distributed by Zeitgeist Films, did fairly well for a black-and-white documentary. Zeitgeist was generous with giving advice — that was important since I was building on the success of *Coming Out Under Fire* and using the rollout pattern of that film as a basis for *Licensed to Kill*.

Another important factor was that I had self-distributed my films to the educational market since 1982 and was familiar with that work. The offers I received for *Licensed to Kill* wanted all markets, including educational, and I resisted that — particularly since I had established strong contacts with the primary users of the film through my collaboration with them during the film's production period.

Finally, the Internet at that time was just beginning to reveal its potential. I think it's more hindsight than foresight, but the Internet sure made it easier to self-distribute than ever before. Of course, that's a no-brainer today, but back in 1997, you have to remember that the Internet was a novelty — spam mail was actually interesting!

When I finished *Family Fundamentals* in 2002, the role of the Internet for marketing was undisputed and I wanted to take advantage of the possibilities. By then I had already used e-commerce and knew it worked. Also, I had purposely crafted *Family Fundamentals* for a more conservative, "red state" if you will, audience. I didn't feel that any distributor was sincerely interested in penetrating that market wholeheartedly.

Q: After your victory at Sundance with Licensed to Kill, *the film had its theatrical premiere at the Film Forum in New York. After that, it played in dozens of venues around the country. Would you have been able to get the same level of bookings had the film opened at another New York theater?*

ARTHUR DONG: Opening *Licensed to Kill* at the Film Forum was important. They handled the promotions, and New York press is a monster, and they pretty much took care of all the details to make sure the word got out. Also, I learned that bookers around the country looked to the Film Forum for programming ideas. So my conversations with programmers were either initiated by them first because they saw it on Film Forum's calendar, or I'd just start a dialogue by saying we grossed "x" amount of dollars at the Film Forum. From that point it wasn't so much a question of whether they would book it, but rather when and what kind of deal to strike. It didn't hurt either that it won a couple of awards at Sundance.

I have to add, however, that *Coming Out Under Fire* opened at the Quad Cinema in New York City in 1994 and that didn't hurt the film's theatrical life at all. So I think while the Film Forum serves as an important barometer, it isn't necessarily the only way to go. Ultimately it's about the grosses and the particular preferences of the programmers. The key goal is to have a strong New York opening. Personally, I hope that mentality gets adjusted because I believe social issue docs can have a different kind of rollout and it's not always dependent on opening weekend numbers. Take the distribution of *Outfoxed*, for example. It started with house parties, cheap DVDs, and Internet transmissions. All that built up the word of mouth, which then thrust the film's distribution into theaters. I think we need to figure out patterns other than those imposed by feature films with bloated P&A budgets.

Q: What were the most rewarding elements of being your own distributor?

ARTHUR DONG: Taking the issue of antigay prejudice to small towns was one of the trickiest but most rewarding parts of self-distribution. My passion to address antigay bigotry was the primary motivator for me to work as hard as I did to bring

Kathleen Brenner
(top) with her gay
grandson David
Jester and her lesbian
daughter Susan Jester
in a 1963 portrait, fea-
tured in Arthur Dong's
documentary Family
Fundamentals. "I
think a distributor
with large overhead
expenses might think
twice about investing
a lot of resources on a
low-paying booking
that only takes in a
minimum rental of,
say, $250 or so,"
says Dong

Licensed to Kill and Family Fundamentals into theaters as well as classrooms. For me, it wasn't so much the box office — although I certainly needed decent grosses to continue — but it was getting the issues out to people who may not be aware of them. Larger towns like San Francisco, New York, Chicago, etc. were critical, but I would actually work harder when we opened in smaller towns like San Antonio or El Paso. It was crucial to get print stories and/or radio interviews since I was using the films as outreach. I figured, "Even if people don't get in line at the theaters and pay their admission, at least they might read and hear about the films and start thinking about the affects of antigay prejudice." That's a start, and change has to begin somewhere.

I think a distributor with large overhead expenses might think twice about investing a lot of resources on a low-paying booking that only takes in a minimum rental of, say, $250 or so. They may not want to expend the energy to make sure that the local press covers the film extensively and to hire a local publicist. But because my overhead was low I didn't have to think about the bottom line all the time. In fact, I often found a kindred spirit in the local theater managers and/or bookers — and sometimes they're the same people — who knew how to handle their community's press and were more than happy to help; after all, they booked the film and certainly wanted good returns. They would sometimes take on the role of publicist themselves or offer leads. It was a win-win situation. In some cities, the managers/bookers hooked me up with local community groups that helped publicize screenings to their constituents and a few even sponsored my travel to be with the film. That was really rewarding — to actually see and hear firsthand what local conditions were like.

Q: *Were there any downsides — emotional, financial, etc. — to being your own distributor?*

ARTHUR DONG: Sometimes I think that if I were more business-minded and savvy about profit making I would have attracted larger audiences. I find that my stubbornness in maintaining a certain level of integrity gets in the way of creating lucrative business plans that may have translated to more people seeing my films.

Also, there were times that I'd think, "Why am I hauling these prints to FedEx again — is this really what I want to do with my life?" But that fades quickly, particularly when I hear that a film garnered good press and drew responsive audiences. But there are moments when I would rather be editing — my favorite part of filmmaking — than making calls to track down prints and overdue payments.

But in the end, I worked for myself and everything that I put in came back twofold — probably more — and you can measure that in both dollars and political outreach. Just to be clear: We're talking minimum wage here! I also knew that my films weren't going to just gather dust on a distributor's shelf because they weren't making enough money to warrant attention. And, I set my own hours and didn't have to answer to anyone. That's not too shabby.

Q: *Will you self-release your upcoming projects? If not, why not?*

ARTHUR DONG: I'm mixed on that one. I think it'll depend on timing; it'll also depend on where the fulcrum sits between the balance of commerce and socially responsible films.

I'm not a filmmaker who always has a new project on the back burner ready to start up as soon as one ends. I like to enjoy the life of a film after it's done. The creative process of making films is an important reason why I'm a filmmaker, but in addition to being an artist, I also want to ensure my films do their jobs to communicate and engage. There's a lot of satisfaction in being with audiences when one of my films works; it's magic and there's no substitution. It's also gratifying when I see that my films can actually address social conditions and contribute to the problem solving. And while I admire a few socially conscious distributors out there, I know that in the end it has to be financially worthwhile for them to invest in a film's marketing. I'm not sure I'm ready to be motivated by profit.

I say that but I also see that marketing for documentaries, especially in the theatrical arena, has changed tremendously in just these past few years. It's become big business and it'd be interesting to see if a self-distributor can compete in that kind of environment. I mean, if you look at newspaper movie sections these days, the ads for some docs are just as big as for studio features. Can you imagine the costs? How can an indie filmmaker put up that kind of P&A?

It's rather ironic, really. I'm a governor of the Documentary Branch at the Academy of Motion Picture Arts and Sciences, which is focused on theatrically exhibited films — versus festivals, television, museums, etc. — and one of the main goals we set five years ago was to put documentaries on par with feature films in terms of their theatrical viability. And now we see that happening. But as a result, corporate interests have crept in and sometimes it overshadows why filmmakers devote their lives to documentaries in the first place. In mainstream publications as well as ones targeted to independents, the coverage often emphasizes grosses as the big news rather than a discussion of social change. I don't know, call me old-fashioned, but I lament the days when our main objective was to get dissident voices heard — not to fill box office coffers.

THE SELF-DISTRIBUTION PIONEERS

As you may have gathered by now, getting a foot in the door with distributors can be difficult. Getting a door in the face seems more likely. And don't think this is the exclusive domain of new filmmakers who are just making their way into the film world. Even someone like Hal Hartley has found himself facing problems with distributors.

Yes, *the* Hal Hartley. In January 2005, Hartley premiered his delightfully offbeat DV sci-fi riff *The Girl from Monday* at Sundance. "It was great to see it in Sundance with large audiences," recalls Hartley. "For so many months professional distributors and sales agents — friends of mine whose advice I sought — were telling me what I've got here is a beautiful but difficult art film, which is not what I thought I was making at the time. It was so consistent that I guess I came to believe this. But at Sundance, the audience was rocking with laughter and enjoying the movie in all sorts of ways. They were having a good time. And they were moved. That gave me a lot of confidence."

While Hartley left Sundance with confidence in his work, distributors did not share his enthusiasm and did not view the film as being commercially viable. Rather than bang on more doors, Hartley took the option of self-distributing his film. But it was not a spur-of-the-moment strategy.

"At a certain point in producing a movie like this — very small, in some ways experimental, with inexpensive equipment and a core group of creative friends — it began to seem like we could consider production and distribution to be the same thing," he says. "Of course it is, in fact, all this speedy technology I was just worrying about that makes this possible. We were already thinking about the production in such radically different terms than is usual with a feature film that crossing the line over into distribution was maybe a little easier."

When it comes to distribution, there is (if you pardon the vivisectionist sentiment) more than one way to skin a cat. In this case, the lack of willing distributors can be replaced with the ultimate in cinematic DIY: being your own distributor. Filmmakers distributing their own work is not, by any stretch, a recent development. In fact, the history of self-distribution stretches back to the latter part of the 1910s and early 1920s, when the concept was molded by a group of Hollywood insiders and one very remarkable Hollywood outsider.

The insiders, who were briefly mentioned earlier in this book, were the quartet who started United Artists: D. W. Griffith, Charlie Chaplin, Douglas Fairbanks, and Mary Pickford (actor William S. Hart was originally part of the process but dropped out early on without making much impact on the plan). The notion behind United Artists was based primarily on money: The four founders felt the studios releasing their respective films were taking more than a fair share of their profits. After consulting with a rather unlikely source — William G. McAdoo, a former secretary of the treasury and the son-in-law of President Woodrow Wilson — the combined Griffith-Chaplin-Fairbanks-Pickford team formed United Artists on February 5, 1919.

Yet United Artists quickly developed from a self-distribution outfit for its creators into a full-fledged distributor for other independent-minded producers. This was a necessity, since the output of the four stellar founders could not float a company (Griffith would later defect to a contract at Paramount, although he returned at the end of his career, and Chaplin took several years before offering his first feature under the United Artists banner, *The Gold Rush*). Over time, United Artists attracted such talents as Samuel Goldwyn, Joseph Schenck (who produced Buster Keaton's classic silent features), Gloria Swanson (during the period when Joseph P. Kennedy was producing her films), Howard Hughes, Walter Wanger, Alexander Korda, David O. Selznick, Hal Roach, and Stanley Kramer. Even the legendary Broadway producer Michael Todd took his sole cinematic endeavor, *Around the World in 80 Days*, to the screen via United Artists.

Obviously, as the years progressed the notion of United Artists being a genuinely independent effort became strained. While the films released under its auspices were technically not studio productions, they nonetheless were well-financed creations featuring major stars and directors. Around the time United Artists was originally taking root, a genuine independent filmmaker was setting new boundaries for self-distribution. During the period he was active, most moviegoers were unaware he existed. Yet in retrospect, his influence has been tremendous. His name was Oscar Micheaux.

Oscar Micheaux is often relegated to a sociological history corner of film studies, since he was a pioneering African American producer and distributor. Yet Micheaux achieved a level of business success that was completely uncommon for its time —

not because he was a black man operating in a white man's industry, but because he was wildly successful in what he did. A one-time shoeshine boy and Pullman porter, Micheaux enjoyed his first success as a farmer in South Dakota, which was no mean feat given he lived in an all-white area. Yet his agricultural know-how impressed the neighbors, especially as his domain grew to 500 acres. During this period, Micheaux wrote a novel called *The Conquest*, which detailed the lives of the South Dakota farmers. He self-published the book in 1913 and sold it door-to-door throughout the state. His foray into publishing was well-timed, as he lost his farm in 1915 (the circumstances behind this turn of events are murky, though Micheaux blamed his father-in-law, a minister, for the disaster).

Micheaux relocated to Sioux City, Iowa, and created his own publishing house. More self-published books were created, and Micheaux expanded his sales further into the Midwest — again, through the door-to-door sales method that he knew so well.

In 1918, the Lincoln Motion Picture Company in Lincoln, Nebraska, received a copy of Micheaux's novel *The Homesteader*, which was self-published the previous year. Lincoln was one of the very few production and distribution companies making films solely for African American audiences. Business must have been somewhat slow, since George Johnson, who handled national bookings from the Nebraska office, held a full-time job as a postal carrier. Johnson wanted to make a film from *The Homesteader*, but Micheaux would not sell the rights unless he directed the movie. Since Micheaux had no previous experience with a camera, Johnson rejected the writer and his property. Undaunted, Micheaux decided to make the film himself.

Going back to the door-to-door approach, Micheaux raised funding by selling stock in his new Micheaux Book and Film Company. Enough funds were raised to enable an all-black cast to be transported (reportedly in a chauffeured limousine) from Chicago to South Dakota for on-location shooting. *The Homesteader* emerged as an eight-reel epic that Micheaux wrote, directed, and produced.

But here is where Micheaux makes his mark in self-distribution. Going from city to city, Micheaux would bring a print of *The Homesteader* and advertising materials. He literally booked his own movie in theaters, but then he would offer publicity stills for what he claimed was his next production. Micheaux used these stills to get theater owners to pay up front for the privilege of screening his next movie, even though the production did not exist beyond a few stills. But the system worked, and Micheaux self-financed and self-released 30 movies throughout the 1920s.

It should also be noted that Micheaux was tackling issues that were mighty sensitive for their day: lynching, interracial romance, violence against African Americans (in the streets and in the courts), economic segregation, prostitution, light-skinned blacks passing for white, and religious hypocrisy (which was memorably essayed with the 1925 classic *Body and Soul* starring Paul Robeson as a corrupt preacher in his first film performance). Not unlike many contemporary indie filmmakers, Micheaux had the daring to challenge controversial subject matter and to fight off attempts at censorship.

Not content with conquering America, Micheaux also hit the European markets. Reports that Micheaux had his own office in London are unconfirmed, but he is known to have sailed for Europe to sell his movies. In a way, this was a fortuitous strategy since nearly all of his films from the 1920s are lost today — but his movies *Within Our Gates* (1920) and *Symbol of the Unconquered* (1921) were recovered in European archives.

We know that Micheaux was not the first independent filmmaker to attempt self-distribution, but he was the first to succeed with a depth and scope of continued triumphs. Most self-distribution up to his time was primarily a one-shot deal or very small scale; Micheaux made himself a one-man distribution operation. This is also significant because Micheaux could only book his films in theaters that played to segregated black audiences. White audiences never heard of Micheaux or his films during his life, and it would not be until the late 1960s and early 1970s that his contributions to cinema were acknowledged.

Micheaux's run of luck came to something of a halt when sound entered the movies. Financial difficulties, coupled with the higher costs of producing sound films, ate away at his profits. He made fewer films in the 1930s and only two in the 1940s (*The Notorious Elinor Lee* in 1940 and *Betrayed* in 1948). By then, the so-called "race films" business was dominated by production and distribution companies run by whites.

But today, the Micheaux model of self-distribution has been emulated (often unknowingly) by filmmakers releasing their own works. Eric Monder, a reviewer for *Film Journal International* and a teacher at Bethany College in Lindsborg, Kansas, delivered two landmark presentations on Micheaux at festivals honoring the filmmaker: at the Oscar Micheaux Golden Anniversary Memorial Celebration in Great Bend, Kansas, in March 2001 about "The Lost Films of Oscar Micheaux," of which there are too many; and again at the Great Bend Micheaux Festival in 2003 about his film *Murder in Harlem*. For Monder, Micheaux is the artist from where today's indie film world has grown.

"Oscar Micheaux inspires me personally as the first true 'indie' feature director and first real film business 'hyphenate': director-actor-producer-writer-distributor," he says. "Moreover, Micheaux has probably influenced and inspired many filmmakers who have never even heard of him. The more I learn about Oscar Micheaux and what he achieved, the more impressed I become. His visionary approach also extends to the sensitive and often controversial topics he tackled, probably at considerable professional and personal risk. I am amazed by his frank, unflinching perspective about race, religion, and gender, among other subjects."

For successful self-distribution, the next filmmaker who picked up where Micheaux left off — and who, prior to Micheaux's belated rediscovery, was assumed to have set the stage for this effort — was John Cassavetes, who was discussed earlier in this book. During the 1970s and 1980s, some (but not many) filmmakers pursued self-distribution. Henry Jaglom found a lucrative niche with his series of eccentric and eclectic comedies;

more recently, his distribution company, Rainbow Releasing, brings other movies to theaters, including the successful commercial re-release of *Monty Python and the Holy Grail.*

Another filmmaker to emerge in the early 1970s, Tom Laughlin — who will be discussed at greater length later in this chapter — was able to enjoy commercial (but not critical) success via self-distribution efforts. Some documentary filmmakers and independent auteurs self-released in one-shot offerings, but for the most part these were isolated endeavors and none of these efforts truly resonated with audiences.

It wasn't until the mid-1990s that self-distribution became increasingly prevalent. This was brought about primarily by default rather than design: With the number of films rising and the opportunity for commercial acquisitions among distributors diminishing, self-distribution has become a more palatable strategy. And in many cases, it is the only way for genuinely original artists to get their works on a screen.

INTERVIEW
ANDREW REPASKY MCELHINNEY, FILMMAKER

One of the most imaginative young filmmakers to blaze across the indie scene in recent years has been Philadelphia-based Andrew Repasky McElhinney. Pushing the proverbial envelope in regard to concept and content, McElhinney has built an impressive canon over the past decade that attracted the attention of the media and audiences. His features *Magdalen* (1996), *A Chronicle of Corpses* (2001), and *Georges Bataille's Story of the Eye* (2004) brilliantly challenge preconceived notions of genre protocol and cinematic niceties. By offering an artistic and mature consideration of the human experience, McElhinney defies the pigeonholing that traps too many artists: He is a genuine original.

Even more impressive has been McElhinney's insistence on theatrically self-releasing his features. By keeping control of where his films are being shown, he has carefully built his reputation in a high-impact and cost-effective manner.

Q: You've theatrically self-distributed your first three features. Was this done by design? Or did you attempt to get an existing distributor to pick up these films for theatrical release?

ANDREW REPASKY MCELHINNEY: I think the most important goal with any releasable feature film is to get it in front of an audience, get it reviewed as much as possible, and channel any momentum generated into finding an appropriate home format deal and into getting another project made.

Often, the process of looking for that ever-elusive "negative pickup" stymies independent filmmakers for undue amounts of time and to diminishing returns. Let's face it, the Kevin Smith/Edward Burns/Darren Aronofsky thing has never happened to any independent filmmaker I know of, no matter how deserving.

With my work, the best way to get it out there so far has been to do it myself. I have relationships with many cinema venues due to my work as a repertory film programmer and being a rabid cineaste who actually goes to all those venues. Happily, I find that once you have a film "on the map" at one place, other venues/festivals seek it out. Then, when you make the next film, you have the relationship to initiate a proposal of screenings.

Q: What was the release strategy on your first feature, Magdalen? *Specifically, which cities and theaters did you initially target for the theatrical release? And what was the eventual scope of that film's theatrical release?*

ANDREW REPASKY McELHINNEY: *Magdalen* was my fourth film project and my first feature. I wrote it in late 1995 and rehearsed/shot it during the summer of 1996. With *Magdalen*, as I would think it would be with any first feature, my goal was to introduce myself as a filmmaker.

By the time the feature was completed in the summer of 1998, I had *A Chronicle of Corpses* scripted and used *Magdalen's* positive buzz to entice talent and crew into being a part of *Corpses*. Often the fact that work is out there, and that there is a body of work, is as important to a director as a project's particular merits.

Magdalen's biggest screening was when Jay Schwartz' Secret Cinema gave the film a theatrical run at Moore College of Art and Design. The film got reviewed and *Magdalen* was on its way.

Q: What was the release strategy on your second feature, A Chronicle of Corpses? *Specifically, which cities and theaters did you initially target for the theatrical release? And what was the eventual scope of that film's theatrical release?*

ANDREW REPASKY MCELHINNEY: I'm not sure how much strategy a self-released independent film can truly have. It's a pretty organic process and requires more than a bit of good luck. You should hope for the best and expect the worst.

A Chronicle of Corpses first screened on Friday, March 24, 2000, at the Prince Music Theater in Philadelphia. The reaction was mixed and the film didn't do anything until September 2001 when John Toner unspooled *A Chronicle of Corpses* at the County Theater in Doylestown, Pennsylvania. The notices were strong and from there I contacted Matthew Seig at the Two Boots Pioneer Theater in New York. He and Phil Hartman, the theater's owner and Two Boots Pizza baron, decided to take a chance on my odd little movie.

A Chronicle of Corpses opened in New York on October 24, 2001, to intriguing notices in the New York Times, Village Voice, New York Post, Time Out New York, and New York Daily News. Seig understood the value of moving *A Chronicle of Corpses* to a Friday and Saturday late-night slot until it was replaced in February of 2002 by Richard Kelly's marvelous 113-minute cut of *Donnie Darko*. By that time, *A Chronicle of Corpses* had been invited to Rotterdam and other venues like the San Francisco Film Festival, the George Eastman House, and the Cleveland Cinematheque of Art.

Unusual films need to find their audience and settle into the world into which they are thrust. Time, determination, and well-allocated resources are the key. To that end, I have never been shy about giving away copies of my films. I have always felt that the more promotional copies are out there, the more people will know about your work. I know I almost never throw out a DVD or a laser disc or a VHS tape and imagine that, like many people, I have a large collection of motion pictures I've heard about and plan to watch. Just having that possibility could lead who knows where, and so if they're legit industry and they ask for a copy, I give it to them.

The other thing I'll add, and this may seem like a simple, obvious thing, but from having worked at film festivals and having programmed screening series I am constantly shocked at how many folks don't put their name and contact information on everything they send out. Even their tapes and DVDs come unlabeled but in a fancy box! Filmmakers want to make it as easy as possible for people to find them and credit their work.

Q: *When you first began approaching theaters to show* Magdalen *and* A Chronicle of Corpses, *how did they react upon hearing from you? Were they receptive to having you self-release your films, or did they state a preference for dealing with an established distributor?*

ANDREW REPASKY MCELHINNEY: It's much harder to self-distribute for the home entertainment market than it is for theatrical. The home entertainment market, without names in your cast, really requires the cachet of a successful theatrical run and something of a promotional push to get it into stores.

Whereas, ostensibly, theatrical venues are always looking for product to screen. There are enough alternative halls over the world that are accustomed to dealing with movies without distributors or even accustomed to seeking out pictures that are otherwise under the radar. I think this willingness to "take a look at a screener" is because they know the worst-case scenario is that they'll have another independent filmmaker begging them to take their money for a four-wall. And if they're lucky, they might stumble onto something worthwhile. My favorite programmers are the ones who book films based on what they want to see, not what they have seen.

The best thing you can do to ease the disadvantage of not having a distributor behind you is to present a press kit that is concise, delivers your message, and looks very good. It takes money to make money. Don't be a slob. Be fussy. Don't cut corners. Make it as easy for people to learn about your work as possible. Communicate clearly. Your screeners and press kits make the first impression and it is to your flick's advantage for them to look and sound their best. Don't spend $1 million on your life's greatest ambition and then scrimp on the promotion or the cost of a few extra screeners.

Finally, have a website. Make sure that when people Google your name they're finding you. Don't be shy.

Q: When A Chronicle of Corpses *opened in New York, what level of marketing assistance did the Pioneer Theater provide you?*

ANDREW REPASKY MCELHINNEY: The Pioneer gave *A Chronicle of Corpses* one press screening and split the cost of an ad in the Village Voice. I made sure that every film critic in town and on the Internet that I could think of received stills, a press kit, and the offer of a screener or screening.

After the reviews hit, and the audience came, the Pioneer assumed most promotional responsibilities and aggressively kept the movie in the public's eye for five months. Matthew Seig and Phil Hartman are a credit to their professions and the best friends your movie could want.

Q: A Chronicle of Corpses *was boosted by an enthusiastic review from Dave Kehr in the New York Times, who later named it among the Ten Best Films of the Year. Was it easier to book the film in other cities based on the strength of the Kehr review?*

ANDREW REPASKY MCELHINNEY: It was easier to book *A Chronicle of Corpses* after the New York opening because of all the notice, exposure, and word of mouth it received from playing well in the West's most magnificent city. Kehr's review in the *New York Times* certainly led the pack and is one of the most exciting pieces of feedback I have ever received. Being number nine on Kehr's Top Ten list solidified his enthusiasm for the picture and encouraged many people who had read about *A Chronicle of Corpses* back in October to make that extra effort to track it down. This second push was more than invaluable and again I feel very fortunate.

Q: What was the release strategy for your third feature, the 2004 release Georges Bataille's Story of the Eye? *Specifically, which cities and theaters did you initially target for the theatrical release? And what was the eventual scope of that film's theatrical release?*

ANDREW REPASKY MCELHINNEY: There are two lives for *Georges Bataille's Story of the Eye*. First, there is the video installation version where the film is splintered into five episodes that loop continuously on five projectors. This edition of the movie premiered at the Philadelphia Fringe Festival in September 2003.

Second, there is the theatrical feature film of *Georges Bataille's Story of the Eye* running 81 minutes and ten seconds. With the feature film I approached every place that had played *Magdalen* and/or *A Chronicle of Corpses* and about two thirds of them were game. Mostly the theatrical venues that were not film festivals embraced *Georges Bataille's Story of the Eye*. They understood it in the tradition of outsider cinema, midnight movies, and porno chic.

The film festivals that had played *A Chronicle of Corpses* and perhaps even muttered sweet nothings into my ear regarding a "lifelong relationship" didn't pan out. I imagine they either found the film too sexually explicit or too radical a meditation on *Georges Bataille*.

Sadly, too, some of the venues that were around back in 2002 have ceased to exist or had their budgets so slashed that they are no longer curating an ambitious film program.

Certainly, the fact that *Georges Bataille's Story of the Eye* got early Internet buzz on *Film Threat*, and in print in the pages of *Filmmaker* magazine via Jeremiah Kipp's interview with me, helped a lot, as did the fact that at the point of *Georges Bataille's Story of the Eye's* theatrical issuing I had a track record as a feature film director. Even a year after the first press coverage came in, *Georges Bataille's Story of the Eye* was still on tour.

Filmmaker Andrew Repasky McElhinney, who has uccessfully self-released three feature films. Says McElhinney: "I'm all for cashing in, but not for selling out."

I've been encouraged that *Magdalen* and *A Chronicle of Corpses* have never really gone away — the former is nearly a decade old! I assume *Georges Bataille's Story of the Eye* will have a long, happy, and healthy life, too.

Q: Georges Bataille's Story of the Eye *features rather graphic sexual footage — more graphic than most commercial releases. Did theaters decline to show the film based on its content? And if they did, was any attempt made to dissuade them from their decision?*

ANDREW REPASKY MCELHINNEY: If people are going to judge a film based on its sexual content, which they often do, there is very little one can do to change their minds. It's important to understand and respect people's "no" and not hold a pass against anyone. Getting a firm "no" is much better than a soft "maybe." You must realize that when you take a risk you're not going to be able to take everyone with you.

I plan to make as many feature films as possible and realize that I need to make them as best as I can and that people will like some of them more than others. Opinions change over time. I know that my films are forever and I am excited at the prospect of the fresh evaluation of each new generation. I just hope not to ever make a mediocre, unmemorable movie that people have no opinion of. That would be sad.

I'm all for cashing in, but not for selling out.

Q: *How would you categorize the entertainment media's level of support for* Georges Bataille's Story of the Eye?

ANDREW REPASKY MCELHINNEY: Dennis Harvey in Variety gave a wonderful review, perhaps my best ever, and called *Bataille* "a punk pornocopia equivalent to *Last Year at Marienbad*." I do not think I could pitch the movie any better. Dave Kehr of the *New York Times*, Johnny Ray Huston of the *San Francisco Bay Guardian*, and you, Phil Hall, have been big champions of the movie. I am profoundly grateful and glad that *Georges Bataille's Story of the Eye* reached you.

In Philadelphia, *Georges Bataille's Story of the Eye* opened at the Roxy Screening Rooms on Friday, December 12, 2003. From there it went to San Francisco, where it played very well. Johnny Ray Huston said the film was "a provocation that hypnotizes, a hallucinatory narcotic." Then it went to New York, where Matt Zoller Seitz said it was "a Rubik's Cube of conceptual porn" in the *New York Press*.

Georges Bataille's Story of the Eye is a film that challenges people, but I am happy to say that most adventurous movie people seem to welcome and embrace the experiment. In many ways *Georges Bataille's Story of the Eye* has been at once the most "out there" and commercially successful film I've made.

Q: Taking the previous question a step further, how do you categorize the level of support that the entertainment media provides to independent films as a whole?

ANDREW REPASKY MCELHINNEY: That's a hard question that I am not sure there is an answer to. But then, these are the questions worth asking. I am more interested in questions than in answers anyway.

Most film critics have an eye peeled for discovering new talent. Most distributors are looking for something they can sell. An American audience now, alas, seems not to know much more that if they "liked it" or "didn't like it," which really, if you think about it, has very little to do with the merits of anything.

We have room in the marketplace for independent films and places they can be shown and for that I am profoundly grateful. But there is still a lot of shit being made and somebody must prefer to see that new remake or that old star in a poorly written vehicle. That lack of risk, that corrupt trust in the familiar, is eating away at the soul of American culture. As a nation we need to move to a progressive place where our national theater, which is the cinema, and evermore TV and cable, forces us to evaluate, self-educate, and grow as people. This should happen each and every time we sit down to watch the little screen or rest among our fellow citizens in the dark caverns of a theater or multiplex. Film and theater must move away from being a tourist destination.

Q: While you've theatrically released three features, you've not self-distributed them for DVD. Why did you opt to have the DVD releases handled by an established DVD label rather than do it yourself?

ANDREW REPASKY MCELHINNEY: I would have sold my theatrical rights to distributors had it been right, rather than do it myself. But it wasn't. My self-theatrical release ignited the interests of home format companies. So I went with it. When it feels right, and I know the movie will be served, I am willing to turn my product over to the industry. Let's face it, the more time other people are at work selling my films, the more time I can spend dreaming up the next one. What's next, and what I've just learned, are most important to me. There is nothing I would rather be doing than making another film.

A FEW BASIC FACTS

Self-distribution can be a fairly complex endeavor, since the filmmaker needs to morph out of the creative state into a business planning mind frame. For filmmakers with no education or experience in business planning, this can be a challenge. But that's not to say it is an impossible challenge.

There are some ground rules for self-distribution that need to be considered:

1. Self-distribution is synonymous with self-financing. Unless the filmmaker has someone else footing the bills, this endeavor will require a personal cash investment to keep the film in motion. If the filmmaker does not begin with a clear and concise budget, there will be chaos in the very near future.

2. If the self-distribution is for a single film, the filmmaking is going to be at something of a negotiating disadvantage. Theater bookers are eager to maintain relationships with established distributors that have a continual flow of commercially viable titles. A self-distributing filmmaker is, for all intents and purposes, a one-shot deal. And unless that shot provides the genuine promise of commercial success, the bookers will view the property with skepticism (if not outright indifference). However, if the filmmaker takes a liking to the process and decides to distribute additional films, this could be the start of a satisfactory relationship between the filmmaker and the theaters.

   The typical negotiation can follow either of a pair of strategies. The first is a straight percentage deal split, with the filmmaker getting anywhere from 10 to 30% of the box office (it is usually closer to the former). The second is the strangely named "house-nut" deal, when the theater owner first takes out all expenses relating to the exhibition of the film, then splits the box office (again in that 10 to 30% range). Signing up for the deal is the easy part. Collecting from the theater can be something of a challenge — and even the established distributors are known to grumble that many well-known theaters are painfully slow in providing either accounting statistics or payments or both.

3. The self-distribution process will (more likely than not) require a "platform release." This means that the film will travel on a city-by-city route, with the film playing anywhere from one to (if Lady Luck is uncommonly benevolent) five cities at a time. The venues that will be interested in a self-distributed film will certainly be the art house cinemas; multiplexes feed exclusively off the Hollywood studios and they couldn't care less about smaller films from self-distributing filmmakers. If the film in question is meant for digital projection, this might limit exhibition choices further because some

theaters (even at this late date) will only screen movies in 35mm or 16mm. And just because a theater has digital projection doesn't mean it will support every imaginable digital format (are we talking DigiBeta, HD, DVD, etc.?).

4. The self-distributing filmmaker will take on new roles that may not have been previously considered. These include: (1) the strategy planner, researching the venues where the film could run; (2) the salesman, pitching the film to the theaters; (3) the shipping manager, keeping tabs on the delivery of the film and all supporting marketing materials to the theaters that agree to show it; (4) the accounts receivable officer, making sure the theaters provide payment for whatever profits are generated; and (5) the accounts payable officer, making sure the various contributors to this endeavor (including publicists, couriers, Webmasters, video duplication shops, etc.) are paid in a timely manner. For filmmakers who approach their craft with the sole concern of making the film, this plunge into Film Distribution 101 can be thrilling or chilling (depending on how one views the less-than-glamorous business aspect of the industry).

5. Self-distribution sucks away the time that the filmmaker can spend on other projects. For example, filmmaker Gene Cajayon spent two years crisscrossing the country with his self-distribution of *The Debut*. And that can be just the minimum amount of time devoted to a complete and total self-distribution odyssey (assuming the filmmaker is looking to take the film to every and any market that will welcome it). "Self-distributing your film means that you'll be living with your film for another one to two years in addition to the two years it took to write and produce it, which means a delay in making your next film and losing your creative momentum," warns Gregory Hatanaka, filmmaker and distributor.

6. Self-distribution will require excessive grassroots marketing. This will be especially relevant if the film plays in markets where newspaper advertising is very expensive (hello, New York and Los Angeles!). Hiring a local publicist can help in getting media coverage, and if a film has appeal to a particular niche audience then it is incumbent on the filmmaker to go after that niche with as much gusto as possible.

SELF-DISTRIBUTION WAR STORIES

One of the most prominent examples of self-distribution came via New York filmmaker Larry Fessenden. Fessenden's first feature, the 1990 production *No Telling*, sort of an updated version of the Frankenstein legend, earned praise from audiences and critics who caught it in its festival run but didn't earn the praise of distributors on the prowl for new theatrical releases. Fessenden, in retrospect, was not surprised at the film's fate.

"*No Telling* is a passionate, serious, and competently made film with a distinct independently minded point of view, and it is a genre film," says Fessenden. "But I guess it isn't hip. I have never forgiven the indie film world for rejecting it so completely."

Yet the film did not meet its fate on a dusty shelf. "We signed a foreign deal very quickly, for which I was grateful," he adds. "It's seen on TV and possibly video in dozens of countries as *The Frankenstein Complex*."

The film finally turned up on American home video somewhat by accident: Fessenden was trying to interest a small (and now-defunct) distributor called World Artists in picking up his next feature, an urban vampire tale called *Habit*. World Artists passed on that film, but grabbed *No Telling* for release — seven years after it was completed.

"As for my efforts, I shopped it consistently during the seven years and no one was ever interested," adds Fessenden. "It was handled by many competent people off and on who couldn't give it away. Talk about feeling like a pariah!"

Fessenden may have experienced a sense of déjà vu with *Habit*: As with his first film, getting distributors to pick up the film was not successful. But this time, Fessenden opted to act as his own distributor. The film opened in 1996 in New York at Cinema Village, a venue that has long been welcoming to self-distributing filmmakers. But unfortunately for Fessenden the film received a negative review from Lawrence Van Gelder, the *New York Times* critic, and that thumbs-down hurt the film's commercial viability.

"Bad reviews make me feel vulnerable: There's someone out there who doesn't see things my way, and they have the power to print their put-downs and prejudice people against me," says Fessenden. "If the review is well written or thoughtful, it's easier to take. But a stupid dis in print curdles my blood. When you have an unknown film, and you're putting it out yourself, all reviews are financially significant, and the bad review from Van Gelder cost me a great deal of money because it caused my exhibitor to share the screen for *Habit* in its second week with another film. I cursed Van Gelder and I cursed the other bad reviews from critics who had supported other projects I'd been involved in."

We need to pause for a moment to note that Van Gelder's negative review had nothing to do with Fessenden's self-distribution. Yet in some sectors, critical prejudice exists towards self-distribution.

"Smart critics know that great films often fail to secure distribution deals," says Ed Gonzalez, editor of *Slant* magazine. "But I also think that a majority of critics think a film can't be very good if it's self-distributed. This has become the sad reality of our profession: With entertainment coverage so inextricably bound to advertising dollars and review space only available to films with distributors, most critics don't even bother seeing a film if they're not getting paid to review it. This is where film-savvy editors can do a lot of good by exercising their clout and devoting special sections in their pages to distributor-less works."

Indeed, many media outlets that celebrate indie cinema do not make the distinction. "I have an open mind while viewing a self-distributed film," says Kent Turner, editor of *Film-Forward.com*, an online magazine focusing on independent productions. "It usually means the film has perceived limited commercial prospects, but it doesn't necessarily have any bearing on the film itself creatively."

But back to the Fessenden story. Despite the dis in the *Times*, Fessenden pushed *Habit* into a platform release. It was a labor, both of love and of pain.

"The joys: knowing that every booking, every ad, every poster, every review, every promotional item, was a result of our own decision-making and hard work by me and my colleague Michael Ellenbogen," he notes. "And so any success we had, we earned. The anguish is knowing that in the end, only money, real studio backing, and the complex publicity machine give you the muscle to stay in theaters."

And the strategy ultimately paid off. Fessenden says the film received "80% good reviews" and he won the Independent Film Spirit Award for *Habit* — no mean feat for a self-released flick. He did not need to push the film further, as Fox Lorber picked up *Habit* for its U.S. home video release.

"The most difficult thing facing an independent filmmaker is the imagination," says Fessenden. "If you have one, it's quite possible no one will give you a chance to exhibit or distribute your picture — let alone compensate you. World Artists and Fox Lorber took chances with my movies, because the decks were stacked against them, with video stores like Blockbuster squeezing out small titles so they can guarantee that the highest-grossing films that have finally left the theaters are now in your face all over again to rent. How pandering and insulting. It's embarrassing to be treated like children by the megavendors."

Yet Fessenden did not have to face childlike treatment from distributors. His next feature, *Wendigo*, was released by ThinkFilm to strong reviews and commercial cheer. And *Habit* has since gained a cult following, with audiences rediscovering its eerie brilliance — but, of course, that discovery would never have occurred if Fessenden had not driven the movie out into the world by himself.

Stephen J. Szklarski is another New York filmmaker who took the self-distribution route. Unlike Larry Fessenden, his decision came after problems arose with the distributor who released his first film, the narrative feature *A Packing Suburbia*. For his 2004 documentary *Union Square*, which focused on the lives of heroin addicts living on the streets of New York, Szklarski took the reins in bringing the film into release.

"When creating the documentary all I thought about was how it would move me emotionally or how it would affect me," he says. "Theatrical self-distribution is always on my mind because I feel that nobody will take the risk with me. I hope in the future some companies will. But I figure if I place it in theaters on my own and get cool reviews and break even, I am happy. It was a great challenge for me with *Union Square* because it had no film festival play, no big stars — it was not a feature but a documentary about the effects of heroin addiction. What theatrical company would place that? I was able to get theaters to play it because I believed in it. To my surprise I got decent reviews from great people and those who did see it gave it a great response."

Szklarski got positive feedback from some distributors, but with knotty strings attached. "The few companies I spoke to wanted these crazy-looking agreements signed, so I turned them down," he adds. "I only pitched distribution companies that did not screw me or screw anyone else. One must go to the film and TV markets and seek out these people. It is a sleazefest sometimes because 75% are out to screw you. But let your gut tell you the truth."

There was also a problem with an independent booker who was hired to place the film in theaters. "Watch out for theatrical bookers, too," he says. "I got ripped off hard-core by a booker who made promises and took my money and did nothing. So I just booked it myself. I would send a screener, then call the theater and beg for it to be screened. Some said yes and some said no. Win some, lose some, it is a gamble all the way. But it is really worth it."

In being his own distributor, Szklarski realized he needed to look and act the part of a distributor. "I started a label called Alliance International Pictures," he says. "I put up a website so it looked cool. I wanted *Union Square* to be the tester for it."

The next strategic move was determining his opening: New York and Los Angeles first. "I wanted to go with theaters that would also play it on digital video only," he notes. "I did not have the funds to make a 35mm print and refused to do it. I shot it on DV so why not screen it on DV? If the content is interesting enough, people will come see it."

In retrospect, this may not have been the best way for the filmmaker to go. "What I learned was the next time I do a release like this, release it in smaller markets first to create a buzz and then book New York and Los Angeles," he says. "Book Boston, Philadelphia, San Francisco, Atlanta, Seattle, then get your press, and then book New York and Los Angeles."

Szklarski also put a grassroots marketing machine into motion. "I created 1,000 letters, 1,000 faxes, 10,000 emails, 200 VHS screeners," he adds up. "I bought phone cards, $20 each, to keep the phone bill down. I called and mailed newspapers, drug treatment centers, colleges. I put together interns for a street team. I hung up posters that I made in Photoshop. I have to give props to Hugh Haggerty for helping me with all the printing. I bought four VHS machines and duped press and film market screeners in my apartment. I placed my own label on them and sent them out on my own letterhead. But the most important thing is your poster. Take it seriously and design a nice one. If you can't make one yourself, find a geeky, cyberpunk movie buff who loves movie posters to make you a poster. Postcards are very important: 4 x 6, worth the investment, cheap to make, and remember all film credits should be universal fonts. I bought them for the computer — that is how I know that. All of this is all trial and error. Once you have it, splatter it everywhere. I made up 2,500 posters and just hung them up after I got the booking in."

How did he plan out the marketing budget for the self-release? "Very carefully," he says. "Ten thousand dollars was all I had to spend. So I stretched it as far as I could. I wanted money for printing. You need to make a trailer for your film that needs to be flat or scope so it can play in theaters one month before the film opens. When it is all done from DVCAM, then a two-minute promo transferred to 35mm with copies in flat and scope comes to $2,500. Theaters run movie trailers in 35mm. I would break it down by percentage: 20% is for film trailers; 20% for posters and postcards; 20% for ads in weekly magazines; 20% for letters, envelopes, and lots of stamps (postage is very expensive); and 20% for the combination of computer equipment, editing programs, rent, and the phone bill. It is a rough breakdown but that is how I did it. And I broke even!"

One self-distributing filmmaker who saved money for himself (and countless filmmakers who followed in his path) was Los Angeles–based Ted Bonnitt. His 2001 documentary *Mau Mau Sex Sex*, which celebrated the history of exploitation cinema, was shot on digital video. Alas, funds for a 35mm transfer were not available for him.

"We did not see getting back the $40,000-plus it would have cost to make a 35mm transfer and prints," Bonnitt recalls. "I also did not want to degrade the final digital image on film. We called theaters around the country and found that sufficient video projection venues existed to play in the cities that we targeted. This is an independent, art house movie and they tend to have more diverse projection equipment and put more effort into promoting your run. However, these being the early days of DV, many theaters did not have video projection equipment, and the cost to rent the projector and playback machine was prohibitive. So, we had theaters wanting to book the movie but unable to do so."

Bonnitt's answer was actually quite revolutionary. "Our solution came from Sharp Electronics, which introduced a high-quality portable LCD projector (P-20) that we were able to ship overnight to theaters," he continues. "We tested it with a DVD player, and the image was remarkably good considering the compression on the DVD. Sharp provided the projector in order to introduce their new product to the theatrical marketplace, and we suggested that theater owners bring their DVD player from home and plug it in. We never had a complaint from a customer, and we received big press reviews in every city we played without

photo courtesy 7th Planet Productions

any mention of how we showed it. It was a successful road-show sleight-of-hand trick! Theaters were even willing to pay for the projector's $100 shipping cost, because after all, their take of the box office sales is in part to cover the cost of their facilities, which we were in part providing to them with projection capability. Necessity is the mother of invention. It represents a new trend, where independents are getting down to business. They'll make their movies on desktop computers and distribute them on DVDs to art house cinemas with smaller and more powerful video projectors that look and sound much better than 16mm. It's an elegant solution that helps dispel the stigma of self-distribution."

Veteran exploitation filmmakers Dan Sonney and Dave Friedman relive old times in Ted Bonnitt's Mau Mau Sex Sex, the first film theatrically released in a DVD format. "We never had a complaint from a customer, and we received big press reviews in every city we played without any mention of how we showed it," says Bonnitt. "It was a successful road-show sleight-of-hand trick!"

And how did the programmers and exhibitors react when Bonnitt told them the film was available for DVD projection? "The typical sresponse was: 'Huh? Really? Wow. Okay, we'll do it,'" says Bonnitt. "Exhibitors are refreshingly down to earth. They'll try anything if they think that it will sell tickets. So, the fact that Mau Mau Sex Sex was the first movie to be distributed theatrically on DVD was no problem for a great majority of them, just a cost-effective solution. And, as a result, theaters are buying the Sharp projector, because it costs less than a 35mm projector, which represents a breakthrough for them. It was a win-win solution for everyone involved, including the audience, who otherwise would never have seen *Mau Mau Sex Sex*. And what was required of theaters to make their projection booths ready for this type of projection? A connection to their sound system, and usually with a simple RCA plug. We included an easy three-page step-by-step instruction manual on how to plug in the DVD player to the projector and point it toward the screen — everything else is automatic."

Bonnitt's film played across North America and in Europe, all via the DVD projection process.

Another New York filmmaker who took the self-distribution route was Michael Prywes. His 2003 comedy (and directing debut) *Returning Mickey Stern* came to the screen through his own efforts. Yet Prywes is the first to admit his efforts were not entirely smooth.

"I actually was not very adept at getting the word out about *Returning Mickey Stern*," he acknowledges. "I got the *Hollywood Creative Directory* and periodically sent out postcards to every last acquisitions person about the movie. I also sent out DVD screeners of the trailer. I had read in a number of books that you should get all the distributors in a room to get one of them to bite. The problem is, how do you do that? I decided to invite distributors to film festival and screening-room screenings, but very few came. I was very against the idea of sending out videotapes, because you can't control the environment in which a tape is watched. In the end, I did end up sending screeners when I was looking for video distribution."

Yet Prywes found getting the videos sent out was actually the easiest part of the process. "Getting it watched was the tough part," he continues. "Most tapes just languish on desks. I did get some ins to a couple of higher-ups at a couple of studios through referrals. The response was generally the same: 'I enjoyed the movie but it's a hard sell, because it's more like a television movie than an indie movie.' My story line is very mainstream, my stars are veteran television stars — including Joseph Bologna, Renee Taylor, Tom Bosley, and Connie Stevens — and the film was shot on 35mm."

In retrospect (naturally), Prywes pinpoints where his strategy should've been altered. "I should not have worked so hard with festivals and concentrated more on markets — AFM,

Cannes, NAB," he says. "Nonetheless, we got some awards, which helped, and I met some wonderful people at the festivals. In fact, I found my foreign sales agent, Barbara Mudge of Worldwide, through a friend from the festival circuit. She introduced me to my domestic television and video distributors. Distributors are always more inclined to look at your product when you are referred by a respected member of the industry."

Prywes also learned a valuable lesson, albeit not in the most positive manner, about dealing with theaters. "When I was doing the festival circuit, I contacted a couple of New York theater owners and asked them if they'd show my film," he says. "This was a partially stupid move, because I did not know that theaters have bookers. I pissed off one of the bookers, Rob Lewinski of Lesser Entertainment, because I went over his head, and he apparently did not love my film, so he decided not to book it at local theaters. Lesser controlled the booking at a whole bunch of New York and Long Island theaters, including North Shore Towers and Kew Gardens, and because my film was made on Long Island and aimed for older audiences, it was at a major disadvantage before it was even advertised. Learn from my mistake: It's okay to meet indie theater owners and entice them with your film, but make sure you don't piss off their bookers!"

THE SERVICE DEAL SOLUTION

Rather than book his film by himself, Prywes got *Returning Mickey Stern* into theatrical presentation through a "service deal." In the realm of self-distribution, the service deal is becoming a very popular option (not to mention financially viable for certain flicks).

A service deal is something of a distributor-for-hire arrangement in which the filmmaker pays an established distribution company to theatrically release a movie. The filmmaker also forks over the funds to handle the costs of prints and advertising (P&A).

A service deal can be viable if a filmmaker already has DVD and ancillary-market sales lined up but still wants to build value from a theatrical presentation. Many distributors will not touch a film unless they can snag the other rights beyond theatrical, so a service deal can still get a film on a big screen — albeit at a price.

During the past half-dozen years, a surprising number of prominent films have been released on a service deal basis. This includes two of the most commercially successfully independently financed films of all time: *My Big Fat Greek Wedding* and *The Passion of the Christ*. Other notable films released as a service deal include *Memento*, *Monster* (for which Charlize Theron won the Best Actress Oscar), *Metallica: Some Kind of Monster*, the Oscar-nominated documentaries *Capturing the Friedmans* and *Twist of Faith*, and the cult favorite *The American Astronaut*.

(Perhaps a bit of stigma still exists here, as Bob Berney, the head of Newmarket, insisted in interviews that *Monster* and *The Passion of the Christ* were actually "partnerships" and not service deals. However, these partnerships looked an awful lot like service deals.)

Many distributors are open to considering service deals. One well-regarded company, Artistic License, primarily focuses on these types of distribution arrangements. "Once the P&A funds are available, Artistic will make a budget that includes all the expenses and a distribution fee," explains Sande Zeig, president of Artistic License. "Some service deals are for a three-city, five-city, ten-city, or fifteen-city release."

Yet a film can open so strongly that a flexible service deal will allow for greater release. In 2003, Zeig experienced that with the documentary *Tibet: Cry of the Snow Lion*. It was slated for a five-city release and wound up playing in more than 100 theaters due to strong critical and audience response.

Zeig freely admits that service deals come with downsides and upsides. "Let's talk about the disadvantage first," she says. "The disadvantage is that filmmakers have to raise additional sources of financing for P&A. The advantage is that filmmakers have much more control over the distribution process. This includes everything from the marketing and promotional materials — posters, trailers, ads — to how that P&A money is being spent. A service deal gives filmmakers the opportunity to work on all aspects of distribution. Some like the hands-on approach. After all, they have been doing everything up until now. Artistic specializes in working closely with filmmakers — we are also filmmakers. Also, once filmmakers have gone through the film distribution process, they will have a better understanding of the business."

Reaction within the industry to service deals is mixed. Filmmaker and distributor Quentin Lee represents those who are not positively inclined. "I wouldn't recommend a new filmmaker sign a service deal unless she or he has a decent P&A — over $250,000 — to work with and a firm understanding about the possible financial downside, such as whether she or he can get any money back at all from the theatrical," he says. "The service distributor charges a distribution fee on top of all the P&A costs, so without a decent budget it would be hard to make a dent in terms of publicity and advertising. With little or no P&A budget, I would personally let a distributor distribute my movie without any advance or distribute it myself rather than hire a service distributor."

Yet Peter M. Hargrove, a longtime distributor in theatrical and nontheatrical channels, feels that service deals have value — as long as the filmmaker keeps on top of everything involved here. "A service deal is fine provided you are prepared to supply everything necessary to exploit a film or pay for it," he says. "You can cut corners up to a point, but a service distributor may be tempted to take the cash and just dump the film, doing the minimum contractually required."

Michael Prywes was fortunate to have an honest service distributor for his feature *Returning Mickey Stern*. "I did a service deal with the now-defunct Metroscape Entertainment, which was started by a friend of mine who had worked in the indie and cable industry," he says. "She resigned from the company shortly thereafter. Vinny Chibber took over the reigns of the distribution and marketing, and Metroscape hired the Los Angeles–based theatrical booking company RS Entertainment, which booked the theaters. I had a $35,000 distribution budget to work with, and I think that is the base minimum you need for a service deal."

Prywes' $35,000 went to the service fee, trailer prints, publicity, advertisements in *Time Out New York*, *Newsday*, the *New York Times*, *Los Angeles Times*, *New York Post*, *New York Sun*, WALK radio, *The LA Jewish Journal*, *Jewish Week*, and *CinemaAds*. "Publicity was the best use of the money. Tom Bosley was in New York at the time of the film's opening, appearing in the Broadway revival of *Cabaret*, and he made himself available for interviews. Radio advertising was probably the least," he says.

Prywes felt this setup would benefit his particular needs for this film. "I recommend a theatrical service deal when you want to retain DVD and television rights — in this case, I knew this would be more financially successful on the small screen, but I hoped that a theatrical release would help DVD sales," he says.

Prywes opened his film in 2003, but its theatrical life was brief (although he did secure that sought-after play date on Long Island at the Malverne, an art house theater). "After its three-theater opening in New York and Los Angeles, we decided not to continue theatrical exhibition," he explains. "We had run out of our marketing money, and theaters require a large amount of advertising in major papers, like the *Sunday Times* in New York and the *L.A. Times* in Los Angeles. One of the reasons many indies don't open first in New York and Los Angeles is the prohibitive advertising budgets. At the time we released theatrically, we had decided to sign with Barbara Mudge of Worldwide Entertainment, primarily because she had been on the executive board of AFMA and was so forthcoming with a references request. Everyone who knows her says she is one of the rarities in the industry: someone not out to screw the producer. Unlike other sales agents, she gave us an estimate of foreign sales projections that was more realistic than 'We'll get you millions upon millions!' We had some interactions with some very shady sales agents, so she was exactly what we were looking for. She brings the film to every market, but more importantly, she has a long history in film sales, so she has people who come to her for product."

TO FOUR-WALL OR NOT TO FOUR-WALL?

Another option within the realm of self-distribution is called "four-walling." It's an awkward name connected to a rather simple concept: The filmmaker leases a theater for the course of an engagement. This could be anywhere from one night for a special screening to a full-week commercial engagement. All of the box office profits from the engagement go to the filmmaker, but the concession sales do not (since, after all, most theaters make their profits from popcorn and soft drinks sales).

Four-walling has a fairly extensive history and has been used by a wide number of independent filmmakers from various parts of the cinematic spectrum. During the 1940s, three film-makers resorted to four-walling to get their respective productions shown. The legendary shlockmeister H. Kroger Babb routinely four-walled grind house theaters to present his seemingly end-less skein of exploitative cheapies to always-appreciative audiences. The groundbreaking avant-garde artist Maya Deren took to four-walling theaters in order to present her collection of experimental short films. And no less a figure than Charlie Chaplin four-walled a Broadway theater and converted it into a cinema in 1947 for the New York premiere of Monsieur Verdoux. While Babb, Deren, and Chaplin might not seem to have anything in common, all three actually shared the same problem: No mainstream theater would present their work. Babb's movies were made outside of the production code, Deren's short films anthology had no perceived commercial value, and Chaplin was under a cloud of alleged Communist sympathies and would have encountered difficulties in booking a regular first-run movie house.

But four-walling on a national scope did not take root until the 1960s, when the Florida-based distributor K. Gordon Murray four-walled neighborhood theaters across the United States for kiddie matinees. Murray offered young moviegoers some rather peculiar treats, most notably the demented 1959 Mexican import Santa Claus, in which jolly Kris Kringle is in a struggle against Satan to ensure a poor little girl remains honest. The success of that unlikely offering encouraged Murray to four-wall additional kiddie matinee titles throughout the 1960s.

But the true commercial value of four-walling on a national level was not felt until 1971, when actor/filmmaker Tom Laugh-lin took control of the release of his feature Billy Jack. Unhappy with how Warner Bros. was releasing the film, Laughlin invested his funds into four-walling theaters and aggressively promoting his movie. Perhaps he rode the cultural zeitgeist with uncanny timing, since Laughlin's offbeat antihero (a karate-kicking, anti-establishment, half-breed Vietnam vet) clicked with audiences. *Billy Jack* became a major event, and Laughlin repeated his good fortune by four-walling his way across America in 1974 with *The Trial of Billy Jack*.

Yet Laughlin's success came too late for others to follow suit. The late 1970s and 1980s saw the slow demise of the independently owned neighborhood cinema. While Laughlin could literally go from city to city and locate stand-alone theaters to run his *Billy Jack* epics, the schematics of the exhibition industry changed dramatically. The old-fashioned single-screen, family-run movie house found itself unable to compete with a new creature called the multiplex, a corporate entity that offered multiple choices of the latest Hollywood offerings. And the emphasis is on *Hollywood* — the bookers for the multiplexes were not particularly eager to present independent productions. It became completely impossible for anyone to duplicate Laughlin's success in this new setup.

But four-walling has not completely disappeared. In at least two major markets, it is still an option for self-distributing filmmakers. In New York, which is the crucial media market for any independent film to play, some theaters will negotiate a four-walling deal. Those theaters include Cinema Village, the Quad Cinema, the Two Boots Pioneer, and the Anthology Film Archives. In Los Angeles, some venues are open to four-walling if a filmmaker wants to have a weeklong local run in order to qualify for Academy Award consideration.

For many filmmakers who want to have their movies play on a big screen but who have been stymied in securing proper distribution and/or exhibition, four-walling is often the last hope. But is it worth it?

"I would recommend the filmmaker try really hard to book it into a theater with an exhibitor on a regular split gross deal before agreeing to a four-wall deal," advises filmmaker/distributor Quentin Lee. "If your budget is limited, for the hefty fee you pay to rent the theater it would be better to spend it on publicity and advertising because ultimately for a first film you would want to get as much exposure as possible. But if four-walling is the only option, then I guess you'll have to decide how important the theatrical release of your film is — and perhaps bite the bullet after all."

Veteran distributor Peter M. Hargrove is even less optimistic. "Four-walling would only work if you have the money and network to promote the film and get an audience out," he says. "Most distributors open films theatrically in New York and/or Los Angeles just to get the press reviews for the video box and they expect to lose money."

Hargrove also notes that the four-walling self-distributor is also facing problems in trying to chase down what little profits four-walling may generate. "Theaters are getting greedier by the day, demanding more and more and returning less and less," he says. "This is not counting those who don't even remit the box office receipts on a timely basis."

Yet filmmaker Antero Alli has used four-walling to find new audiences for his productions. Alli does not use four-walling for commercial theatrical releases, but rather for limited special events designed to showcase his distinctive experimental filmmaking.

"Over the last 15 years I've had art house cinemas and venues receptive to one- or two-night exhibitions of my work," he says. "They actually exist. I appear in person, along with my films and sometimes my LCD projector, and field audience questions afterward. I promote these events through the media at large, my own website (*www.verticalpool.com*), word of mouth, and the old-fashioned way of canvassing the streets with home-made flyers. The venues that have screened my work include the UC Irvine Film Series (Irvine, CA), the Pacific Film Archive (Berkeley), Mills College Concert Hall (Oakland), the Fine Arts Cinema (Berkeley), the Red Vic Moviehouse (San Francisco), CELLspace (San Francisco), A.T.A. (San Francisco), the Parkway Speakeasy Theater (Oakland), the Hollywood Theater, (Portland), the Clinton Street Theater (Portland), The Guild at the NW Film Center (Portland), 911 Media Arts (Seattle), the

photo courtesy Davis Gang Films

Mexican illegal aliens casually scale a fence into Texas in Tommy Davis' documentary Mojados: Through the Night. *"If a theater calls I'll send it to them, and I've set up enough stuff that I can just mail them a package," says Davis about unsolicited requests to screen his film. "But I don't have the time to seek out theaters."*

Crest Theater (Sacramento), Abundant Sugar (Los Angeles), 21 Grand (Oakland), Oakland Black Box (Oakland), Danzhaus (San Francisco), The Jazzhouse (Berkeley), the Live Oak Theater (Berkeley), La Pena (Berkeley), The Artship (Oakland), Magic Theater (Nevada City), the Finnish Brotherhood Hall (Berkeley), Midnight Special (Santa Monica), Velvet Elvis Arts Theater (Seattle), Colourbox (Seattle), Weathered Wall (Seattle), and the Endocrine Company Warehouse (Oakland)."

Filmmaker Andrew Repasky McElhinney adds that four-walling can answer one important question, albeit at a price. "While a fast way to lose money for sure, a four-wall is often the best way to kick-start a movie's momentum or prove once and for all that you have something without an audience on your hands," he says. McElhinney is shooting a new film and is not ruling out four-walling to get it shown. "I would like to premiere my fourth feature in a major film festival/market environment. From there I will hope for a negative pickup deal but I'll have plans laid for a New York/Los Angeles four-wall if all else fails."

OPPORTUNITY KNOCKING

Strangely enough, there is also the rare case when self-distribution takes place even if the filmmaker had no plans to pursue commercial presentations. Texas-based filmmaker Tommy Davis enjoyed festival success in early 2005 with his documentary on illegal immigration, *Mojados: Through the Night*, and had already secured a DVD deal through Vanguard Cinema when an unexpected phone call arrived from the programmer at the Two Boots Pioneer Theater in New York, requesting that he consider playing his film there for a week's run.

"To be honest, when the Pioneer called I was surprised," recalls Davis. "But I knew it was justified given the word of mouth in New York. When I was offered the New York screening I was thrilled that my friends and other people in New York could see the movie. But it's a lot of work. If a theater calls I'll send it to them, and I've set up enough stuff that I can just mail them a package. But I don't have the time to seek out theaters. After the Pioneer put it up on their site, I got a call from Minneapolis and played there after New York."

photo courtesy Possible Films

Tatiana Abracos in the title role of Hal Hartley's self-distributed The Girl from Monday. *"The main idea is to eventually distribute other people's films," says Hartley.*

James Fotopoulos has also found himself getting screen dates without initiating contact. On several occasions he was invited to show his films at New York's Anthology Film Archives. "I've had a few shows in 2000, 2002, and 2004 at Anthology," he says. "They all came about much the same way. I am friendly with the people there and the programmers support what I am doing. In 2002 when Facets wanted to do their booking tour, I talked to the programmer about it and they said yes."

(Though unlike most filmmakers, Fotopoulos did not keep tabs on audience reaction. "I really don't know how the audience reacted," he adds. "I was only there for the first day and then I went out to a bar or something with some friends, so I don't recall if I was there when the shows ended.")

And sometimes, the self-distribution thrill can prove to be a lucrative route to new business endeavors. Hal Hartley eventually plans to move beyond the self-distribution of his work and to incorporate the presentation of films by other artists.

"The main idea is to eventually distribute other people's films," he says. "But all we have to work with right now are mine. It's true, though, we don't feel very original in doing this. At a certain point — given the kind of things I want to pursue in my filmmaking — it just made sense. I'm sure a lot of filmmakers feel the same way."

Perhaps programmer and filmmaker Matthew Seig sums up the subject best: "In the end it may come down to this: self-distribution, some kind of service deal, or a deal with a very small company. It may be a matter of what you can afford, and can you afford not to give self-distribution a try? Getting a theater to show your film can be hard, and getting some attention from the press can be hard. You've got to be comfortable promoting yourself and your film, and you need to get good at it. Think one step in the future. Distributors are often hoping just to break even theatrically and even lose money in markets like New York. Theatrical exhibition is an investment, and if money is made it will often be put right back into advertising and publicity. You have two goals. One is to create awareness of the film for sales to cable and home video. The other goal is to create awareness of yourself as a filmmaker. Right now you may be selling one single film, but ultimately you are developing your career. Self-distribution is not for everyone. Sometimes it is better to get on with the next project."

INTERVIEW
NICK DAY AND MAURIZIO BENAZZO, FILMMAKERS

Anyone involved in the indie film world cannot help but notice that a growing number of filmmakers are self-releasing their movies. This is often done by default rather than by design, but often it proves to be an effective strategy to ensure the film is receiving its proper due.

An excellent case in point is *Short Cut to Nirvana: Kumbh Mela*, a wonderful documentary that made its way across the United States during the course of 2005. Filmmakers Nick Day and Maurizio Benazzo captured the depth and scope of India's Kumbh Mela, the world's oldest and largest religious festival (it draws 70 million pilgrims ranging from the Dalai Lama to the average wisdom seeker).

While the subject matter was clearly compelling and the finished production was highly compelling, Day and Benazzo had problems securing a proper distribution deal. Taking an entrepreneurial approach, the duo opted to release the film themselves. To date, it has been a serendipitous decision.

Q: Was theatrical self-distribution always under consideration when you were creating your film, or did this arise over time during your attempts to get the film released?

NICK DAY: When we got back from India we weren't even sure whether we had a full-length feature or a 60-minute television documentary. The shooting had gone well and we knew we had some great footage, but we had changed our plan significantly during the three weeks we were at the Kumbh Mela, and we knew what we'd got wasn't going to be a standard journalistic-style piece. The first assembly came in at about 100 minutes, which was quickly chopped down to about 88, but even then we were undecided about whether it could stand up as a feature. It was, even by our standards, an unusual film: more a sensory experience of an incredible event than a conventional documentary.

We could have tried to re-cut it and made it more generic, but we liked it and felt it could work. Then, after the first few test screenings, we knew our instincts were correct.

Audiences were responding using language we hadn't expected, with people repeatedly telling us the film had touched their hearts and made them feel blessed!

This was something we hadn't anticipated. Next, the film was honed and polished down to 85 minutes and we began the long journey to bring it into the world. But as this was our first feature, we only had a vague notion of what to do next, so we started entering film festivals hoping that eventually we would be "discovered" by a distributor, and if that didn't happen we'd go straight to video. It would be fair to say that our expectations were modest at that point.

It was reasonable to assume that a small film about an obscure festival in India might not be an obvious choice for theatrical distribution.

Q: How many distributors did you contact for possible pickup of the film? And how did you pitch them on the film?

MAURIZIO BENAZZO: We talked to a few companies who weren't sure they could market a film on this subject and seemed to be waiting for someone else to take the plunge first.

This put us into a period of uncertainty and it constrained us. But then we'd suddenly have bursts of energy and everything would move forward again. We decided to four-wall two consecutive Thursday nights at the Two Boots Pioneer Theater in New York, which were both sellouts. This gave us an enormous boost and we decided to gear up for another round with distributors.

Q: *Your film was under consideration with a distributor as a service deal. Looking back, do you consider this approach to distribution as being beneficial to independent filmmakers?*

NICK DAY: The service deal offers some potential for a small film where larger distributors have passed and there's not much money in the pot. It gives smaller films a chance to get a place at the table. For us, the service deal could have been okay but we discovered what many small filmmakers eventually find, that the distributor is focusing more effort on other films, or that they don't fully understand who the audience is and therefore how to convince theater bookers to take a chance. We had several months of waiting for something to happen but it seemed as if we'd lost momentum yet again. At some point we realized we could do better ourselves, so we made the radical and quite scary decision to take the film back and go on alone.

It may not be the right decision for everyone but for us it was the beginning of something much bigger.

Q: *Doing self-distribution, how did you plan your release strategy? And specifically, why did you decide to begin on the West Coast and work your way East?*

MAURIZIO BENAZZO: There was a time when our strategy was forever shifting depending on our level of expectation. At one point we were even thinking of four-walling a small theater in New York for a week and another in San Francisco, and at that time we would have been happy with that! In the end we were incredibly fortunate.

Our big break came through a connection we made at the Newport Film Festival that eventually led us to Landmark Theaters, the leading national independent theater chain. We sent them a screener and they initially gave us four cities to get an idea of how well the film would perform. The first of those was Boston, where we opened at Kendall Square, so we actually started in the East and then moved West, to the Bay Area and after that Los Angeles. Because we did well in all those markets, with a run of five weeks in San Francisco and then hitting top of the *IndieWire* chart on a per-screen basis in L.A. — although they mistakenly missed us off their list that week! — we were offered the rest of the Landmark chain over the next few months.

So there hasn't really been a regional strategy in place as such, as we've been playing these cities in the order they were given to us. Ideally we would follow up a run with another opening close by, but at some point the number of openings was threatening to overwhelm us and we decided to thin them out. That's one of the many challenges of self-distribution, to be able to support every market adequately. Friday comes around very quickly and you have to have a lot of things in place.

Q: What level of grassroots marketing are you doing for the film?

NICK DAY: Our film is about the biggest spiritual festival in the history of humanity, so it appeals mainly to people who have an interest in Eastern traditions, those who are on their own spiritual path and practice yoga and meditation, and then others who might be members of the Unity Church, which is very open to other traditions. The film also features the Dalai Lama, who is the second-most recognized spiritual figure after the pope. So our grassroots campaign is designed to inform as many people in these communities as possible. We generally start several weeks ahead and identify yoga studios and meditation centers in a particular area and then contact them, asking them to place flyers and postcards in their center.

We also try to be present for Q&As at as many opening weekends as we can, as we value contact with the audience very highly. We always ask people in the audience to help us connect with others and it also gives us a chance to build a community by gathering email addresses.

Later we're able to send an email blast to let everyone know we're opening in another town, and they can tell their friends and families.

Q: You worked with Sasha Berman, one of the best-regarded publicists in the indie film world. How crucial has the PR effort been in bringing people to your film?

NICK DAY: We were extremely fortunate to find Sasha. Not only has she been an excellent publicist for us in the two major markets, but also she's become our guru in understanding the nuances of distribution. We knew nothing about this business just eight short months ago and have had to learn a lot very quickly. Sasha has been our mentor and advisor, and we would not have come this far without her.

Q: How did you plan out your marketing budget for the self-release? And is opening the film in some cities much more expensive than in other cities?

MAURIZIO BENAZZO: Again, with no previous experience in this we've had to find our way and learn through a mixture of trial and error and common sense. The biggest single cost is print advertising, and choosing the size and frequency of ads in the dailies and the weeklies is something we've had to learn. We discovered early on that a city tends to dictate its own terms. Los Angeles and New York are both very expensive in everything from press ads to rental of screening rooms. Smaller markets are often a lot cheaper but we tend to spend less on them anyway.

Ironically, in our best market to date, San Rafael in Marin County, California, we only had a fairly low-cost weekly ad running, and here the grassroots efforts and word of mouth were by far the most effective.

Q: Which markets have been most responsive — in terms of media attention and box office receipts — to the film? And to what do you attribute your success there?

NICK DAY: Our film has a natural audience among spiritual seekers and people who are open to other cultures and traditions, and while these people can be found in every part of the country, they tend to be more concentrated in West Coast cities than anywhere else.

It's maybe not so surprising that our film did better in Los Angeles and San Francisco than, say, Dallas or Houston. While those Texas cities still have an alternative community, they are much smaller and not so easy to reach.

photo courtesy Mela Films

Maurizio Benazzo (left) and Nick Day join forces with a sadhu during the production of their documentary Short Cut to Nirvana: Kumbh Mela. *"We don't want to be distributors!" says Benazzo.*

Q: From your experiences in self-distributing your film, are you emboldened to pursue distribution for your future projects or for other people's films?

MAURIZIO BENAZZO: We don't want to be distributors! However, to take it on and have success has been an extraordinary and unique experience and has completed our filmmaking education. Distribution is a tough and demanding game and most filmmakers would rather be making films than constantly calling theaters, tracking print circulation, and chasing late payments. For our next project we would much prefer to let the experts work their mojo. But if it comes to it, at least we know what to do.

❧

LISTEN TO WHAT THE MAN SAYS

Self-distribution, not unlike pursuits such as mountain climbing or lion taming, is clearly not for everyone. But the schematics of today's film industry often give filmmakers no choice but to take their movie on the road. If you go this route, here are some very practical considerations you need to keep in mind:

1. Make sure you have the financial resources to cover a self-distribution strategy. Everything is coming out of your pocket, and if the pocket isn't deep, then the self-distribution route will be very short and unsatisfactory. If you cannot afford this, don't do it. There is no joy in being broke.

2. If you are plotting a self-distribution strategy, New York must be a part of the strategy. New York is the media capital and getting reviewed by that city's media can make a film. Bad reviews won't help, of course, but they are not the end of the world (remember Larry Fessenden and *Habit*). If a film doesn't play in New York, the industry probably won't know it even exists.

3. Working with theaters that boast in-house PR mechanisms may or may not be a blessing. Sometimes the theater's PR team is brilliant in the quality of coverage they generate (New York's Film Forum is the tops here). Other theaters, however, take a more leisurely approach to their PR. Don't be surprised if the theater's publicist simply sends out screeners for review purposes and makes no attempt to generate interviews or other feature coverage. In cases like this, you'll wind up doing the publicist's work — while the theater takes your money for PR services!

4. If you are going to spend advertising dollars, try to focus on the newspapers and broadcast outlets favored by your core audience. A film with an ethnic slant would find a more appreciative audience in a local ethnic weekly —

not to mention lower ad rates than a daily or alternative weekly. And don't forget the gay media. Even if your film is not gay-oriented, the readers of local gay publications are often very loyal to the advertisers in their favorite weeklies. Sometimes art house theaters can be found in neighborhoods with significant gay populations (such as the Quad Cinema in the heart of New York's Chelsea district), and the idea of "keeping it local" is attractive to the readership of these publications.

5. Be serious about considering a service deal. It is often the best of all worlds: The film is being booked by professionals who know the exhibitors and who can secure the most appropriate venues. Exhibitors are more comfortable in dealing with professionals they know and respect (and from whom they get repeat business) than in taking unsolicited inquiries from newcomers whom they may never see again.

6. I have to agree completely with Peter M. Hargrove's comments on the subject of four-walling: "Four-walling would only work if you have the money and network to promote the film and get an audience out." Again, if you have the money and can afford to take a financial loss, then it should be considered. I am unaware of any person who makes money on four-walling (Tom Laughlin's success was three decades ago and, quite frankly, was just a happy fluke of a hippy-dippy time).

IS "DIRECT-TO-VIDEO"
SYNONYMOUS WITH FAILURE?

My strength lies solely in my tenacity.
— Louis Pasteur

6

As you may have gathered by now, the majority of films being produced today do not get released in theaters. Many don't even get the chance to be projected on any sort of a big screen. But this is not to say that these films go unseen. Many films find their way into the world via a route known as DTV, or direct-to-video for those who prefer English to acronyms.

(Yes, I know that video has given way to DVDs. But as far as the industry goes, the home entertainment market is still known by the "video" name. No one is talking about sales of VHS tapes, in case you are wondering.)

There are no numbers available on the number of DTV titles in release each year, and you'll understand why such accounting is impossible as this chapter progresses. DTV titles span the entertainment industry, from no-budget endeavors by unknown filmmakers to pricey productions made by name talent and released by major companies. There is no one-size-fits-all here. But there is one stigma that blankets this entire genre: the question of whether or not DTV titles are inherently inferior to flicks that get theatrical release.

For Lawrence P. Raffel, editor of the online magazine *Monsters at Play*, there is a clear and succinct answer to that question: "Generally speaking, no. And it's worth noting that there are quite a few reasons why a film would or could be sent straight to home video. There are the films that are designed to go straight to video for a quick cash-in. It's cheaper than mass-marketed theatrical distribution in just about every way. Films like these can be studio films or independently made. Then there are the films that are made — or picked up — by a major studio and wind up sitting on a shelf. These films sit — and sit — and none of the marketing heads know what to do with them, so they eventually throw them straight to video. Granted, I'm sure that there are other scenarios that could see a film hit video rather than the big screen, but these points would tend to be the most important."

Raffel adds another key point: "The value of the film should never be judged by its distribution, or lack thereof. Shot on video, shot on film, released theatrically, mass-distributed on home video, or only 100 manufactured for home video, it doesn't matter. The film should speak for itself. And if it's a good film, that's all that should matter."

Christopher Bligh, a writer with *Ain't It Cool News* and *DVDAuthority.com*, agrees. "I had gone to the 2005 Tribeca Film Festival and was amazed at how many good undistributed movies there were while the one dud, in my eyes, was the one that already had a distribution deal," he says. "So I felt just because you have the deal doesn't mean you've got it made."

In concept, all titles are equal in the DVD format. "DVD is the great equalizer, since the studios don't have much ability to produce cheaper discs than indies," says Christopher Null, editor for *FilmCritic.com*. "Their only tools are advertising and the name recognition of the theatrical release."

Yet having a theatrical release prior to a DVD release can help raise awareness and sales. Steve Kaplan of Alpha Video has released both DTV titles and films with theatrical play dates into the home entertainment channels, and he notes that there is a difference when it comes to commercial considerations. "Theatrical release is a real plus, no question about it," he says. "There is a 'history,' no matter how short, for the film. But the [DTV] films are not inherently inferior. I've seen some real classics that just haven't gotten off the ground yet. If they played in the theater and got reviewed, it would be safer for a distributor to sink money in them."

Another distributor, Greg Ross at Go-Kart Films, also finds the DTV market to be a profound challenge — not only from a distribution standpoint but also from the movie lover's mind frame. "I think that people are more accepting of the direct-to-video movie, especially in genres like documentaries, but I still think the average movie lover will rent the latest Hollywood blockbuster before they take a risk on a smaller, less-known flick," he says. "There are a few factors here. We have all been burnt by the smaller movie that looks great on the shelf but sucks when we play it at home. We could say the same about the Hollywood blockbuster, but since most Hollywood movies follow simple formulas, the risk is less. Also, most people don't want to be challenged by their entertainment. This is true for music, television, and movies. People may complain about mediocre crap that Hollywood produces, but there is also some comfort in having an idea of what you are getting before you watch it, so they keep going back to what they know."

DTV, YESTERDAY AND TODAY

Just how did the DTV market come about? Well, let's pedal back to the 1980s for a quick but amusing history lesson of the home entertainment market and its effects (for better or worse) on the motion picture industry. Our guide to this history tour is Randy Pitman, publisher and editor of *Video Librarian* magazine, a trade journal that covers home entertainment titles for an audience of library purchasing officers.

"I wouldn't necessarily say that direct-to-video is the world's third-oldest profession, but DTV titles have been around since the beginning," says Pitman. "In 1986, VCR penetration stood at about 30% of American homes, but already by that time video store shelves were flooded with what were called 'B' and 'C' movies, because the technology was still very new and the vast majority of studio catalogue titles had not yet been released.

Remember, the studios initially fought heartily against the VCR and were reluctant to release many of their prize properties on video — 1975's cult classic *The Rocky Horror Picture Show*, for example, did not show up on VHS until the early '90s. But in 1987, among the numerous DTV titles on the shelves of my local video store, I was able to find *Redneck Zombies*, a backwater horror flick made on a shoestring by some people in the library field I knew who were using pseudonyms. My general sense is that the number of DTV releases subsided a bit in the late '80s, but began to rise once more with the advent of DVD in the mid-'90s and continues to grow due to a combination of plummeting prices on digital video cameras and relatively cheap costs of Internet marketing. Of course, that doesn't mean that any more than a sliver of these films are either being purchased for rental by video stores or being reviewed in the press, mainstream or otherwise."

Pitman notes it is difficult to keep track of this market. "I'm sure someone must track the number of DTV releases each year — not me — but as of the end of April 2005, IMDb lists 318,540 theatrical releases and 35,302 DTV titles," he says. "And I know from experience that a large number of DTV titles are not listed on IMDb."

Pitman's magazine receives numerous DTV titles for review consideration. "For any review publication, selecting the titles that are covered is a juggling act," he continues. "At *Video Librarian*, we review approximately 225 titles in each bimonthly issue and an additional 50 titles online during the same period. Of those, approximately 60-70 are feature films — although a conservative estimate of the number of video movies that are submitted for review for any given issue would easily be well over 100. I suspect most video review editors would say that they aim to provide comprehensive coverage of mainstream releases while bringing to readers' attention various potential sleepers that might have slipped through the distribution channel cracks. Of course, as in most walks of life, there's a certain amount of disparity between the ideal and the real, and due to space and time constraints, editors are forced to take certain logical shortcuts to weed through submissions. At *Video Librarian*, mainstream titles do take priority, for two reasons: First, our audience — librarians — have a responsibility to provide their communities with a wide variety of recreational, educational, and informational materials in all formats. Libraries carry the works of John Updike, of course, but they also carry the novels of John Grisham, and from a circulation standpoint, Grisham is a much bigger mover — if not a better writer — than Updike. Two hundred years from now, people will still be reading Updike, while Grisham is likely to be long forgotten, but that doesn't change the fact that a library's mission is to respond to readers' and viewers' needs today. Granted, libraries have a bit more flexibility in this regard than video chains or mass-market merchants since they are not driven by the financial bottom line, but rather a mandate to build a balanced collection. Even so, libraries, like politicians, ignore the will and taste of the people at their peril."

Pitman notes that in video circles, familiarity doesn't breed contempt — it actually breeds audience appeal. "The second reason that mainstream titles receive attention first is that readers are far more likely to notice the glaring absence of a review of *The Lord of the Rings* series than, say, *Mosquito Man*," he continues. "However, even after the pressing business of adding one's kick in print to a turkey like *Seed of Chucky* has been seen to, there's still room for lesser-known independent and foreign fare, and this is where the Internet has absolutely revolutionized the way films are selected for review — among many other things. Thanks to websites such as IMDb, Metacritic, and Rotten Tomatoes, which aggregate review sources, editors can quickly find out whether many seemingly obscure titles are worth reviewing. Direct-to-video titles, however, which often have not been seen by any critic, are a much tougher call. DTV titles tend to fall into five categories: exploitation genre films such as action, horror, erotic, etc.; sequels, both live-action and animated; films that the studios shelved for some reason — not always artistic — that they wheel out on video when a tie-in appears, such as another feature film with similar subject matter or the sudden rise of one of the film's stars; films considered too controversial for theatrical release; and non-studio/home video label titles that filmmakers try to distribute independently, often on recordable DVD (DVD+R or DVD-R), marketed on the Internet. Most of these titles can be dismissed or dealt with very quickly. You know what you're getting with *Animal Instincts 3* or *The Land Before Time XI* or the cheesy 'early' films of newly minted Hollywood stars. But others without obvious marketing hooks are a little harder to judge, and then it simply becomes a matter of how much time an editor has to pop in a title for a quick peek. And, to be honest, some titles — such as the whole film-students-making-films-about-film-students-making-films genre, which is the cinematic equivalent of '60s navel gazing — have such a low payoff ratio that I don't even bother to check them out. So, I guess the bottom line is that DTV titles do have a tougher row to hoe, so to speak."

But has the DTV world produced any classics, to date? Pitman acknowledges the answer is not easy to figure out.

"There's a long-running joke in literary circles to the effect that the Great American Novel has already been written, it just wasn't published," he explains. "Of course, the technology for the printed word and film are universes apart: People may judge a book by its cover, but they rarely judge one on the basis of its typeface. In other words, the medium has not truly changed all that much since Will Shakespeare first put quill pen to parchment 400-plus years ago. People do judge films, however, by their look as much as — if not more than — their narrative content, so there's a bit more required of filmmakers than simply a great story or script. Of course, as 1999's *The Blair Witch Project* (budget: $35,000), Shane Carruth's 2004 *Primer* (budget: $7,000), and Jonathan Caouette's 2003 *Tarnation* (budget: $218) demonstrate, you don't necessarily need to have either the wealth of the Vanderbilts or the filmmaking acumen of Stanley Kubrick to make a fine or successful film. That said, I'm hard-pressed to think of true direct-to-video classics off the top of my head. Of course there are a whole slew of wonderful films that play for a week or less in Podunk, Wherever, before being shuffled to video, but these do not technically qualify as direct-to-video titles, although in terms of visibility they might as well be. *Toy Story 2*, ironically, was initially going to be a DTV release, until Disney realized that it was infinitely superior to, say, the *Aladdin* spin-off, *The Return of Jafar*. Also, believe it or not, Marlon Brando's next-to-last film, 1997's *Free Money*, was a DTV release — and costarred Donald Sutherland, Charlie Sheen, Thomas Haden Church, and Mira Sorvino! Given the ever-increasing venue for independent work to be screened and evaluated — ranging from Sundance to Slamdance—my gut feeling is that there are not a whole lot of really great films going absolutely unnoticed. I suspect that the best stuff that is being missed — and the most promising for the future — is in the documentary category."

INTERVIEW
DOUG PRATT, AUTHOR, *DOUG PRATT'S DVD*

When it comes to the world of home entertainment (ranging in the format spectrum from Betamax to VHS to laser disc to DVD), few people have the depth of knowledge of Doug Pratt. Pratt began reviewing films in 1976 and in 1984 he made the transition from writer to publisher with his breakthrough offering *The Laser Disc Newsletter*. The publication changed its name, for obvious reasons, to *The DVD-Laser Disc Newsletter* in 1999, but its mission was still the same: cogent reviews of all new home entertainment titles, running the gamut from grand opera to "B" Westerns, from Hollywood's grandest extravaganzas to the smallest features imported from the smallest countries.

Pratt's knowledge has not gone unnoticed: The *New York Times*, *Newsweek*, *Time*, and *Rolling Stone* have acknowledged Pratt's indefatigable pursuit of the subject (he has been known to watch up to six films a day and listen to every commentary track on every DVD he gets). No less a figure than Roger Ebert praised Pratt's DVD writing as being "the best on the subject."

Pratt has, to date, authored three books on laser disc releases and two on DVD releases. His most recent, *Doug Pratt's DVD* (HEP Publishing), is a massive two-volume collection with in-depth reviews of more than 7,000 titles. If anyone knows video in general and direct-to-video in particular, it is clearly and obviously Doug Pratt!

Q: For the longest time, DTV was considered a dumping ground for less-than-stellar movies. How and when did DTV become commercially viable?

DOUG PRATT: Basically, what happened was that as the theatrical market for, say, cheap horror movies, dried up in the 1980s, a parallel market for those very same horror movies expanded in the straight-to-video market to the point where such films became more profitable than ever before, even if they did not "break out" to become big hits. The reason, once again, being that their availability increased through the efficiency of home video distribution in a manner that theatrical distribution could never imitate. The same thing happened very rapidly to porn, which shifted almost overnight from a niche theatrical market into an enormous straight-to-video industry.

By the late 1980s, the major film studios began to recognize that they could still recover costs from turkeys that they could not afford to market theatrically by giving them an organized video release. Usually the films were tried out in theaters first, test-marketed here and there before the goat was given up, so to speak. An example would be MGM's 1990 release *Daddy's Dyin'... Who's Got the Will?* Such films were virtually straight-to-video and proved that there was a market for more.

I can't tell you offhand what the first titles were, but veteran "B" movie producers such as Roger Corman quickly recognized the altered economics of the industry and adapted to it rapidly.

Q: Was there a particular moment when direct-to-video suddenly became a legitimate option for quality films?

DOUG PRATT: I can't speak for the film companies, but to me the title that really turned things around was Columbia Tri-Star's 1992 release *Red Rock West*. The film clearly gave a boost to John Dahl's career, and may have even helped Nicholas Cage clear away the misapprehensions that had accompanied some of his earlier performances. It was an ideal home video movie, because the story grabbed you immediately and held on to you all the way through. The performances were terrific and it was shot really well, so you could see that it had some class. At the time, Cage didn't quite have enough box office draw to justify a theatrical release, so Columbia TriStar dumped it onto the home video market and it became a deserved cult hit. You could say the trend culminated in 2003, when one of the best-produced films of 2002, *Ripley's Game*, was released straight-to-video in America, although it had a theatrical run in Europe.

In the 1990s, however, you saw more and more films coming out that weren't just severe genre pictures, more mainstream dramas and that sort of thing. When Alfred Hitchcock first began shooting his TV show, he justified the effort by explaining that he wanted to do stories for television that wouldn't be popular in theaters, and that is what has happened with the straight-to-video market. Genre films can reach their fans, dramas with tough subjects and obscure but talented performers can have the time to build an audience, and independent filmmakers can achieve the low-level financing they require to practice their art.

The 1994 direct-to-video sequel produced at Disney, *The Return of Jafar*, was enormously profitable and demonstrated the viability of creating modestly budgeted and artistically compromised product for the home video market. It was still a well-written and effectively executed, funny cartoon, even though it was not produced to theatrical-level standards. Since then, Disney's cartoon video feature releases have been uneven, some of them so good that they should have been released theatrically and others simply glorified pilots for potential TV series, but I believe almost all of them have scooped up the cash in gobs.

Q: From your professional viewpoint, do you automatically judge direct-to-video films as being inherently inferior to films that first had a theatrical release?

DOUG PRATT: Of course not. You always let every film speak for itself. You do not expect to see enormous special effects budgets, though CGI costs have come down so much that a well-made made-for-video sci-fi film, particularly one from a big studio, can have better-looking effects than a major motion picture from a decade ago. If somebody told me that one box had nothing but theatrical movies in it, and another had nothing but made-for-video films, I would expect that the theatrical box would have more entertaining titles as a whole, but there are going to be some real gems in the made-for-video box, and perhaps a few future superstars.

It can go both ways. A direct-to-video movie can be blander, or it can be edgier. It can have such a compromised budget that production values impact its entertainment value, or it can cost so little that its producers have stayed out of the way and allowed the filmmakers to realize their visions unhindered by market-conscious meddling. Both types of movies are out there, and the only real problem is that they aren't sufficiently differentiated in the critical forum.

Q: From a commercial standpoint, can direct-to-video titles compete against higher-profile theatrical releases when they appear on DVD?

DOUG PRATT: I don't think they need to. I think the market is big enough for both. I doubt it is any filmmaker's ultimate dream to have the No. 1 direct-to-video title. It is a stepping-stone toward the motion picture pantheon, though as Dahl demonstrated, it is a viable route. On the other hand, there are filmmakers like Fred Olin Ray who are perfectly content to grind out their video product and make a decent living from it. If anything, the programs enrich the market as a whole, and even the worst ones expose viewers to the pleasures of a given genre and encourage further exploration.

Q: Do you see the number of direct-to-video titles rising? If so, or not so, to what do you attribute this?

DOUG PRATT: With more cable channels and increasingly cheaper digital video production costs, the trend is only going to go in one direction, which brings us to the world of *CustomFlix* or *BuyIndies.com.*

Q: What is your opinion of services which allow filmmakers to independently distribute their own titles on DVD?

DOUG PRATT: I think it's the next Sundance. Again, the real problem is just one of getting the word out — there is so much product available that the traditional critical vetting cannot occur, and this is where the online critic community will begin to play a wider and more important role, once a few truly centralized critical sites are established — or better yet, a loosely linked net of critical sites, so that if a quality title does bubble up, word can get around quickly.

❧

ONLINE SALES SUCCESS

Okay, we need to pedal backward again. Doug Pratt mentioned services that enable filmmakers to self-distribute their own DVDs. If you are not familiar with how this can be achieved, your DTV knowledge needs some fine-tuning — because the Internet has changed the face of the DTV market.

Not every film being aimed for the theatrical market gets into cinemas. Likewise, not every film being aimed for the DTV market gets a distributor. And then again, not every distributor can get its titles into the major retail outlets. A case in point is Go-Kart Films, which offers a vibrant mix of tough-edged documentaries and insouciant comedies on DVD — the Go-Kart output is wonderful for those who love provocative and daring films, but some people have rather quotidian tastes. And as luck would have it, those people tend to be in positions of determining which DVD titles to pick up for retail placement.

"We have not had any success with Blockbuster and Wal-Mart in the U.S., but we have in Canada," says Greg Ross, president. "I don't think a lot of what we do is appropriate for them, and really, I don't see them as having success with most of our product. An amazing documentary like *Orwell Rolls in His Grave* would never be sold in Wal-Mart. They would find the subject matter too controversial — ironic that the truth is controversial. Wal-Mart also demands pricing that is much better than anyone else. I have a problem with that. I would rather support the chains that support us all the time than a company that picks and chooses like Wal-Mart. We have had titles in Hollywood and Movie Gallery, but not in huge quantities. Companies like Tower and Virgin have been really supportive as well. They realize that they need to stock what Wal-Mart and Blockbuster don't." But if support in the traditional brick-and-mortar video outlets is spotty, Ross has a solid level of enthusiasm within e-commerce. "The online companies like Netflix and GreenCine have been very supportive, as have the online distributors like Amazon," he adds. "Our titles are perfect for them because they aren't as easy to find at traditional retailers. Thanks to the Internet, they are."

Netflix, with more than three million subscribers, is clearly the most sought-after retailer online. Some filmmakers are even using Netflix for exclusive distribution deals: Tim Robbins' *Embedded Live* and Hal Hartley's *The Girl from Monday* were first released on DVD exclusively through Netflix. In September 2005, the Cinequest Film Festival of San Jose, California, announced the launch of a DVD label offering indie films exclusively through Netflix.

Even smaller releases vie for a spot on Netflix. Stephen J. Szklarski, who took his documentary *Union Square* into theatrical self-distribution, took his self-distributed DVD to Netflix. For him, there were no ifs, ands, or buts about it.

"I wanted placement on Netflix, for sure," he says. "I spoke to the buyers at Netflix and sent them ten screeners with the press kits including the theatrical reviews attached. The reviews helped out, because that is how I got on Netflix. Netflix is a very important placement for a documentary or indie film because they are great at getting rental DVDs into the hands of people who want these types of films. Netflix knows how to match up films that have the same theme or interests and that helps a lot. Their customers watch everything and are looking for new content that is hard to find on a local shelf. Netflix provides that."

While Netflix was aimed at consumers, IndieBuyer Inc. was an Internet-based e-commerce wholesaler that brought DVDs to retailers. IndieBuyer Inc. took a lesson in Netflix-style exclusivity in early 2005 when it announced it was the only wholesale source for the DVD version of David Lynch's 1977 cult masterpiece *Eraserhead*. Prior to the IndieBuyer deal, the *Eraserhead* DVD was only available for direct retail purchase of $34.94 plus an average of $11 shipping and handling costs from David Lynch's website — and that price applied to both consumers and retailers. According to a statement by Lynch's spokesman Eric Bassett to the trade journal *Home Media Retailing*, the iconoclastic filmmaker chose IndieBuyer because it enabled a "unique ability to reach the best sales force for independent film and our ability to retain ownership of the film."

For filmmakers who lack a DTV-DVD distribution deal, the Internet has become a cyber-opportunity for being seen. For Boston filmmaker John Farrell, the Internet became a saving grace for his digital feature *Everyman*, a modern-dress adaptation of the classic 15th century morality play. As you may imagine, *Everyman* was an unusual endeavor that did not lend itself to immediate commercial possibilities.

"I must say I didn't have any immediate plans for *Everyman* once I finished the digital remastering," recalls Farrell. "It's a modest movie, and from my initial marketing program — years ago when it was first completed as a 3/4-inch master for VHS distribution, which I sold through Catholic newspaper ads — I didn't think the market would be huge. The Catholic ads approach basically broke even. I took out ads in *Our Sunday Visitor* and one other paper, thinking the movie might appeal to traditionalists and family viewers. But that was years ago. When I remastered it in 2002, it was during a time of Internet growth and there was a rising presence of colleges online. I thought it would be an obvious seller to schools and colleges, where the text of the play is still studied. But I didn't have the time or the patience to mount an email campaign. Direct mail wouldn't have been worth the investment."

The answer for Farrell was a new online service. "And then I heard about CustomFlix," he continues. "I seem to recall clicking on a link to them after a story I saw at either *Streamingmedia. com* or some other Web news portal. It may be that Nels Johnson at *DV* magazine put me onto them. In any case, I did know about them for about six months to a year before I looked at their terms more closely, before I had the ability to master my own DVDs. Then I realized that *Everyman* would make a great initial foray, a test case for the new model of independent film distribution. That's what it has turned out to be. I knew that I was getting constant traffic to my website from students and teachers looking for the text of the original play online, which I have on my site. So I figured there would be a natural link to show them the trailer and send them to the DVD site for sale."

CustomFlix combined the jobs of DVD duplicator and e-commerce retailer. "Your film has to be finished, with a master tape or DVD that CustomFlix [used] for distribution," explains Farrell. "I did DVD only for Everyman because, as a remastered digital from 3/4-inch video, the DVD was as good as seeing the original. Everyman was originally shot with a JVC 1900 — still a great little camera and you can still find them for sale online — and a JVC KY-310 (if I recall correctly) with the portable deck, the old workhorse that used 20-minute 3/4-inch cassettes. The whole thing was mastered on 3/4-inch, and if you screened it in that format, it looked great. VHS dubs, though, never looked that good — not for resale purposes. When I remastered it, I found that VHS, while better from a digitally remastered tape, still just didn't cut it as far as I was concerned. So I decided the movie would only be available in its best format. I authored a master DVD in iDVD and sent it to CustomFlix. They pound on it, make some dubs to make sure it's dependable, including a review copy for you to check on your own player — then you send them some high-resolution art and text for your box cover and for your DVD label. They have a great template you can use yourself… right online. Which I did, since I have a lot of design experience with Photoshop. That was a lot of fun!

"[This] took place over about a two-month period. I did the initial application and setup in May 2004 and had the thing ready in June. My first sale was in July. The only month that nothing sold was October. Every month since December has been six to seven sales per month. Once I sent them the DVD and uploaded the labels, the movie went for sale within just a couple of weeks. Bearing in mind that *Everyman* is a very-special-interest video — I mean, how many people want to kick back and try to follow dialogue in English that was just one step past Chaucer and not yet at Shakespeare? I expected to sell maybe one a month. In fact, the movie has averaged six sales per month — and I started getting modest little royalty checks right from the start. I do know who's buying the movie, which is also very powerful information to have, because now you can begin to build a database of buyers, people who are interested in your work — who they are, where they come from, etc. As I figured, most of my buyers are from schools and colleges. Which is great. I'm not finding them. They're finding me. This is really the ideal model for an indie filmmaker. You produce your movie, and you have a low-cost, high-quality means to offer it to anyone anywhere in the world. I've had people from South Africa and Korea buying *Everyman*. And there is no selling your soul to a third party for distribution."

In 2005, *Amazon.com* purchased CustomFlix; the service was later folded into CreateSpace. "You don't have to do the extra legwork to get it on Amazon yourself," adds Farrell. "They do it for you. You don't make as much net on sales through Amazon, but on the other hand, you get wider exposure; you sell more. I know sales of *Everyman* went up because of it — so it's worth taking the cut in your percentage."

The do-it-yourself element of DVD releasing has brought mixed opinions. Scott Weinberg, an online writer whose work appears at Cinematical and eFilmCritic, is enthused. "I think it's a great approach, especially for those who really are trying to break out of obscurity by making good films," he says. "There's a lot more talent out there than there are available gigs, so anything that enables an indie filmmaker to get his movie seen and, hopefully, appreciated is an important asset. True, there will always be a glut of low-end junk piles that flood this kind of service, but as in any sort of film distribution, the cream should be given a chance to rise to the top. Mediocre filmmakers don't need these outlets to act as encouragement; crap films will pour forth from every nook and cranny of the film industry. One piece of hidden treasure is worth a dozen head-slappingly awful experiments."

Randy Pitman's *Video Librarian* is among the relatively few industry trade journals that regularly review the titles offered by these services. "The growing proliferation of DVD burners coupled with the reduced cost of recordable DVDs has led some companies to adopt the equivalent of what's called 'lightning' publishing in the book world (in the video world, this is literally video-on-demand, as a copy is produced for each order) for less-than-blockbuster-status titles," he says. "For $10.47, for example, you can purchase a title called *Brian and Veronica's Wedding*, which is described as 'the wedding of Brian and Veronica Melcic on December 1, 2002,' and — judging from a brief preview clip — appears to be precisely that: a proverbial wedding video, not even a more indie variation on *My Big Fat Greek Wedding*. Companies like *BuyIndies.com* or Microcinema International show a bit more discretion in their acquisitions, but even here there is a real leaning toward short films and experimental art — and as Marcel Duchamp discovered, one man's urinal is another man's art exhibit when labeled 'Fountain'."

Yet distributor Peter M. Hargrove has no use for these services. "They are all incompetently run," he says. "They are the equivalent to product reps or sales agents, just under another guise. It's not as if they're doing any work to hype your title. You'd be better to list it on your website and accept PayPal."

Another online site being used by filmmakers (usually the self-distributing creators of special interest titles) is eBay. Selling via eBay tends to be on single DVD units, but even this one-at-a-time approach has been known to generate sales.

Typical of the eBay approach is Paul DeSimone, a Boston-based bodybuilding champion who created three documentaries highlighting his intensive training regimen. For the past few years, DeSimone has been able to sell from eBay and to use his eBay sales platform to call attention to his websites, where he sells more videos and other merchandise.

photo courtesy John Mitchell / BBPics.com

Says DeSimone: "eBay is a great way to advertise. And the most positive element is that you get a direct connection with the consumer, who gives you a better idea of how to market your product. It also gives you an idea of how to improve each movie. The direct feedback also makes you feel like what you're doing is actually worthwhile."

Bodybuilding champion-turned-filmmaker Paul DeSimone has successfully sold his documentaries via eBay. "The most positive element is that you get a direct connection with the consumer, who gives you a better idea of how to market your product," says DeSimone.

While this may seem like a laborious and potentially unproductive pursuit (DeSimone usually sells one video at a time), it seems to be working in covering the costs of his filmmaking. "I can't really say I made a profit from the videos, but I can say they ended up paying for the production," he says. "So that's not bad in itself. As long as you can cover all your expenses with what you're making, then you can keep on making new videos. If I became a pro bodybuilder, I think I would probably sell about ten times as many videos as I have sold now."

Another bodybuilding champion, Michigan-based Daniel C. Przyojski, has taken a page from DeSimone to sell his special interest title *Full Body Workout: Instructional Training DVD* via eBay. "I first produced the movie as a VHS for my mail-order business," he says. "I have fitness clients around the country and many do not have access to experienced trainers who know how to properly train the body with weights. I sold the video to gym members and made it accessible to customers who had purchased my books. I really never put much thought into selling on eBay. Then in July 2005 I had the idea to see if one of my books would sell on eBay. It sold at the end of the week and I thought, 'Not bad — nothing great but at least it sold.' While talking to my Webmaster about my experience, he said I should sell my instructional video on eBay. His opinion was that it would sell faster if I had it made into a DVD. We converted the video into a professional DVD with a menu that would allow you to pick any subject from the movie and go right to it for viewing. We put the DVD for sale on his eBay site at 11:00 in the afternoon and by 10:00 that night it was sold. We were both very surprised."

Przyojski never considered pursuing professional distribution for his DVD, but his eBay sale (and more sales of the same title followed) did whet his appetite. "I have never tried any other means of getting my DVD distributed," he adds. "I am totally new to the aspect of the DVD business and just finding out about the need for such DVDs. Since this experience I am now researching the business and marketplace to learn the potential and see if it interests me enough to make a deeper dedication to getting more DVDs in the marketplace."

Like DeSimone, Przyojski also sells his titles from his website. Of course, that is a viable option: Filmmakers can either arrange for payments via PayPal, as Peter M. Hargrove stated earlier, or go through their bank to set up a merchant credit card account. No matter how it is accomplished, *Video Librarian's* Randy Pitman sees the Internet as a commercially viable solution for DTV titles.

"When you stop to consider all of the production, marketing, and distribution costs of theatrical films — many of which fold and lose millions of dollars after a mere week or two in theaters — compared to the relatively inexpensive under $10,000 productions that can be marketed by companies such as CustomFlix or *BuyIndies.com*, or build word of mouth through other Internet venues, then the possibilities for substantial return on low overhead are certainly there," he says. "In the audio world, I think of singer/songwriter Aimee Mann — well known to film fans for the *Magnolia* soundtrack — who grew frustrated with her record company and finally started self-distributing her records on her own website, and built quite a following. So, yeah, hope springs eternal — and that's one of the most wonderful things about the human species."

DOING THE NONTHEATRICAL CIRCUIT

One area of the DTV world that was originally in an orbit unto itself is the nontheatrical market. As its name would suggest, non-theatrical encompasses distribution separate from commercial releasing (including theatrical exhibitions plus festivals, home video, and television presentations).

So what's left? There are, in no particular order: film societies and museums, grade schools, colleges and universities, libraries, professional organizations (including labor unions), fraternal and social organizations, religious organizations, nongovernmental organizations, nonprofits, and government agencies at municipal, state, and federal levels.

Nontheatrical became a DTV offshoot by default rather than design. In the years before video, nontheatrical was strictly a 16mm affair. Videocassette recorders killed the 16mm market and the majority of nontheatrical outlets switched from 16mm projectors to video projection. The 16mm films were often thrown away, though some wise cinephiles (most notably the celebrated archivist Dennis Nyback) were able to rescue scores of very rare 16mm reels that were discarded in the rush to embrace video. Of course, some years later there was another rush-and-jettison when DVD came in and VHS fell out of favor.

Today's nontheatrical market consists of two unequal parts. The first involves films that were originally in theatrical release. This is obviously not an example of direct-to-video, but it is also the smaller of the two parts. In fact, it gets smaller as years go by. Distributors have primarily found more money taking films from theaters into home entertainment channels and the majority of films playing on the big screen bypass the nontheatrical market completely.

The second and larger part involves films that are made exclusively for nontheatrical release. It is surprising that many professional and aspiring filmmakers are totally unaware that such an outlet exists. And for that matter, they are also unaware of how lucrative this niche can be.

Filmmaker Leszek Drozd has enjoyed lucrative commercial success creating films exclusively for the nontheatrical market. "It is hard to ignore the market for special-needs educational videos when there are 55 million people who suffer from disabilities in the U.S. alone!" says Drozd. "Strangely enough, every filmmaker I know ignores nontheatrical filmmaking — Hollywood is still a magic word. I truly believe nontheatrical filmmaking is a very rewarding career possibility.

Filmmaker Leszek Drozd runs Story Tellers Productions and he has created films exclusively for nontheatrical release to health professionals. His titles include *Overview of Speech* and *Language Pathology and Hypnosis: The Power of Your Mind*. If you never heard of Drozd's films, that's okay — the people who need to know about them are more than aware of his output.

"Nontheatrical filmmaking is a fantastic alternative to theatrical filmmaking," says Drozd. "It is hard to ignore the market for special-needs educational videos when 55 million people suffer from disabilities in the U.S. alone! Strangely enough, every filmmaker I know ignores nontheatrical filmmaking — Hollywood is still a magic word. I truly believe nontheatrical filmmaking is a very rewarding career possibility. Nontheatrical filmmaking gives you satisfaction, experience, a great resume, your own network of contacts, and possibly money. And the biggest plus is that you can do your nontheatrical filmmaking everywhere — no trip to Hollywood is needed!"

Did you catch that phrase "possibly money" in Drozd's quote? One way a nontheatrical filmmaker can harvest profits is through the same means that many commercial filmmakers have employed: self-distribution.

"There are many reasons why self-distribution is the best solution," continues Drozd. "First of all, most nontheatrical distributors actually are catalogue companies, with no solid network of distribution. Usually, especially in educational videos, such distributors are independent filmmakers/producers who are interested in expanding their offer to small audiences by adding outside work into their list of videos for sale. Simply and straightforwardly: You as a filmmaker can do the same, so why share profits on the scale of 80% to 20% with the distributor — you get 20% — while losing all rights regarding your project for a minimum of three years with late royalties, if any royalties?"

Among the filmmakers who've used nontheatrical distribution to keep a title alive is Nick Day of the documentary *Short Cut to Nirvana: Kumbh Mela*. After the film ran its theatrical course in New York in the summer of 2005, Day successfully booked the film in a local nontheatrical venue: the Rubin Museum of Art, a cultural institution celebrating Central Asia. But unlike the case with most nontheatrical presentations, Day opted to advertise the Rubin screenings, thus turning a nontheatrical exhibition into a quasi-commercial release.

"The Rubin engagement was seen as an opportunity to reach another audience that might not necessarily go to the movies," explains Day. "The museum setting is quite unlike a theater, and our film is received differently by audiences as a result. Also we were able to negotiate a lengthy run of two months, which gave us an opportunity to invite groups from places such as yoga and meditation centers to attend special screenings. The hope was to further raise awareness for the film, which will help with eventual DVD sales."

But for those who prefer to let someone else do the distribution grunt work, there is no shortage of nontheatrical organizations that handle the release of these films. National Video Resources, based in New York, is one of the most prominent nontheatrical organizations operating today. But whatever you do, don't call them a "distributor"!

"We are not a distributor," explains Brian Newman, executive director. "We curate packages of films and take them out to broad audiences. For example, our *Human Rights Video Project* took 20 human rights videos to 350 cities, mainly through public libraries. Fifty of these sites collaborated with human rights groups in their towns to hold public screenings. We purchased all of the DVDs in the series at reduced, bulk rates with public performance rights from distributors — and at times from the filmmakers directly — and disseminated them to the venues we worked with. We considered over 200 videos to pick the 20 for this series."

However, Newman is not optimistic on the overall state of distribution. "I view the state of all film releasing, not just nontheatrical, as dismal," he says. "Theatrical distributors have been shrinking and consolidating. While it can seem like a crowded marketplace of distributors, look at how many have folded and how many have been absorbed into larger institutions. On the nontheatrical side, the few distributors who exist today have been able to do so largely by following an institutional sales model. In some senses this is great — their doors are open, a few filmmakers get to a broader audience, albeit through institutions, and the better of these distributors — such as Women Make Movies — truly care about their filmmakers, know their markets, and are great partners to their artists. On the other hand, most filmmakers make their films for an audience, and hope for a large public to see their film. Nontheatrical distributors, for the most part, don't encourage consumer sales, due to the belief that this will erode institutional sales. So the larger public remains underserved due to this dilemma. Furthermore, many of these distributors are small, and cash-strapped, meaning that they can't afford the costs of moving their libraries to DVD. Numerous titles sit on the shelf because they lack funds to digitize them and feel there is too small a market."

Newman's advice for filmmakers is to use the tools of the trade to full advantage. "Enterprising filmmakers can do a fest tour, use a blog, website, and other online means to get the word out," he advises. "Then make the film available on DVD in each city the day after festival screening and for rental via Netflix right after your festival tour, and then make the film available for VOD download through *GreenCine* or a similar group. And don't forget to have a teaser and script for your next film, because if you play this new game right, you can start building audiences and funders for your next film based on the audience you find for this one."

The bit about having a teaser and script for the next film will remind you about the foundations built by Oscar Micheaux so many years ago. But what is Newman referring to when he says "VOD" and "GreenCine"? As luck would have it, that subject comes up next....

SELECTED MOVIE, COMING UP

VOD means "video on demand." As the name suggests, it allows for programming to be viewed at any time via Internet-based video streams or a cable download tat can go to a computer or a television. VOD also provides functions similar to a VCR or DVD player: pause, forwarding and rewinding at different speeds, jumping between scenes, etc.

It is not a new concept — it actually began in Hong Kong in the early 1990s when Hong Kong Telecom came up with the idea of making a selection of films available via a pay TV format. At the time, however, there was no call for it and the system flopped. So did Hong Kong Telecom, which was acquired by Pacific Century Cyberworks in 2000. But as time went on and high-speed connectivity became commonplace, VOD caught on. In the United States, nearly all major cable television providers have VOD services and programming selections.

Not surprisingly, most cable providers also fall back on high-recognition Hollywood output for their VOD selections. On the Internet, however, indie cinema is the major force among the VOD channels. Online entities such as *GreenCine, Cinequest Online*, and *CinemaNow.com* have brought together a remarkable collection of independently produced cinema offerings.

Of course, the threat of piracy has always haunted any Internet-based film presentation. But perhaps the pirates are following in the footsteps of what Napster and other music download pioneers did: creating a culture of using the Internet to seek out entertainment. As more and more people use the Internet to gain forbidden (and, quite frankly, illegal) copies of the current theatrical releases, there is no reason to think they won't shift their browsers to sites offering an intriguing mix of properly promoted DTV fare.

"We're firmly in an age now where people are freely downloading theatrical releases on the Internet," says Rory L. Aronsky, who reviews original online movie content for *Film Threat*. "While the MPAA goes after them with 800,000-plus guns blazing, they are completely ignorant of the fact that this could be beneficial for the industry and not only for Hollywood. Stay with me on this. These people may be out there for the big releases, but imagine where that could go for online films! Users download these movies, but the Internet being the Internet, they become more curious about what else is out there. It's just like with any other pleasure on the Internet, be it porn, poker, or chat rooms. Once in a while, only one dab'll do you, but other dabs seem just as interesting. Therefore, if Hollywood can show a little leg to the other side of the filmmaking sphere and allow them to partner up somehow, without sacrificing quality, there's a real chance to bring film lovers not only toward what they want to see, but what they may very well be curious enough about to click on. Put simply, a comedy or any other genre is good enough for everyone and the latest releases from Hollywood are like big, hulking magnets for some, with their brains and emotions being pulled toward them. But what if, for example, besides the film you want, William Shatner decides to go nuts and indeed perform *Julius Caesar* as he described in *Free Enterprise*? It's morbid curiosity, but there it is online. *AtomFilms* and *iFilm* can do a lot with a Hollywood partnership. I'm not sure of profit sharing, or even if Hollywood would share when the day comes that they do offer new releases legally online. Hell, I'm just a young, hopeful idealist. But for the love of film, there should be more love on both sides. Technology keeps going the way it's going, Internet connections become faster, and the day will come when people may very well see just as many feature-length and short indie films as they do with Hollywood's output. I hope it'll happen."

INTERVIEW
MICHAEL LEGGE, FILMMAKER

Michael Legge is a filmmaker who has a considerable cult following, which is remarkable given that none of his films has ever been in theatrical release. Legge specializes in ultra-low-budget horror comedies — there have been witches, zombies, aliens, and assorted gasp-inducing nasties on the prowl in his films. For nearly two decades, Legge's output has been strictly small screen and DTV — he has a long-running and mutually profitable relationship with the distributor SRS Cinema LLC — but neither filmmaker nor fans are complaining that his work is absent from the local multiplex.

Wearing the quadruple crown of writer/director/producer/actor, Legge offers films that are satires of both the horror/sci-fi genre and contemporary American society. *Working Stiffs* (1989) solves the problem of troublesome employees with a unique approach to personnel considerations: hiring the undead. *Loons* (1991) brings back the Salem witch hunt through a cross-generational curse of mental lunacy placed by a doomed witch on the family of her judge. More recently, his films *Honey Glaze* (2003) and *Democrazy* (2005) have taken good-natured swipes at the James Bond fantasy world and the George W. Bush version of American government, respectively. *Democrazy* won Legge the Best Screenplay Award in the 2005 B-Movie Film Festival, where the movie was also nominated for Best Picture.

Q: When you began making films, what were the distribution plans you had for your films? Did you feel they would ever play theatrically, show up on television, or be sold on home video?

MICHAEL LEGGE: When I was young and stupid, in my early 20s, I think my aim was to be your run-of-the-mill mainstream filmmaker; getting my movie picked up by a distributor, eventually playing on TV, etc. At that time there were no VCRs all over the place, so video didn't enter into it. I made a 16mm feature in the early '70s called *Down the Rabbit Hole*, which was the first feature-length movie I'd attempted. Up until that time, I had been making 8mm and Super 8mm shorts since I was 16, but those had initially been for fun, and then I simply became addicted to the whole process. From the beginning we — and "we" means my brother and friends — made comedies, or I should say parodies, since any movie I particularly liked I would write a parody of. Not to make fun of it, but because I liked it, and parody is easy to do because you already have the plot and characters supplied. Along the way, I started to write short films that weren't parodies and that became an odd mix of spoof and satire. I had gotten to the point where I wanted to take the plunge, and saved the money to rent an Eclair camera, Nagra recorder, and rolls of 16mm Reversal film — with a horrendous light index of 25, which means you needed a small sun to light the sets. We knocked it off in three or four weekends, and then I had the nightmare of editing a black-and-white work print and then A and B rolls out of the original. No way could I afford a pro to do this. I hated it with a passion. Looking back, it was kind of astonishing that I got it made, especially an approximately 90-minute film, done with no budget and using friends as actors. I can't look at it now, it's god-awful, but at the time, it seemed like it had potential.

I had dreams of an art house type of distributor picking it up. *Monty Python and the Holy Grail* had just come out, and I thought we were in that category. I tried to get it shown in the Boston area first. I remember going to some ersatz movie/coffee house to show them my masterpiece. I can still see the owner's expression watching it; a block of unsmiling chiseled granite. He looked like his soul had transported itself elsewhere and left his body behind to take the punishment. He was justified, of course: In general, the movie was awful in all aspects and I had a lot of gall to show it to anyone. I screened it again to some other people and they suggested cutting it — the film, not my throat! I'd listen to anyone then, so I went ahead and whittled it down to an hour. Now it was a shorter bad movie. I sent the streamlined one to someplace in Cambridge that returned it with a polite no thanks.

The worst was to come. Through a friend of mine, I was going to get it screened at his college in Dartmouth, Massachusetts. I would finally be able to see and hear an auditorium of people reacting to my first film. The night came. It was a double feature. Also showing was Arthur Penn's film, *Little Big Man*. It was shown first. *Little Big Man* ended and mine started. The audience got up and walked out. Myself and couple of friends sat there in this big empty auditorium while the movie played. We did spot a young couple who stayed for the whole movie, although they were a distance away. As they walked out after it was over, I stood and said to them, "Bless you."

My youthful enthusiasm was crushed. It was the turning point in every moviemaker's life. Your first time out and people don't like your movie — and with comedy it's even more punishing because not hearing laughter is the worst silence in the world. This is when you either give it up or try again. One thing had helped me. When I had gone to get the movie soundtrack mixed in a studio, the engineer who worked on it with me was laughing at the movie. I always remembered that. Somebody thought it was funny.

Q: To date, how and where have your films been released? Have any played theatrically?

MICHAEL LEGGE: I had made a second 16mm film, a short this time, which came out much better than the previous one. I submitted it to a film festival somewhere, I can't remember where, and not only did they show it, but it got an honorable mention. I felt more justified to call myself a filmmaker. A good friend of mine suggested that I really didn't have to waste all my money on 16mm anymore because the medium of Super 8mm had grown up into quite a professional medium. I checked out his suggestion and he was right. Now there was Super 8mm sound film, sophisticated cameras, decent mikes, editing equipment, and more. I could make a dozen Super 8 features for the price of a 16mm one. I invested in the equipment and entered the world of Super 8mm. It was the smartest thing I ever did. Other than the money factor, the idea that I could turn out many short films and try to get my bearings as a filmmaker was tremendously helpful. Another big help was discovering Brodsky and Treadway, enthusiastic advocates of Super 8mm, who also did professional transfers of Super 8mm to 1-inch videotape. They became my first real fans and pointed me in more friendly directions to get my films screened.

I started submitting short films to film festivals all over the world. I got movies screened domestically in Ann Arbor, New York, Florida, North Carolina, and Puerto Rico, and internationally in Australia and Venezuela. To my astonishment, I started to win awards. During this time, the USA network had a great late-night program on called *Night Flight*. They showed all kinds of weird stuff, music videos, short films, features. I submitted a short I had made, *The Lemon Man*, and they paid me a flat one-time fee to air it. I'll never forget the night it came on the air and it hit me that the whole country could see me making a fool of myself.

Now it was time to make my first feature in Super 8mm, *Working Stiffs*. It was a horror comedy, and I wanted to show zombies in new light that was actually an old light: zombies as mindless slaves, not flesh-eating monsters. They are used by a temp agency for cheap labor; something I know that if it were possible it would be done. It was a long road to get my first real distribution deal. I had to go through a couple of crooks at first, just to get an idea of what the business was really like. I had scoured all the magazines and books I could find about distributors who were willing to look at movies that weren't made by the "big boys." The first bozo I hooked up with supposedly was willing to take on the movie but did nothing with it. The second guy was worse. He seemed very sincere — I suppose John Wayne Gacy did, too — about getting my films distributed. We had a contract and he promised big things. Then he stopped answering calls.

This I had gotten used to with the first dipstick I had a contract with. But this time, this guy had all my printing materials in a lab in Texas. The short story is I had to hire a lawyer to break this guy and get all my stuff back to me.

In spite of these setbacks, I was getting encouragement from different places. On the strength of *Working Stiffs*, I was able to get an NEA grant to do my second film, *Loons*. That movie, in turn, got me yet another NEA grant to do *Cutthroats*. My favorite story from this process is that one of the panel members who gave the grant told me what a breath of fresh air it was to see my movie after watching all these documentaries and heavy dramas. So I had some positive vibes going, but three movies that had no distributor.

Q: How did your relationship with SRS Cinema — formerly Sub Rosa Studios, formerly Salt City Home Video — begin? And have your films been released by other companies?

MICHAEL LEGGE: Although I can't remember exactly, I think my relationship with SRS Cinema was a lucky coincidence. I believe I had found Ron Bonk's website and emailed him to ask if he was interested in viewing my films for possible distribution. He already knew who I was through Hugh Gallagher, who publishes *Draculina* magazine and who had written some positive reviews about my older films. Ron ended up seeing all I had done up to that point and he liked them. Initially he acted as a go-between: He listed and promoted the movies, then if anyone wanted to buy them, he'd order from me. Eventually he started to finance the distribution end on some films, primarily when DVD came into its own. He coupled two old features, *Loons* and *Cutthroats*, and my newest movie, *Honey Glaze*, was paired with *Braindrainer*. Since I hooked up with SRS, I've never tried to find any other deals, since my primary aim was to find somebody I could trust, not someone who would lie through his crooked teeth, promising me great things and delivering nothing.

Q: Do you feel that you've achieved your professional goals in getting your films released on DVD/home video? Or are you hopeful your films will be shown on a big screen someday?

MICHAEL LEGGE: Strangely enough, in today's viewing environments everything can get on a big screen! But I know what you mean is if I hope for mainstream release and find myself in some multiplex somewhere. First of all, I don't believe that will ever happen. I don't make mainstream movies. I make a kind of retro comedy; to me, modern comedy for the most part has degenerated into lame-brained exercises in vulgarity and grossness. I know I sound like a prude, and I'm not — I can watch and enjoy all sorts of depraved things — but I like to see some semblance of wit behind it. I fully admit to being old-fashioned. I am a big fan of all the old comedy teams; the Marx Brothers, Laurel and Hardy, Abbott and Costello, etc., plus I like silly

Ed Eck and Michael Legge prepare a cerebral meal in Legge's comedy Braindrainer. *Says Legge: "I rarely encounter indifference. The people who like me cut me a lot of slack for my decided lack of production values."*

and/or wild humor like Monty Python, SCTV, Kids in the Hall, Black-adder. I have a special fondness for the dry, absurd humor of Bob and Ray and consider them a great influence. I don't think for a minute that if some producer handed me tons of money to make a movie that I'd be allowed to do what I want. I've seen too many great comedians come from an off-the-wall background and become absorbed into conventional movies, consequently losing what made them special in the first place.

Case in point: John Candy, a wonderful comic actor with SCTV, who broke off and became a "big-time" movie star. With few exceptions, he ended up making a lot of crap movies, completely wasting his talent. I am very happy to have gotten as far as I have. I have national distribution and while I would wish more people would become aware of my work, at least I have an outlet.

Q: What is the level of feedback that you've received from your films?

MICHAEL LEGGE: I rarely encounter indifference. The people that like me cut me a lot of slack for my decided lack of production values. I've always considered my strong suit to be the writing. I don't consider myself a great or even good director. I know from years of doing live theater that I do have a talent for performing comedy, and even people who may not like the movie will say something nice about that. When reviewers don't like the movies, they really seem to hate them. I'm sometimes taken aback by really mean-spirited reviews; I envision the writer drooling while he's tapping the keys. If someone doesn't find a movie funny, that's okay with me. What irks me is the ones who say "this is not funny" in the tone of "I know what's funny and not funny." I'll listen to a reviewer who qualifies the criticism by saying that a person's sense of humor is a very individual thing.

I know that what other people will think is hilarious I might not find funny in the least. Of course, there are the trolls who have their own websites or who make moronic comments at the IMDb; you can tell their age from the words they use; they are to be ignored. I do get good reviews and feedback. I think I hit about 50-50 in the good versus bad. Usually, if someone likes the first thing they see from me, they're probably going to like them all. If nothing else, I don't feel you'd mistake one of my movies for someone else's.

Anyone who appreciates wry, absurd humor with a touch of surrealism should like my movies. The more-insightful critics like Rob Firsching see the humanity underneath the nonsense. He characterized me best by saying my movies were "quirky and strangely heartwarming." Rob is a fan of mine but I have a funny story about him. The first thing he ever saw of mine he absolutely hated. I had done a short segment for an anthology movie. I did a tongue-in-cheek horror story called *Dryer Straits*. It was about an older woman who keeps finding larger and larger amounts of lint in her dryer. The lint eventually accumulates enough to produce a lint monster who tries to kill her. Rob really disliked, if not hated, this segment. He trashed it as silly and dismissed the whole thing. Later on, I guess Ron sent him my newest feature at the time, *Braindrainer*. Rob did a turnaround and really liked it. He compared it to *Rocky and Bullwinkle*, which I consider a high compliment. In general from then on he's been very supportive of me and I appreciate all the good things he's said. To me, *Dryer Straits* is an example, albeit a quickly thrown together one, of what I do. It hit him wrong the first time, but he changed his mind about me later. I wonder if he ever watched *Dryer Straits* again to see if he still hated it.

Another unusual reaction was at a film festival. In the 1980s I had a short film shown at the Ann Arbor Super 8 Fest and I was able to attend it. The movie was called *Joe X* and was a Hitchcock-like spoof of an innocent who gets dragged into dire doings. One of the gags in the movie was a variation of something you've see in old film noir flicks. The hero is trying to keep the heroine from following him into danger, so he clips her on the chin, knocking her out. "Sorry I had to do that, baby, but it was for your own good." In my movie, my character does the same thing. He hauls back and lets loose with a right cross to his lover. She jerks back from the blow, but it didn't affect her at all. She stands there looking at him like nothing happened. So he decides she can go with him. I'll add this got a good laugh from the audience. After the screening, I was accosted by two or three young female college students who were rather miffed at me for making a joke about violence toward women. Obviously that wasn't my intention; I was lampooning an outdated attitude from old movies and I tried to explain it to them the best I could. They seemed mollified but it was an example of how you never know how someone will react to you. The corker is that mainstream movies revel in violence toward women. What I did was nothing.

Q: *What professional advice can you share with aspiring filmmakers who are eager to get their movies into release?*

MICHAEL LEGGE: Patience. Tons of it. If you don't have that, give it up now. The easiest way to get something seen is to get it on the Web. There are websites where you can get short films shown, or you can even create your own website. Plenty of people are jumping right into digital filmmaking and creating sites that map a film's progress and then offer a trailer or even sell it online. If you're looking toward big-theater release as your goal, your only remote chance is to make a film and submit to places like Sundance or similar places that get scouted for potential releases to the public. However, I would say the worst thing to do is sit down and make a movie with a big-screen release in mind. I have always believed you have to make the movie for yourself and then hope that others will appreciate it. I could never in a million years sit down to write a script and think, "I want this to be like *American Pie VII*."

Look up the smaller distributors like SRS Cinema and others that are open to indie product. There's nothing wrong with having a DVD release only. More and more people are converting their homes into mini-theaters. This is where the small, personal, no-budget films will continue to find an audience, not in the multiplexes. You have to decide what's worth more to you, the almighty buck or... (*Mwahahahahhahaha! Cue the lightning!*) **your soul!?!**

❧

LISTEN TO WHAT THE MAN SAYS

The chapter began by asking if DTV is synonymous with failure. The answer is a big fat "No!" But to get a better idea of the DTV world, here are some tips on proceeding further:

1. Subscribe to the media that covers this aspect of distribution. *Video Business* and *Home Media Retailing* are weeklies that focus on the home entertainment world. They are well-written and entertaining publications and they provide a comprehensive view of the trends and troubles in this sphere. *Video Librarian* is a monthly publication aimed at the librarians who purchase DVDs and videos, but it offers the best guide to both the commercial and nontheatrical titles being released.

2. Be aware that many popular consumer publications do not review DTV titles. If you are fishing for reviews, do not waste your time going after media outlets that only give coverage to the DVD versions of Hollywood titles. There is no shortage of highly regarded media that will consider DTV titles. These outlets are mostly online, although some magazines like *Phantom of the Movies' Videoscope* and the aforementioned *Video Librarian* will give equal coverage regardless of the lack of theatrical release.

3. When negotiating a deal with a DTV label, ask hard questions about their depth of distribution. Where can you find their titles? How do they promote them? What is the average level of their returns? How many units need to be sold before you start to see a profit?

4. If you are going the route of the DVD duplicator services, take the time to seek out the filmmakers selling their titles through these services. Ask them about their feelings on these services. And, again, be as frank and honest in your questioning as you can.

5. Believe it or not, selling DVDs via eBay is good idea. Paul DeSimone has sold his bodybuilding documentaries via this method and managed to build up a fairly considerable audience of new fans. DeSimone's comments are worth repeating: "The most positive element is that you get a direct connection with the consumer, who gives you a better idea of how to market your product. It also gives you an idea of how to improve each movie. The direct feedback also makes you feel like what you're doing is actually worthwhile." Hey, can you believe that — a filmmaker who actually listens to viewers without rancor and happily takes their advice?

USING THE INTERNET TO CALL ATTENTION TO YOUR FILMS

The Internet is the world's largest library.
It's just that all the books are on the floor.
— John Allen Paulos

7

As mentioned earlier in this book, the 1990s came to a dramatic end when the low-budget horror flick *The Blair Witch Project* tapped into the potential of the Internet to create a word-of-mouth buzz that resonated all the way to the box office. As the twenty-first century rolled around, the Internet saw the rise of a new selection of websites and services designed to expand and redefine the concept of communication and self-promotion. Several of the new sites and services were specifically designed for the motion picture world, but others proved to be versatile enough that filmmakers incorporated them into their efforts. Today, their ubiquity is a commonplace part of the online environment.

However, these sites and services are frequently used incorrectly, thus diluting their effectiveness. Too often, the level of usage is so low that it is impossible to make any positive impact. However, there is also the other extreme, where too much recklessness is put into play.

Admittedly, this is all relatively new territory for many people, and the mistakes that are made are rarely lethal to one's career or output. Nonetheless, understanding how to make the most of these important online tools has become crucial for spreading the message about your work.

BLOGGING

The concept of the blog — the word is a derivation of the term "web log" — originated in the early 1990s. In many ways, the blog appeared as a contradiction to the community-building aspects of the early online experience — the original forms of online communication, Usenet forums and Bulletin Board Systems were specifically designed to encourage dialogue rather than monologues, while the chat room features of online services such as America Online encouraged the free exchange of real-time conversation.

No one is quite clear who the first blogger was — the *New York Times* Magazine called Swarthmore College student Justin Hall the "founding father of personal blogging" based on his 1994 online diary — but in any event, the use of the Internet as a forum for the individual rather than the community took root and blossomed.

Blogs have evolved over the years from online diaries that recorded daily ennui and odd observations into full-throttle promotional tools to keep all interested parties abreast on new developments. Independent film distributors have used blogs as quasi-press rooms that promote films, screenings and other activities. This approach is used most successfully in the blog operated by Facets Multi-Media, the Chicago-based media arts organization.

"Facets started its blog (*facetsfeatures.blogspot.com*) in 2006," explains Phil Morehart, writer and editor for the blog. "It serves multiple purposes: it allows our very talented staff an outlet to write about cinema and to explore a variety of film-related topics at length (via reviews, film festival reports from Berlin, Cannes, Chicago, Pusan and beyond, film lists, interviews); it's a venue for us to link to and discuss current film news online; and, most importantly, it provides an opportunity for our customers, members, and readers to connect with the people behind the scenes at Facets."

Morehart notes that having control over the creation and release of this information has benefited Facets in many ways.

"Reaction to the blog has been absolutely positive from day one," he continues. "In addition to being linked on various film-related blogs and websites, we've also received multiple mentions in the *Guardian* (or rather, on the *Guardian's* film blog) praising our annual "31 Days of Horror" video clips feature. Based on feedback, our readers are genuine lovers of all cinema, reacting to and commenting on posts be they about Bela Tarr or Bela Lugosi."

However, maintaining a blog is very similar to maintaining a houseplant: if you fail to provide the proper level of care and attention, it will ultimately wither and die. According to Nielsen Media Research, there are approximately 126 million blogs across the World Wide Web, but the vast majority of these blogs are rarely, if ever, updated.

Furthermore, blogs should not be considered as standalone islands in the World Wide Web. Independent filmmakers should be linking blog content to other sites.

"At the moment," says New York filmmaker Mark L. Feinsod, "whenever I post something on my blog (*feinsodville. tumblr.com*), it automatically posts the same contact to my Twitter account."

And speaking of Twitter…

TWITTER

Twitter represents a new landmark in minimalist communications: conveying messages with a limit of 140 typographical characters. The idea for such a strategy began in 2006 at a podcasting company called Odeo, where Twitter developed as an internal service among employees who wanted online chat that was more succinct than instant messaging. Several of Odeo's employees acquired the company and its assets in October 2006, and by April 2007 they launched Twitter.com as a standalone company.

Twitter actually has a connection to the independent film world: the first major demonstration took place at the 2007 South by Southwest (SWSX) festival. Twitter found itself on display with a pair of 60-inch plasma screens that offered the constant streaming of Tweets (a.k.a. the Twitter messages — as with any technology, Twitter encompassed its own colloquialisms). And in typical film festival fashion, the Twitter team received an award from the SXSW for its contributions to the event.

In a relatively short period of time, Twitter has evolved into the de facto platform for instant messages, press statements, and news announcements. When singer Michael Jackson died in 2009, the sheer volume of Tweets relating to his unexpected death caused *Twitter.com* to experience a temporary shutdown.

Independent filmmakers and distributors are still wrestling with how to best use Twitter. For some, it means building a community among like-minded Twitter addicts who keep tabs on the latest Tweets from their favorite indie sources.

"We're using it as a means to connect with our customers and members, linking to online content that we find interesting to hopefully create a dialogue," says Facets' Morehart. "We also use Twitter to promote events, but that is not the sole purpose. Creating a personal experience for our patrons and Twitter followers is the prime goal."

Connecticut-based filmmaker Joel Vetsch relies on Twitter to promote his work.

"I started using Twitter in 2009," says Vetsch. "I have a fair amount of followers now, and have used it to advertise screenings of my movies, links, and on Twitpic I can put photographs up as well. I hope to build the amount of followers I have on Twitter, and use that to market my projects, expose them to people, and generate buzz."

For others, though, Twitter remains a tool that might be able to solve problems, once the problem of figuring out its full potential is solved.

"I like Twitter and I have an account with a decent number of followers," says Mark L. Feinsod. "But I have yet to figure out how to utilize it to most effectively promote my work as a filmmaker."

However, not everyone is fully convinced. Berkeley, California–based underground filmmaker Antero Alli expresses concern that the minimalist nature of Twitter actually restricts the free flow of communication.

"I'm a neo-Luddite in love with the immediacy of life and cautious about the immediate gratification that Twitter delivers," he explains. "Most people lose touch with the authentic immediacy of existence as their experience becomes increasingly and excessively mediated by external technologies. The convenience of immediate gratification replaces the spontaneity of direct experience. There is something about Twitter that serves and feeds the epidemic of infantile narcissism and frustrated creativity amongst its users who become addicted to posting notes about whatever they're doing, assuming that someone out there cares enough to read it. Unfortunately that assumption is fulfilled and feeds a false sense of self-importance and entitlement. There's also something paranoid about the whole Twitter world and schizophrenic in the way so much information gets crammed into such a small space. Like, how many times did you Tweet today?"

And then there is independent director/producer Thomas Edward Seymour and his approach to the subject: "The most important way that I use Twitter is to link it to both Facebook and MySpace — when I Tweet, it will update my Facebook and MySpace pages."

Which now takes us into...

MYSPACE AND FACEBOOK

In the beginning of the social networking world, there was Friendster. This site was launched in 2002 and headquartered in Sydney, Australia. But Friendster's popularity was initially slow in taking off; while it is still online, many people often refer to it as an example of a pioneer that never truly controlled the sector.

The site that was responsible for stealing Friendster's thunder was MySpace, which was launched in August 2003 by employees at the Internet marketing company eUniverse (later Intermix Media Inc.). eUniverse had the advantage of tapping into a database of 20 million e-mail subscribers, which enabled MySpace to catch on fairly quickly.

Initially, MySpace's popularity centered on independent bands eager to promote themselves on a free site. Soon, a larger variety of MySpace subscribers began to come along. MySpace's growth and influence became so pronounced in such a short period of time that Rupert Murdoch's News Corporation, the parent company behind 20th Century Fox and the Fox Broadcasting channels, successfully purchased MySpace and its parent company for $580 million.

While this was going on, another social networking site turned up. Facebook, an operation created by a group of Harvard University students, found its way online in 2004. By June 2008, the privately owned Facebook matched MySpace's subscriber base with approximately 115 million people on each site. By January 2009, Facebook passed MySpace in the quantity of subscribers.

Over the past few years, a MySpace versus Facebook rivalry has consumed many Net surfers — not unlike the Windows versus Mac or Coke versus Pepsi challenges that inevitably occur when two powerful brands try to dominate a single industry. The preferred site depends on which person you are talking to.

"Facets is active on both MySpace and Facebook, with a heavier lean towards Facebook," says Morehart. "Again, the results have been great. Much like our blog, Facets uses these social networking sites to connect with our customers and members, creating a dialogue either through direct interaction using their provided messageboards or by linking to online content (current film news, reviews, etc.) to hopefully spur a conversation via the comment fields. Luckily, our 'fans' eat it up. The personal connection element is key, and it's one that exists both between Facets and our fans and also between the fans themselves. Ultimately, our Facebook page is a large community, and we're merely guiding the conversation."

"Facebook has been very helpful in terms of cementing connections with contacts I've made along the way," says Mark L. Feinsod. "It's never gotten me a job or anything, but it places you firmly in somebody else's orbit and vice versa."

But MySpace has its fans, most notably indie icon Kevin Smith. When Smith was putting together his 2006 comedy *Clerks II*, he created a MySpace account for the film that featured a unique contest: the first 10,000 MySpace users who added *Clerks II* as a "friend" would see their name in the closing credits. The 10,000 quota was reached within two hours.

Oklahoma-based filmmaker Jonathan Grant also used MySpace to create an alternative universe for his 2008 comedy *No Burgers for Bigfoot*.

"We love MySpace because it gave us a chance to allow audiences to experience the 'world' that the film takes place in after the movie is over," explains Grant. "Several of the main characters in the film have MySpace pages, and they were filled out as the characters would have filled them out. All the characters in the movie were fleshed out and brought to life by the actors, so they made their own pages. The characters publicly commented on each other's pages and created a nice little fantasy world for audiences to find. The main character's MySpace page is linked to from our film's website, *noburgersforbigfoot.com*."

But for those who don't want to play favorites, there are tools that enable both sites to be treated equally. "There are social aggregators like *Bebo.com*, *Socialthing.com* or *Stands.com* that allow you to check all of your social sites (Facebook, Twitter, MySpace) in one place and update them all as well," says Thomas Edward Seymour.

WIKIPEDIA

One of the most ambitious — and, later, controversial — online do-it-yourself projects has been Wikipedia, a free information reference site that bills itself as "the encyclopedia that anyone can edit."

Founded in 2001 by Larry Sanger and Jimmy Wales, Wikipedia's popularity as an Internet destination was quickly established and its influence as both a reference source and a media outlet expanded with unprecedented speed. Today, it is among the top ten visited sites on the Internet.

Unfortunately for Wikipedia, the do-it-yourself aspect of the site enabled a multitude of severely unqualified people to become part of the editorial community. A combination of incompetent input and deliberate vandalism has taken its toll on Wikipedia's credibility and quality control efforts. Many articles that appeared on the site have been identified as either being intentional hoaxes or improperly referenced, while others have been used to promote distinctive political, religious and sexual agendas. In a scandal that damaged Wikipedia's credibility in many quarters, the site was faulted for being too slow to catch user-contributed vandalism that rewrote the biography of distinguished journalist John Seigenthaler to include phony claims that he was a figure in the assassinations of John F. Kennedy and Robert F. Kennedy.

Nonetheless, many people who are unaware of or unconcerned about the site's long-boiling problems view the notion of being the subject of a Wikipedia article as a confirmation of importance. Many independent filmmakers have viewed a Wikipedia article as being a key to establishing credibility for themselves and their work — in their view, an article on Wikipedia is the closest thing that the online world has to a stamp of approval.

Furthermore, Wikipedia doesn't require a film to be a classic in order for it to merit an article. If the subject has adequate reference sourcing in recognizable major media, it can make the grade. Thus, new films and (in certain cases) productions awaiting distribution can find their way into Wikipedia.

In keeping with the entrepreneurial nature of independent films, many creative artists do not want to wait for someone to write a Wikipedia article about them. Instead, they take it upon themselves to create their own entries. However, the resulting efforts usually create more headaches than glory. Gregory Kohs, a research practitioner with a Fortune 100 company who also consults with individuals and organizations about Wikipedia, explains that too many people approach Wikipedia without being cognizant of the site's surprisingly Byzantine editorial governing policies.

"Most of the people motivated to participate in Wikipedia for the purposes of self-promotion will fail in their efforts, and it's largely for one key reason: they don't do their homework beforehand," he says. "At the bottom of the food chain, many individuals or enterprises come upon Wikipedia, read the mythical slogan 'anyone can edit,' and just start creating a delightful page about themselves. These pages will typically be deleted within hours or even minutes because the editor will have broken any of a number of Wikipedia policies including 'Notability,' 'Conflict of Interest' and 'Single Purpose Account.' Higher up in the food chain, some will take more care to learn, honor, and obey Wikipedia's various rules about content inclusion, and they will rigorously craft a Wikipedia article that they believe passes all of the policy checks. But, about half the time it seems, they will end up sadly disappointed when their article gets deleted anyway."

Some independent filmmakers who took this approach discovered that the hard way. "Wikipedia is a whole other entity, run by the people for the people — unfortunately," says award-winning director Eric B. Hughes, who fought a good fight to get content relating to his work on the site. "In the case of Wikipedia, you have very fussy hands-on people who, if they don't like what you are posting, will remove it. Anyone can do that, and some people go a little overboard."

Hughes' initial endeavors in publishing information relating to himself and his work on Wikipedia resulted in an overzealous site administrator disabling his account. However, Wikipedia's sieve-like system (the free registration requires no formal identification process) allowed Hughes to start a new account and restore his material with links that confirmed the notability of his work. To date, the articles relating to his career remain undisturbed.

Mark L. Feinsod had his own hit-and-miss experiences with Wikipedia. "Putting articles about my work on Wikipedia hasn't been without problems," he confides. "They do have people who monitor the site, and they take that work very seriously. Which is good. But back in the early days of Wikipedia,

I put up a listing for *A Sense of Entitlement*, my first short out of film school, which has some legitimacy because it was reviewed in the *New York Times* by Dave Kehr and numerous other publications, and it has played around the world. That helped. I also have a listing for *Virginal Young Blondes*, but for whatever reason the article about my next film, After an *Autumn Day That Felt Like Summer*, was removed. If I remember correctly, the site monitors didn't think the movie was noteworthy enough. Which is a shame, because I think it's a good movie. But then again, I like the idea of Wikipedia being a source of information and not a depository for PR professionals to write garbage about whatever products they're hawking. If the price of that is having the occasional micro-budget short be scrutinized very closely, then so be it."

A key mistake among self-promoting filmmakers who approach Wikipedia for the first time is openly identifying themselves as being the creative artist whose work is the subject of the article. This runs afoul of the aforementioned "Conflict of Interest" and "Single Purpose Account" guidelines, thus setting up the new article for immediate deletion. Yet Kohs points out that some Wikipedia editors that routinely review new articles have their own agenda that require them to seek the removal of certain text.

"Some powerful Wikipedia crusaders may take offense at the new subject's promotional tone," he continues. "It's all a big saga to stamp out self-promotion on Wikipedia, and if your article gets caught up in that saga, just kiss it goodbye."

However, Kohs offers professional advice on how filmmakers can get their articles on Wikipedia without running afoul of suspicious editors. But be forewarned that this requires somewhat more time and energy than many people would plan to volunteer.

"If you want to successfully integrate your content with Wikipedia, you do what the expert manipulators do," advises Kohs. "You create an account from a new IP address not tied to your identity (don't try this at home, or at the office); a perfect spot is the public library or the corner coffee shop with Wi-Fi access. You build up a fake reputation for authentic, altruistic editing contributions. You'll want to constructively edit at least ten different articles over several days, not directly related to your ultimate self-promotional article topic.

"Then, you'll strike. Have your article fully prepared in advance, complete with properly formatted reference citations and an infobox to lend the topic an aura of credibility. Then, over the course of about 30 to 45 minutes, you should publish small sections of the prepared article, piece by piece, so it looks like you're really working on this thing as a 'knowledge-sharing' process. Then, continue to work on two or three other unrelated articles. Then shut up and wait. Don't announce your new Wikipedia article in a blog. Don't trumpet your Wikipedia success story in a press release. Don't encourage your employees or friends to go check out the new Wikipedia listing. Just keep quiet and wait. If someone asks you about your Wikipedia article, say, 'Oh, is there a Wikipedia article about me? Fancy that!'"

However, be aware that Wikipedia is *not* the only do-it-yourself encyclopedic reference site on the Internet. The most notable rival involves Wikipedia co-founder Larry Sanger, who left the project shortly after its inception to helm Citizendium, which has far stricter editorial requirements for publication.

For his part, Kohs operates MyWikiBiz, a Wiki-style directory that allows people and enterprises to fashion their own content without facing the editorial chaos that often surrounds the internal Wikipedia operations.

"The key advantages MyWikiBiz holds over Wikipedia (especially if your content has been unceremoniously removed from Wikipedia) are that MyWikiBiz does not restrict content based on notability — an article about your dog, or even your dog's red collar, is welcome there — and MyWikiBiz pages that are properly formatted with semantic tags will do better on search engine results than Wikipedia's tags. And you are welcome to advertise and promote your business or film on My-WikiBiz, keeping 100% of the revenue for yourself. It's not just free web hosting — it is pay-yourself web hosting!"

photo courtesy Milestone Film & Video

Henry G. Sanders in Charles Burnett's 1977 classic Killer of Sheep, *distributed by Milestone Film & Video. "We sometimes start or contribute to the Wikipedia pages that deal with Milestone's films, but on the whole, the public does a good job," says Dennis Doros of Milestone.*

However, some people in the independent film world do not give much thought to getting on Wikipedia — after all, there are many eager Wikipedia contributors who actively go out of their way to ensure that their favorite independent films and filmmakers receive coverage on the site.

"A very talented artist and photographer in Germany, Misha Evstafiev, started our Wikipedia page, and that speaks on the international benefits of the Internet," says Dennis Doros of Milestone Film & Video. "We sometimes start or contribute to the Wikipedia pages that deal with Milestone's films, but on the whole, the public does a good job."

"I honestly do not know how I got onto Wikipedia," exclaims Antero Alli. "A friend told me I was on there and I couldn't believe it. Though I am an underground filmmaker with a loyal but smallish West Coast following, I sometimes forget that I am also a published author with eight books in print. It could have been anyone familiar with my books or films that believe in me and wanted others to know about my work."

Alli, however, adds that he is uncertain just how to react to being part of Wikipedia's vast collection of articles. "My Wikipedia page has served as a kind of generic bio that has been useful on those occasions I want to impress someone with the broader range of what I do and have done," he says. "But it's still odd. When I look at it and read it, it's as if I'm reading the story of someone who has already died. I mean, don't you have to die first before getting listed in an encyclopedia or your face plastered on a postage stamp?"

INTERNET MOVIE DATABASE

So far, all of the websites and services presented here are open to anyone with Internet access. Filmmakers and distributors are able to use them, of course, but these are not trade-specific tools. A number of sites are aimed primarily at the motion picture world, and being involved on their pages is critical in order to spread the word on a new film.

The most important is clearly the Internet Movie Database (IMDb). This monster site, which covers the full motion picture spectrum from the Lumière Brothers to current preproduction endeavors, began in 1989 with two different lists compiled for the "rec.arts.movies" Usenet newsgroup — one list consisted of films rated on a one-to-ten scale by the newsgroup subscribers while the other offered a somewhat subjective listing of actresses by physical beauty. The following year, a British engineer for Hewlett-Packard named Col Needham combined the two lists and began adding new lists. This grew into the rec.arts.movies movie database, which migrated from Usenet to the World Wide Web in 1994 under the peculiar name *Cardiff Internet Movie Database*. (The reference to the Welsh capital in the site's name was inspired by having the database hosted on servers at Cardiff University's computer science department.)

Originally inspired as a volunteer effort, the database project became so large that Needham incorporated it in 1996 as the Internet Movie Database. While the information provided to the IMDb came from volunteer contributors, the advertising and partnerships generated by the site enabled Needham to hire an editorial team to help keep the site's contents organized and updated.

In 1998, IMDb was purchased by Jeff Bezos' Amazon.com. The site continued to exist as an Amazon subsidiary, expanding further in 2002 with the creation of its subscription-driven IMDbPro for film industry professionals and in 2008 with its acquisition of Withoutabox, a web-based service that enables filmmakers to submit their work to over three thousand film festivals around the world. Also in 2008, IMDb created a German-language version of its database, and versions in other languages will probably arise in the near future.

Unlike Wikipedia, where information immediately goes online and is then judged for accuracy, people presenting new information or correcting existing data need to have their submissions vetted before anything is published online. There is, however, something of a problem here: the submission process is often erratic and inconsistent. Films that are in the preproduction or even the development stage have been able to get listed in the IMDb while completed films that are in release are excluded from coverage.

For Eric B. Hughes, the troubles he encountered in navigating the Wikipedia environment were the equivalent of a week at the seashore in comparison to his efforts in getting the IMDb to acknowledge his 2010 feature *Pacing the Cage*.

"Being an independent filmmaking has its advantages and its disadvantages," he says, ruefully. "The one major disadvantage is that I'm not shooting the next film for Universal Pictures — so with anything I do, I need to spread the word on my own. In writing, producing and directing *Pacing the Cage*, trying to get it listed on IMDb didn't come easy. Somewhere along the way, IMDb stopped taking title submissions from just anybody, and it has become more and more difficult for the indie filmmaker to get their title listed, because IMDb editors have to verify the accuracy of the title/submission. I even know established filmmakers who have had to fax letters-of-intent from actors who are starring in their film, just to get it listed on IMDb. This was never the case several years ago."

Still, Hughes isn't entirely unsympathetic to the IMDb's operation. "In a way, it's a good thing, because more and more people were padding their filmography with titles that didn't exist — vanity projects," he continues. "So, that part is good — it is ridding the site of that element. However, it's harder for an indie filmmaker to get his or her title listed because the verification procedure is harder now. At the end of the day, I had another project in the works, and someone who is involved with that was able to get *Pacing the Cage* listed. And because of that, I am able to now go on there and edit my current and future projects."

Jonathan Grant also has his IMDb-related war stories when *No Burgers for Bigfoot* was being exhibited.

"It was not easy at first," he recalls. "I'm not sure what the problem was, since we had won festivals and had filled out all the questions. But it had been almost a year and we still weren't up while others we knew who haven't even finished filming were up. I ended up submitting about three times. Soon after the third time, we were up."

While getting on the IMDb was a struggle for Grant, using the site to promote the film was another challenge. "The biggest problem with IMDb is the rating system," he continues, referring the manner in which IMDb readers can offer their own opinion on the listed films by voting on a star scale that stretches from one to ten. "Few people ever rate a film, but we've gotten several ratings all of which were either nine stars or ten. Only one rating was lower, as someone gave it a four. Somehow, IMDb decided that the average star rating for our movie was four! That makes our movie look terrible, when that isn't the case at all."

Nonetheless, Grant recognizes that the IMDb provides filmmakers with a free promotional platform to sell all of the aspects of a production — including links to external reviews, video clips and official websites, plus unique information on the creation of the film.

"I took advantage of the quotes and trivia aspects of the IMDb site," he says. "Our movie, *No Burgers for Bigfoot*, has been very quotable, according to the audiences we've had. We kept hearing from people how often they'd quote it. So, we put a few quotes up there that we thought would raise interest in those who read them. And we had some pretty interesting trivia about the movie, the cast, and how it was filmed, so we put some of that up as well. We just tried to make every aspect of everything about the movie we did as funny and entertaining as the movie itself. The people who have seen it want to experience more, so we try to give it to them."

Sharing the pain is Mark L. Feinsod, who found his IMDb submission efforts to be "excruciating," particularly when an entry for a feature film called *The Deafening Silence of a Very Bright Light* was listed for some time before being removed without notice or explanation.

"Why this is the industry standard is beyond me," he complains. "Why their submission process is so ancient makes no sense whatsoever. I don't think they've updated it in any fashion since I first started to make movies in 1999. It's nonsensical."

However, Feinsod eventually experienced a happy ending. "If you submit a film to the festivals through Withoutabox, you automatically get an IMDb page," he says. "I've submitted to one festival, so we got our page back."

ONLINE VIDEO SITES

During the 1990s, the slower speeds of Internet transmission made the presentation of online video difficult — pixilated imagery, muffled sound, and frequent screen freezing were par for the course. But the breakthroughs in broadband transmission helped make the online video experience easier on the eyes and ears. And the traditional computer monitor is no longer the only online video venue. Handheld devices, including cell phones, can double both as a mini-screen for watching videos and a camera for capturing live footage — one of the most famous examples of a cell phone video that gained international recognition was the so-called *Bus Uncle* incident involving footage of a real-life altercation between a young man and a somewhat stressed-out older man on a Hong Kong bus in 2006. The six-minute video was uploaded to a number of video sites around the world, and helpful Net surfers provided subtitles to help non-Chinese viewers decipher what was being said (or, in this case, yelled).

Most people came to see *Bus Uncle* on YouTube — the video racked up 1.7 million hits within three weeks of being posted to that website; this was almost entirely from word of mouth, since the video was an amateur effort with no marketing behind it whatsoever. The YouTube-based popularity of *Bus Uncle* helped to confirm YouTube's rapid dominance of the online video sector.

YouTube was created in February 2005 by a trio of employees who previously worked at PayPal, an online financial transaction enabling service. Within a very short time, YouTube became the go-to site for offbeat viral videos such as *Bus Uncle* and for video clips ranging from amateur home video to scenes taken out of classic film and TV productions (often without clearing the copyrights from the companies that maintained the rights to these works). By November 2006, YouTube was such a hot property that the search engine giant Google Inc. successfully negotiated its acquisition for $1.65 billion.

YouTube has become a significant source for filmmakers eager to spread the word about their films, and the site has been blanketed with trailers for independently produced feature films. Yet the site has received some criticism for both its quantity and quality of videos.

"YouTube is good for college humor — shtick and gimmicky stuff like a two-minute clip of a college student eating dog food from a bowl, compared to someone who is trying to get their filmmaking out to the masses," says Eric B. Hughes. "You have to use this medium wisely, especially if you want to be taken seriously."

The proliferation of videos on YouTube can also result in not easily standing out from the crowd. Independent director/producer Haim Silberstein learned this when he posted a couple of videos on YouTube to build interest in *Vice 101*, a Net-exclusive series that he co-created.

"For us it was to try and get out there," he says. "We had our own dedicated site for the show, *Vice 101.com*, and wanted to generate some kind of buzz and navigate traffic our way and get noticed. We tagged the clip with lots of keywords that are from the clip topic and rank high with online searches. We also wanted the clips to be short, so not to bore the viewer."

And what kind of feedback did Silberstein get after posting the videos in January 2010? "Very little," he says. "Really!"

Other video sites have come forward to challenge YouTube's dominance in this area. The most notable might be Vimeo, which actually predated YouTube by a year. Unlike YouTube's enabling of anyone to post videos (including copyright protected material that is being presented without proper authorization),

Vimeo requires posted material to be created by the individual that is putting it online.

Furthermore, video hosting capabilities can be found at a number of portals, Internet service providers and social networking sites including Google, Yahoo!, America Online, MySpace, and Facebook.

"I think that on the surface, these sites seem like a good tool for an indie filmmaker," states Eric B. Hughes. "However, these sites are inundated with content, so your work almost gets lost sometimes. That's why I find it better to target specific people on Facebook than a mass of people on YouTube."

Still, there is the trial-by-error element that requires filmmakers to discover what works and what doesn't. Joel Vetsch eventually found his groove after experimenting with a large number of online video sites.

"In the beginning, when I started uploading films online, I went wild and put them on many sites — up to 18 blog sites, viral sites, and embeddable sites," he recalls. "Recently I have learned where the audience is, and I now focus my efforts on a few sites, primarily Vimeo, YouTube, and Facebook."

Vetsch adds that his efforts have paid off. "To date, my films have been seen almost a million times online and have been featured on certain sites like MySpace, Yahoo! Video and CNN, getting tens of thousands of views per day!" he says. "I have had very interesting experiences with my films online. The BBC showed one of my short films in one of their shows last year, and a TV channel in Germany broadcast the same short on a TV show this year. They discovered that short film, entitled *Do-It-Yourself Hovercraft*, online. The Guardian newspaper in the UK chose one of my films as among its five top online videos to see in June of 2007, alongside a Will Ferrell viral video, and a London radio station used the audio of my film *Skiing in Iran* on one of their podcasts! It has really been an effective way to get my films out there for people to watch, give me feedback, and also purchase the rights for broadcast!"

However, the online video sites often come with problems. Chicago-based filmmaker Leszek Drozd notes that some sites place specific digital limits on what a person can post.

"Since most of the sites with free uploads are limited in video size up to 100 MB, you may want to consider the option of preparing a five-minute-long clip that links directly to your website," he says. "With this approach, as the website owner, you can provide more information there about your film, your company and your projects."

But for anyone who is new to online video, Drozd warns that digital pirates are sailing the online waves. "The Internet is an anonymous public place, and viewer will embed your video and use material from it any way that they please," he continues. "And sites with uploaded videos can also be sold to a third party. So, please, secure your copyright and feel free to use all the tools and options available to prevent the copying of your video to sites that you do not wish to be featured on."

Also, having an online video is no guarantee that people will be watching it. Joel S. Bachar, president of the San Francisco-based Microcinema International, experienced that problem when his company arranged for an online screening in 2008 of the indie film *Encyclopedia Asthmatica* via the Imeem social network service.

"To be honest, I don't recall the web traffic, but it was poor," he says. "This could have been a problem of PR — not something we did wrong, but our partner did." (Founded in 2003, Imeem ran into financial troubles by 2008 and was acquired by MySpace in 2009, which shut down the service and redirected its users to MySpace Music.)

Still, Bachar believes that online video has potential that is still not being tapped. "We very much want to do online screenings, but I think they sort of need to be a 'value add' to what we are doing with our DVDs — sort of like there are extra features on a DVD that one might buy," he adds. "We could think about having Internet-only video clips, outtakes, shorts, behind the scenes footage, interviews, etc, which drives people to the site on a daily basis for a certain number of days leading up to the DVD release."

There is also the question of charging people to watch films online. A number of sites including YouTube, Hulu, Cinema Now, EZTakes, and iReel require people to pay to watch special video content. The 2010 Tribeca Film Festival inaugurated an online program that made eight feature films available for online screening within the continental United States during the festival's run; the festival charged $45 for subscribers.

Haim Silberstein believes that more innovations will be forthcoming in the very near future. "Online video is a work in progress and no one knows what makes a clip more popular than others," he says. "I think you can't go wrong here unless you're naked in the clip and later in life you want to run for public office — but even that might be a positive these days!"

INTERVIEW
JAMES L. HENNESSY JR.,
PUBLIC RELATIONS/MARKETING EXPERT

When it comes to the various aspects of the promotional sphere, James L. Hennessy Jr. has been there and done that — and got plenty of T-shirts, too! The San Diego–based managing director of Strategic Vantage, a boutique marketing and public relations agency, is also a veteran journalist, novelist, and screenplay writer. There isn't much that he hasn't seen within the realm of publicity and marketing.

For Hennessy, the recent emergence of social networking media offers more than a little déjà vu. Yes, the tools are different and their reach is far wider than earlier promotional vehicles. However, he points out that the basic do's and don'ts of your father's promotional push apply with equal vigor to today's environment.

Q: *What is your take on social networking media, as it applies to the motion picture industry?*

JAMES L. HENNESSY JR.: If ever there was a perfect application for electronic social media, it is independent cinema. Truly, this innovation, this Web 2.0, is a match made in heaven for the indie filmmaker. They go together like pie and coffee, politics and pork, Gable and Lombard. Social media, and only social media, has the ability to put the indie filmmaker in the same league as the Gucci-shod studio distribution guy by reaching an amazing number of people and creating more buzz than a flotilla of wood chippers. The difference, of course, is that social media makes it all cheap. Indie filmmakers understand cheap.

Q: You sold me! But, seriously, how does a newbie indie filmmaker get started… or, to be more specific, get started correctly?

JAMES L. HENNESSY JR.: You want to do it right. The good news is that even if you do it wrong, you still get a benefit. But it's better to do it right and it's not that hard.

Electronic social media is all those websites you've heard about, like Facebook, MySpace, LinkedIn, as well as Twitter and by some definitions, e-mail. It is also YouTube, especially if you create that lightning-in-a-bottle "viral" video, the YouTube item that everyone just has to see. By combining the various components like the elements of an effective scene, you can accomplish some amazing results with virtually no upfront costs. I'm not saying it is easy, but you already accomplished something far more difficult when you wrapped that independent film.

Q: Okay, let's accentuate the positive before we eliminate the negative. What are the some considerations that you need to focus on?

JAMES L. HENNESSY JR.: First, do your homework. Start by getting your company and/or your film established on Facebook, Twitter, and LinkedIn, for starters. This will mean investing a day or so, but you might well speed up the process by asking someone among your cast or crew if they have done this before. It's a lock that someone has. MySpace was an early big player in this arena, but its fortunes fell roundly to Facebook a few years ago. MySpace seems to be gearing up again, so it may soon be worthwhile for your purposes once more. YouTube is the perfect place for clips, trailers, interviews and anything else visual.

Then, use your imagination. You're all about making statements — otherwise you'd be an accountant, not a filmmaker. Don't let your creative juices go to waste, especially when they can become an inundation, a veritable tsunami of metaphor and hyperbole to describe what is amazing about your film project. People respond to social media much the way they do to movie trailers, and when it comes to indie films, they are trained to expect things to be over the top. So your project is not just a superb character study, it is something far, far more. Your horror film isn't merely scary, it is a new standard in cinematic blood-curdling-ness that will haunt viewers and plague their sleep into generations yet unborn. Be bold, colorful and perhaps a bit outrageous.

Next, use your address book. It's okay — you're not pushing life insurance. Unless, of course, that's your day job when you're not hunting up film stock or bartering whole life policies for a better digital video camera. But assuming it's not, don't be afraid of using your address book. These sites often want to send notifications to everyone in your existing address book on your computer, and sometimes that's not a good thing.

For announcements about your film, however, it probably is. You see, the whole thing about social media is that it is exponential in its reach. You reach out to Aunt Gladys and she has the capability of turning on everyone in her address book to your message with a couple of clicks of the mouse. With a word from her, all those who receive her message can do the same thing, and so forth, and so on.

So your message saying, "I've finished a film! Check it out at 'TheMonsterFromTheMauveLagoon.com!'" can go from your address list of a hundred recipients and within days be seen by 10,000 people who might be interested in a fun film website. Of course, you don't want to do that if you don't have a website to send them to. But you get the idea.

Next, be innovative and clever. Your message should be crisp, like your film. Cute may not work as well with a social media message as with, say, a trailer or a poster. There's heavy competition for attention in social media, so clever and innovative goes further than shocking and squishy. For example, you'll have a tougher time getting audiences to become interested in a film that's dark and serious with a message that says, "Hey, we're dark and serious," than one that says, "What does a person do when faced with a choice between unending solitude and lifelong despair? What would you do?" Pose a "What if?" and intrigue your potential audience. Perhaps this is a bad example, but it's the thought that counts.

Finally, respect the medium. You may not have grown up in a digital society, but you're living in one now. Youth, particularly, is able to switch back and forth between real life and digital life effortlessly, and does not consider social media a toy. It is every bit as much a tool for life's functions as an automobile, a coffee maker — or a film. The incredible power to send a message via social media is unlike anything seen before on earth, and deserves to be respected with proper use, etiquette and technique.

Q: All of that sounds good. Now, what are the mistakes to avoid?

JAMES L. HENNESSY JR.: For starters, don't spam! Spam is something like pornography — it's not the same for everyone, but everyone knows it when they see it. For others it takes repeated viewings just to be sure, but eventually it becomes clear what is worthwhile and what is not. The best way to lose the attention of the people you're trying to interest is to send out too many messages with too little content. I get at least a dozen different foreigners trying to sell me generic E.D. medicines each day. I just turn them off after a while, and it doesn't matter that they might be offering something meaningful because they've lost me. The same can happen from any source. So even if you've got something of great interest to disseminate, consider that one message might be better than sending 20 in a single day.

Next, don't be overly wordy. Keep your messages short and sweet. Many people see social media on little tiny screens and in situations where they don't want to do a lot of reading. Twitter limits you anyway to 140 characters. Use no more than a few sentences on alerts and general messaging. Like dialogue on film — most of the time, anyway — less is more.

Then, don't be a crashing bore. It's the same thing when you're making your film — the worst thing you can do is bore your audience. Try to use action verbs and high-energy thoughts in your messaging, including the "what ifs" mentioned earlier. "A uniquely stimulating cinematic experience awaits the discriminating viewer, blah, blah, blah" will be less effective than something like, "You've seen *Avatar*, you've seen *The Hurt Locker*. Our picture is nothing like them, but it's a great time!" I know it seems obvious, but it's never a good thing to overlook the obvious when you can put it to good use for yourself and your film.

Also, don't forget attitude. Gen Xers like attitude and don't mind confrontation as much as others, so it's okay to have a bit of an edge on the message. Where would *The Onion* be if it weren't for attitude? That doesn't mean you should use offensive language or images, of course, but it is definitely okay to be edgy. Sure, "edgy" is an imprecise word, but seeing as how it is usually applied to the independent film world as a hallmark, you probably know what it means better than just about anyone else. When defending a message from just about any criticism, just say you were going for "edgy," and all is usually forgiven.

Finally, don't be afraid of criticism. On Facebook and elsewhere, the purpose is not only to inform of an upcoming showing or release, it's to engage. This means encouraging discussion, and if your project is like any other film that's ever been made, there will be those who won't like it. They will also comment, given the opportunity, and it won't be like a one-time appearance in a newspaper, but on a virtual wall for all visitors to see. Others will defend against the criticism, so don't be afraid of the discussion. You put the film out there, and the chances are good that it will have fans that will spread the word, just as it will have critics eager to express themselves. In general, any discussion about your film or your company brand will end up benefiting you. Unless, of course, you are making and distributing really, *really* bad films, in which case I wish you'd pass my phone number along to your investors.

Q: Ultimately, can all of this work to promote an indie film to the proverbial bigger and better?

JAMES L. HENNESSY JR.: Social networking media is changing just about all the paradigms about advertising and marketing, which is another way of saying we don't really know where its outer limits lie. Some people believe it will ultimately replace television, newspapers, books, and movie theaters, and they may be right. But I just don't see that happening anytime soon. I think we are going through the "Gee whiz!" phase at the moment, much the way we did ten or twelve years ago with the Internet. The dot-com boom and subsequent bust occurred because people got all hot and bothered over the prospect of the new emerging medium's taking over life as we knew it. That has happened, of course, but to a far lesser extent than the hype predicted back in the late 1990s. We still have retail stores, we still have supermarkets, and we still go to movie theaters.

The brilliance of social media for me is threefold. Its immediacy is amazing, with messages reaching recipients very swiftly and having attention paid them. Unlike the incessant Viagra ads and email from those pesky people from Nigeria wanting me to help them cash huge checks for a piece of the action, social media messages are typically read instead of being instantly deleted.

Secondly, social media has the potential to be truly viral, and not in the sense of making people sick. So many people can end up seeing a message that directs them to an interesting You-Tube link — and they can pass it on to dozens or hundreds of others in a trice — that the numbers can be staggering. It made a career for Susan Boyle, so think what it could do for you!

Lastly, it is free. I know I don't have to add anything to the wonderment of something's being free, especially for indie film people. It is really incredible when you think about it — and well worth a short time investment to put it to work for yourself and your project.

❧

LISTEN TO WHAT THE MAN SAYS

So, you think that you know everything that there is to know about social networking media, Wikis, Tweets and other on-line communications strategies and services? Well, here are a few more things to mull over.

1. Don't forget the real world. It is too easy to become addicted to Twitter, Facebook, Wikipedia, or the next too-popular website. Social networking media is an aspect of the sales and marketing effort, but it should never be seen as a replacement for the old-fashioned concept of person-to-person networking.

2. Recognize the problems in online communications. Everyone who has ever communicated by e-mail, in-stant messaging, and online forums knows that it is too easy for words to be taken out of context. The absence of sound dilutes whatever humor or irony you are trying to get across — and an innocuous comment can easily be mistaken for a slur if the reader is in the wrong frame of mind.

3. Don't create a free forum to unpleasant people. While some people accidentally create ill will, others do it on purpose. Don't be surprised if you become the target of such sour people. When posting videos online, always disable the commentary function that would allow people to leave messages with your videos. More often than not, some less-than-funny character will show up with rude and revolting thoughts. Likewise, make sure that any unsavory comments left on your social networking pages are deleted — the "delete" function is there for a reason, so don't be shy about using it when you feel that you are under attack.

4. Think twice about leaving intentionally negative mes-saging. Words that are left online don't disappear in to the digital ether — they often have a way of being reprinted

elsewhere. Thus, any harsh or abrasive commentary and complaints may come back to haunt you on other websites. If you are sending Tweets, leaving Facebook and MySpace messages or trying to communicate with the powers that be at the IMDb or Wikipedia, accentuate the positive. Calling people names or making unkind remarks will not reflect well on you, and the residue from these poorly chosen words will be very difficult to wash away.

5. Stay tuned for further details. Yes, this is all an evolving process, so don't be premature in claiming any degree of expertise in regard to online promotion. For all we know, the IMDb or Facebook of the next decade is currently being created in some unlikely corner of cyberspace. Thus, it is crucial to keep abreast of what is happening in the online world — you honestly never know what the next big thing is going to be on the Internet!

WHO'S WHO, WHERE THEY ARE, AND WHAT THEY ARE LOOKING FOR

Victory belongs to the most persevering
— Napoleon Bonaparte

8

INTERVIEW
MARK CUBAN, PRODUCER/DISTRIBUTOR

The film business has never been lacking in larger-than-life visionaries, but even by the industry's standards there are few people with the imagination, vision, and spirit of Mark Cuban. Having conquered the worlds of high tech (via *Broadcast.com*, which he and Todd Wagner sold to Yahoo! in 1999 for $5.7 billion) and sports (as the owner of the Dallas Mavericks basketball team), Cuban has set his sights on the world of motion pictures.

Cuban's business savvy, when it comes to films, is peerless: He is involving himself on every possible level. Through his 2929 Entertainment (created with Todd Wagner), Cuban has built a sophisticated operation involved in the funding and production of films (via HDNet Films), distribution (via Magnolia Pictures), exhibition (via the Landmark Theaters chain), and even cable television (via the HDNet channel).

Cuban is also doing something that many people have talked about but few people have accomplished: pushing motion pictures beyond the 35mm film format into HD production. He is also reconfiguring distribution patterns to accomplish the simultaneous offerings of theatrical, DVD, and cable broadcast presentations (this was successfully achieved earlier this year with the acclaimed documentary *Enron: The Smartest Guys in the Room*).

Q: What is your opinion of the current state of independent film production? Specifically, how do you feel about the quality of the indie films being made today?

MARK CUBAN: The quality of films is always subjective. It's like music. Everyone thinks what they are doing is phenomenal and everyone else sucks. Personally, I think the important item is that the cost of production tools continues to come down.

Q: What is your opinion of the current state of independent film distribution? Do you feel that the distributors — both the "classics" divisions of the studios and the boutique distributors — are doing an adequate job of bringing independent films to audiences?

MARK CUBAN: It kind of depends on where you are in the food chain. If you are producing movies in the $5 million to $10 million range, as an indie you have a shot to get distributed. You can make less expensive films and get them released theatrically if you have connections and attach a star to them. If you scrounge up the credit you and your friends have available on your credit cards and make a movie with local talent, unless you have a movie that is incredible to everyone who watches it, you are going to have a hard time getting released theatrically.

I know with Magnolia Pictures, our distribution arm, we watch everything that comes our way. We don't discriminate by budget or format. However, we have to be realistic. There has to be a way for us to sell it to theaters and to the movie-going public. Movies that can't find a distributor have a very difficult time getting seen. There are lots of ways to make movies available, via iFilm, Netflix, and other websites, but driving any revenue becomes very, very difficult.

Q: What advice would you give to filmmakers who want to get funding from HDNet Films? And are you open to unsolicited submissions or would filmmakers need to approach HDNet Films through agents, sales reps, and other third parties?

MARK CUBAN: We are open to reading scripts. My suggestion, however, is for filmmakers to be brutally honest with themselves. Just because you wrote it, or will direct it, doesn't make it good. Find someone who has made movies and have them read it and give you notes. We are also looking for unique projects. There is nothing worse than getting a submission about poker with a pitch saying that "poker is hot." Don't try to present us what you think is hot and currently selling tickets. Give us something that is personal, unique, and different.

photo courtesy Magnolia Pictures

Kenneth Lay smiles in the face of adversity in a scene from Enron: The Smartest Guys in the Room. Says Magnolia president Mark Cuban: "No one ever counts how many times you have failed. You only have to be right once. Do what you love and have fun doing it. If it hits, great. If not, you had a blast along the way."

Q: What type of films are you looking to fund and/or distribute? Are there particular or specific styles, genres, or points of view that will pique your attention immediately? Or are you open to all titles?

MARK CUBAN: We are open to anything and everything. We want unique concepts that we think we can find a market with.

Q: The vast majority of independently produced films never get released. What professional advice — or personal advice, if you wish — can you give to filmmakers who've been rejected by festivals, distributors, and exhibitors?

MARK CUBAN: No one ever counts how many times you have failed. You only have to be right once. Do what you love and have fun doing it. If it hits, great. If not, you had a blast along the way.

Q: Have you had the urge to direct your own movies?

MARK CUBAN: No. I'm a sales and marketing and technology geek. I have a good sense about what kind of small–budget films can be commercially successful — relatively speaking. I will leave directing to those with talent.

THE STATE OF FILM DISTRIBUTION, AS OF TODAY

If you've made it this far into the book, two words need to be stated: "Congratulations!" and "Continue!"

"Congratulations!" are in order since you've shown you are ready, willing, and able to pursue the dream of getting your film released. This is, admittedly, a difficult endeavor and too many people are not up to the challenge.

"Continue!" is the order to move ahead and to seek out the distributors who would be most interested in your work.

Before we dive into the pool of distributors operating in today's independent film world, let's pause to pay tribute to those who are no longer with us. It should be noted that film distribution is not a business that is chiseled in stone. Over the past 30 years, many influential distributors, both large-scale and small-scale, went out of business despite highly regarded releases (including Oscar-winning classics and box office hits). The distributor graveyard includes the likes of the American Film Theatre, American Home Entertainment, Aquarius, Artisan Entertainment, Avenue Pictures, Cannon Films, Cinema V, Cinecom, Cowboy Booking International, CQN Releasing, IDP Distribution, IRS Media, Independent Artists, Island Alive, Jour de Fete, Kit Parker Films, Libra Films, Lot 47 Films, Madstone Films, Meridian Home Video, New World Pictures, October Films, Orion Pictures, Phaedra Cinema, Sceneries Distribution, Shooting Gallery Film Series, Stratosphere Entertainment, United Artists Classics, USA Films, World Artists, and World Northal.

One needs to be aware that it is not uncommon for smaller distributors to abruptly go out of business. Likewise, new distributors have a way of popping up out of the blue. The following list is up-to-date as of May 2010.

ALIVE MIND EDUCATION
http://www.alivemindeducation.com
This non-theatrical distributor offers documentary programming to the educational market.

ALPHA VIDEO
http://www.oldies.com

Although primarily focused on presenting classics and older curios, this DVD distributor has found room for cult-worthy contemporary indie productions including Andrew Repasky McElhinny's *A Chronicle of Corpses* and *Magdelan*, Mark Redfield's *Dr. Jekyll and Mr. Hyde*, Georg Kozulinksi's *Blood of the Beast* and Jacque Boyreau's *Candy von Dewd*.

ALTERNATIVE CINEMA
http://www.alternativecinema.com

This home entertainment distributor aims for the low-budget horror market, and is best known for offering a wide selection of titles starring the alluring B-Movie goddess Misty Mundae.

ANCHOR BAY ENTERTAINMENT
http://www.anchorbayentertainment.com

This company offers a wide mix of titles, ranging from fitness videos to kiddie programming to classics of the horror and sci-fi genres.

APPARITION
http://www.apparition.com

Created in the summer of 2009, this distributor's initial offerings included the U.S. indies *Black Dynamite* and *Boondock Saints II: All Saints Day* plus the Oscar-nominated imports *Bright Star* and *The Young Victoria*.

ARAB FILM DISTRIBUTION
http://www.arabfilm.com

As its name would suggest, this distributor focuses on films relating to the Arab world. American films that focus on Arab history issues have been among the titles presented for theatrical and non-theatrical release.

AREA232A

http://www.area232a.com

Founded in January 2010, this theatrical distributor places a special emphasis on social issue and music performance films.

ARKADIA DVD

http://www.arkadiadvd.com

This division of Arkadia Entertainment has primarily focused on music-themed documentaries.

ARTISTIC LICENSE FILMS

http://www.artlic.com

This company has been responsible for the service deal theatrical release of many notable features and documentaries, including the Academy Award–nominated documentaries *Twist of Faith* and *The Sound and the Fury* and the popular cult title *The American Astronaut*.

ARTMATTAN PRODUCTIONS

http://www.africanfilm.com

This theatrical distributor focuses on global black cinema, with a heavy emphasis on films from Africa and European filmmakers focusing on African themes. American filmmakers have been a part of the company's annual New York African Diaspora Film Festival, which brings the best of the genre to appreciative audiences every November.

ASYLUM

http://www.theasylum.cc

This feature film distribution company covers American and international releases ranging from the artistic to the extreme.

THE AV CAFÉ

http://www.theavcafe.com

The AV Cafe is a non-theatrical distributor aiming at public libraries in the U.S. and Canada.

BALCONY RELEASING

http://www.balconyfilm.com

This distributor focuses on theatrical distribution strategies for independently-produced documentary features. It is best known for the Academy Award–nominated *Daughter from Danang* and for the critically-acclaimed features *The Same River Twice* and *Stolen Childhoods*.

BRAIN DAMAGE FILMS

http://www.braindamagefilms.com

This DVD distributor mixes goth, horror, shockumentaries and blood-tinged "reality" movies into its line-up.

BREAKING GLASS PICTURES

http://www.breakingglasspictures.com

A DVD distributor offering, in its words, "a wide range of provocative and challenging films from all genres." Its specialty label Vicious Circle Films is "dedicated to extreme material."

BRIMSTONE

http://www.lindenmuth.com

Another DVD distributor going for the scare tactics, this company has vampires, werewolves and aliens as its main attractions.

BRINK DVD

http://www.brinkdvd.com

A DVD distributor that aims for fans of off-kilter, cult-worthy titles.

BULLFROG FILMS

http://www.bullfrogfilms.com

This non-theatrical distributor focuses on documentaries relating to the environment and ecological issues, economic development, the rights of indigenous people, cultural diversity, and the celebration of the performing arts (primarily music and dance).

CALIFORNIA NEWSREEL
http://www.newsreel.org
Founded in 1968, this theatrical and non-theatrical distributor is the oldest non-profit film and video production/distribution center in the United States. The company focuses on titles relating to "social change" and its output is primarily in the documentary sector.

CELEBRITY VIDEO DISTRIBUTION
http://www.cvdistributes.com
The company bills itself as a "one-stop" distribution service for independent movie producers and video retail buyers.

CINEMA EPOCH
http://www.cinemaepoch.com
A DVD distributor that specializes in edgier, low-budget independent and international productions.

CINEMA GUILD
http://www.cinemaguild.com
This venerable distributor has primarily focused on American documentaries and features from the global cinema.

CINEMA LIBRE STUDIO
http://www.cinemalibrestudio.com
Billed as "The Haven for Filmmakers with Views," this distributor reaches theatrical, home entertainment and television markets with its edgy mix of features and documentaries.

CULT EPICS
http://www.cultepics.com
This DVD distributor provides an outlet for outré titles (Manson Family Movies is among their most sedate offering!).

DISINFORMATION
http://www.disinfo.com
Launched in 1996, this distributor focuses exclusively on left-of-center documentaries released to the home entertainment market .

DOCURAMA

http://www.docurama.com

This DVD distributor, as its name suggests, focuses exclusively on documentaries (including many films which were not in theatrical release).

ECHO BRIDGE ENTERTAINMENT

http://www.echobridgeentertainment.com

This home entertainment distributor includes independent features as part of its mix of releases.

ECHELON STUDIOS

http://www.echelonstudios.us

A DVD distributor specializing in horror and action/adventure titles.

ECLECTIC DVD

http://www.eclecticdvd.com

With titles ranging from *Dracula's Great Love* to *My Life with Morrissey*, this DVD distributor certainly earned its name!

EMERGING PICTURES

http://www.emergingpictures.com

This distributor has focused on presenting independently-produced features (and some foreign imports) in art house venues.

FACETS VIDEO

http://www.facets.org

The home entertainment distribution subsidiary of Facets Multi-Media, this distributor brings independent features into the home entertainment market.

FANLIGHT PRODUCTIONS

http://www.fanlight.com

Nontheatrical distributor that specializes in documentaries relating to medical, sociological and business ethics-related issues.

THE FILM-MAKERS' COOPERATIVE
http://www.film-makerscoop.com
Billed as "the largest archive and distributor of independent and avant-garde films in the world," this company was created in 1962 as the distribution branch of the New American Cinema Group and currently has more than 5,000 titles in its collection.

FIRST INDEPENDENT PICTURES
http://www.firstindependentpictures.com
This indie distributor focuses on releasing four to six features per year in the theatrical market.

FILM MOVEMENT
http://www.filmmovement.com
Created by Larry Meistrich, the force behind the ambitious but doomed Shooting Gallery Film Series, this distributor initially planned to present independent American features and foreign imports in a simultaneous DVD and (in selected cities) theatrical release. That did not quite work the way the company hoped, so the company successfully reinvented itself as a DVD distributor.

FILMS FOR THE HUMANITIES & SCIENCES
http://www.films.com
This non-theatrical distributor presents documentary titles to colleges and universities.

FIRST LOOK MEDIA
http://www.flp.com
This distributor provides theatrical, home entertainment and international sales for independently produced features.

FIRST RUN FEATURES
http://www.firstrunfeatures.com
Founded in 1979, this theatrical and home entertainment releases (according to its web site) "12 to 15 films a year in theatrically and 40 to 50 videos and DVDs annually," ranging from gay and lesbian titles to documentaries to cult-ready offerings.

FOCUS FEATURES
http://www.focusfeatures.com
The "classics" division of Universal Pictures, this distributor (and occasional producer) released the Oscar-winning films *Lost in Translation*, *The Pianist*, *Brokeback Mountain* and *Milk*.

FOX SEARCHLIGHT PICTURES
http://www.foxsearchlight.com
The "classics" division of 20th Century Fox, this distributor brought the Oscar-winning *Sideways* and the cult favorite *Napoleon Dynamite* into release.

FRAMELINE DISTRIBUTION
http://www.frameline.org
This company is unique since it is the only educational distributor solely dedicated to the release of gay, lesbian, bisexual, and transgender (GLBT) film and video titles in the non-theatrical market. The company is also the presenter of the annual San Francisco GLBT Film Festival.

GKIDS
http://www.gkids.com
This distributor specializes in global cinema, including the Oscar-nominated Irish animated feature *The Secret of Kells*, though it did pick up the U.S. theatrical rights to Nina Paley's 2008 animated feature *Sita Sings the Blues*.

GO-KART FILMS
http://www.gokartfilms.com
This DVD distributor aims for politically motivated documentaries and offbeat cult-ready titles.

HARGROVE ENTERTAINMENT
http://www.hargrovetv.com
This boutique distributor specializes in politically edgy documentaries. Its 2002 release *Yugoslavia: The Avoidable War* made

international headlines when it was cited (albeit out of context) in the war crimes trial of former Yugoslavian leader Slobodan Milosevic.

HALO-8
http://www.halo8.tv
An independent film studio specializing in iconoclastic and music-driven cult movies and their related soundtracks

HBO FILMS
http://www.hbo.com
This division of Home Box Office has placed a few productions into theaters, though most of its efforts have been concentrated on cable television and DVD release.

HOME VISION ENTERTAINMENT
http://www.homevision.com
This DVD distributor tends to aim for international and classic cinema, but also offers contemporary independent features.

ICARUS FILMS
http://www.icarusfilms.com
This distributor's focus comes in providing documentaries to the non-theatrical market, although occasionally it snags theatrical play dates for some of its titles.

IFC FILMS
http://www.ifcfilms.com
The theatrical arm of the Independent Film Channel, this distributor is best known for bringing *My Big Fat Greek Wedding* to a big fat box office bonanza.

IMAGE ENTERTAINMENT
http://www.image-entertainment.com
This DVD distributor offers a range of titles including art house theatrical releases and gritty action/thriller offerings.

INDICAN PICTURES
http://www.indicanpictures.com

This theatrical and DVD distributor provides a playful mix of genres, ranging from the serious art house fare of *Boondock Saints* to the playful tomfoolery of *Bare Naked Survivor.*

INDIE-PICTURES
http://www.indie-pictures.com

This DVD distributor presents a mix of narrative and nonfiction features.

INDIEPIX FILMS
http://www,indiepixfilms.com

Home entertainment distributor specializing in DVD and download presentations.

KINO LORBER
http://www.kino.com

In December 2009, the highly respected art house distributor Kino International was acquired by Hidden Treasures Inc., the holding company of Lorber HT Digital. The new entity combines Kino International Films and Lorber Films, as well as Lorber's Alive Mind documentary subsidiary.

LANDMARK MEDIA
http://www.landmarkmedia.com

A nontheatrical distributor that serves the educational market with subjects ranging from advertising to zoology.

LEO FILM RELEASING
http://www.leofilms.com

This distributor originally focused on art house releases, but lately has placed its chips on horror, exploitation and urban thrillers.

LIBRARY VIDEO NETWORK
http://www.lvn.org

This non-theatrical documentary distributor began as a consortium of Maryland public libraries and is currently under the auspices of the Baltimore County Public Library. As its name suggests, its customer base consists of libraries.

LIONS GATE FILMS
http://www.lgf.com

This company is among the most highly influential independents operating in today's motion picture industry — it picked up Michael Moore's *Fahrenheit 9/11* after Disney forced its Miramax subsidiary to drop the title. The company has a unique gift for picking up low-budget indie titles and pushing them to box office and home entertainment success: *Monster's Ball* (starring Halle Berry in her Oscar-winning role) and the thrillers *Saw* and *Open Water* are among their most notable triumphs.

LONELY SEAL RELEASING
http://www.lonelyseal.com

A division of Westlake Entertainment, this company specializes as a theatrical and non-theatrical distributor.

MAGNOLIA PICTURES
http://www.magpics.com

Magnolia is the distribution arm of the entertainment operation run by Mark Cuban and Todd Wagner, a pair of deep-pocketed extroverts who also run the Landmark Theater Chain and the HDNet Films production company. Magnolia has released the Academy Award–nominated documentary *Capturing the Friedmans* and the surprise commercial hit *Woman Thou Art Loosed* from Bishop T. D. Jakes. Magnet Releasing is the genre division of the company.

MAINLINE RELEASING
http://www.mainlinereleasing.com

This company specializes in DVD titles, mostly of an exploitative and titillating nature.

MATSON FILMS

http://www.matsonfilms.com

This boutique distributor launched its first release in 2005 with the British import *It's All Gone Pete Tong* and followed up with a number of U.S.-based indie productions.

MAVERICK ENTERTAINMENT

http://www.maverickentertainment.cc

This DVD distributor offers a wide mix of genres, ranging from comedy to action to erotic thrillers to gospel music titles.

MEDIA BLASTERS RELEASING

http://www.media-blasters.com

This distributor specializes in Japanese imports (mostly anime and action flicks), but it went stateside in producing and distributing Terry M. West's 2003 *Flesh for the Beast*.

MENEMSHA FILMS

http://www.menemshafilms.com

The small distributor is primarily focused on global cinema imports, although it did present the well-regarded indie documentaries *Shanghai Ghetto* and *The Life and Times of Hank Greenberg*.

MICROCINEMA INTERNATIONAL

http://www.microcinema.com

The pioneer online film distributor presents DVD releases of nonfiction and narrative films.

MILESTONE FILM & VIDEO

http://www.milefilms.com

This boutique theatrical and DVD distributor has been honored by the National Society of Film Critics (twice!) and by the New York Film Critics Circle for its contributions to film preservation and for bringing long-lost classics back to the big screen. The company's contemporary release focus has primarily been within global cinema, though occasional American features have made it into their mix (films by Alan Berliner, Philip Haas, Fred Parnes and Eleanor Antin have been presented under the Milestone banner). In June 2005, Milestone Films announced the formation of Milliarium Zero, a new company specifically created to acquire and distribute films of strong political and social content.

MONTEREY MEDIA
http://www.montereymedia.com
Founded in 1979, this pioneering company continues to supply the home entertainment market with independently produced films ranging from children's productions to "mature" offerings.

MOONSTONE HOME ENTERTAINMENT
http://www.moonstonefilms.com
This distributor offers a mix of global imports and offbeat American indies.

MPI MEDIA GROUP
http://www.mpimediagroup.com
A home entertainment distributor that specializes in both art house and popcorn fare. MPI Home Video and Dark Sky Films are the company's subsidiaries.

MTI HOME VIDEO
http://www.mtivideo.com
This home entertainment distributor actually operates six different genre-specific labels, which mostly cater to action and adventure titles, though an occasional art house title has been known to pop up in its mix.

MUSIC BOX FILMS
http://www.musicboxfilms.com
Founded in 2007, the company offers distribution in all formats, although its emphasis is primarily on international cinema titles.

MUSIC VIDEO DISTRIBUTORS
http://www.musicvideodistributors.com
While the company has primarily focused on concert films and music-related documentaries, it occasionally releases narrative features.

NATIONAL FILM NETWORK
http://www.nationalfilmnetwork.com
This non-theatrical distributor focuses exclusively on presenting documentaries.

NATIONAL VIDEO RESOURCES
http://www.nvr.org/content.php?pro=about
This not-for-profit organization, established in 1990 by the Rockefeller Foundation, brings independently produced film and video (documentaries, features and even experimental films) to non-theatrical channels.

NEOFLIX
http://www.neoflix.com
A DVD distributor offering "an integrated solution for e-commerce, order fulfillment, and customer service created for filmmakers and film distributors with multi-channel sales strategies."

NEW DAY FILMS
http://www.newday.com
This filmmakers' cooperative (currently representing 50 artists) presents documentaries to the nontheatrical market.

NEW VIDEO
http://www.newvideo.com
A distributor specializing in cutting-edge documentaries, independent films, collectible television series, sports and classic kids programming available digitally and on DVD.

NEW YORKER FILMS
http://www.newyorkerfilms.com
This distribution company was founded in 1965 by Daniel Talbot as an outgrowth of his celebrated (but, sadly, long-gone) cinema, the New Yorker Theater. The company, which was acquired by Aladdin Distribution in February 2010, has one of the widest and most-respected theatrical, nontheatrical, and home entertainment libraries.

NORTHERN ARTS ENTERTAINMENT
http://www.northernartsentertainment.com
This theatrical distributor specializes in global cinema, although on occasion an American independent release gets on its slate (most notably Joan Micklin Silver's *A Fish in the Bathtub* starring Ben Stiller and Jerry Stiller).

OSCILLOSCOPE LABORATORIES
http://www.oscilloscope.net
An independent theatrical and DVD distributor founded by Adam Yauch of the Beastie Boys.

OVERTURE FILMS
http://www.overturefilms.net
Created in November 2006 as a subsidiary of Liberty Media, the company is a theatrical distributor that also produces its own titles.

PALADIN
http://paladinfilms.com
Film distribution veteran Mark Urman launched this theatrical distribution company in the summer of 2009.

PALM PICTURES
http://www.palmpictures.com
Priding itself in offering "true independents," Palm Pictures offers a range of narrative and nonfiction titles for theatrical and DVD release.

PANORAMA ENTERTAINMENT

http://www.panoramaentertainment.com

This boutique theatrical distributor specializes in off-beat independent features, most notably including Joe Mantegna's film adaptation of David Mamet's *Lakeboat*.

PASSION RIVER

http://www.passionriver.com

Provides theatrical and DVD release of independent features and documentaries.

PATHFINDER PICTURES

http://www.pathfinderpictures.com

This theatrical and DVD distributor has primarily focused on Asian imports, but it has presented several American independent features.

PHASE 4 FILMS

http://www.phase4films.com

A theatrical and DVD distributor specializing in art house, action and children's titles.

PLEXIFILM

http://www.plexifilm.com

This DVD distributor defines its mission as expanding "the variety of films available on DVD and to champion lesser-known-yet-amazing indie directors." The company has a particular interest in music-related documentaries, most notably the documentary on They Might Be Giants entitled *Gigantic (A Tale of Two Johns)*.

R-SQUARED FILMS

http://www.rsquaredfilms.com

This independent distributor brings a mix of horror, action and comedy titles to DVD, download and pay-per-view channels.

RED FLAG RELEASING

http://www.redflagreleasing.com

Created (according to its founders) "out of a desire to create new paths and opportunities for independent filmmakers in this age of ubiquitous technological change," this distributor was created in early 2010 with the documentary *8: The Mormon Proposition* as its first release.

REGENT ENTERTAINMENT

http://www.regententertainment.com

This theatrical distributor offers an eclectic mix of titles, ranging from comedy concert films to gay-oriented features.

ROADSIDE ATTRACTIONS LLC

http://www.roadsideattractions.com

This theatrical and DVD distributor seeks out off-beat and provocative films, most notably the and the Oscar-winning documentary *The Cove*.

RUMUR RELEASING

http://www.rumur.com

A multimedia company that distributes feature films, webisodes, music videos, mini-series, industrial commercials, and web applications.

SCREEN MEDIA FILMS

http://www.screenmediafilms.net

Screen Media Films acquires rights to high-quality, independent feature films, for all of the US and Canada, with distribution in theaters, on home video; and to all television outlets.

SEVENTH ART RELEASING

http://www.7thart.com

This distributor is concentrated on presenting documentaries in first-run theatrical release, including the Oscar-nominated *Balseros*.

SHADOW DISTRIBUTION

http://www.shadowdistribution.com

This company announces that it is interested in "unusual, specialized films," with a particular focus on documentaries such as the Oscar-nominated *The Weather Underground*. The company also runs the Railroad Square Cinema in Waterville, Maine.

SRS CINEMA LLC

http://www.b-movie.com

This distributor, originally known as Salt City Home Video and then Sub Rosa Studios, is primarily focused on DVD releases relating to horror and sci-fi, although on occasion it has put forth art house titles including John Farrell's adaptation of Shakespeare's *Richard the Second*. The company also produces the annual B-Movie Film Festival in Syracuse, New York.

STRAND RELEASING

http://www.strandreleasing.com

This theatrical and home entertainment distributor was initially concentrated on gay and lesbian titles, although in recent years it has branched out into other genres within the independent film world.

SUMMIT ENTERTAINMENT

http://www.summit-ent.com

This production/distribution company is best known for offering moviegoers the *Twilight* franchise and the Academy Award–winning Best Picture of 2009, *The Hurt Locker*.

SUNDANCE CHANNEL HOME ENTERTAINMENT

http://www.sundancechannel.com

As its name suggests, this is the DVD branch of the cable television network specializing in contemporary indie movies. If you've seen a flick exclusively on this network, there's a good chance you may see it in DVD retail outlets from this label.

TARTAN USA
www.tartanfilmsusa.com
The American branch of the British entertainment giant consists of the theatrical distributor Tartan Films and the home entertainment provider Tartan Video (whose titles are actually distributed in stores via TLA Releasing).

TEMPE
http://www.tempevideo.com
This DVD distributor keeps its concentration on offbeat and outrageous horror and sci-fi titles.

THINKFILM
http://www.thinkfilmcompany.com
This theatrical and home entertainment distributor takes aim at both narrative and nonfiction titles.

TLA RELEASING
http://www.tlavideo.com
Founded in 1981 in as a repertory cinema, this Philadelphia-based group branched out into video retailing in 1985 and later moved into theatrical and home entertainment distribution and even festival operations (it runs the Philadelphia Film Festival). Much of its focus is on gay and lesbian titles, and it also conducts the annual Philadelphia International Gay and Lesbian Film Festival.

TRIBECA FILM
http://www.tribecafilm.com
Robert De Niro and Jane Rosenthal announced the launch of this new distribution company in March 2010 as a spin-off from their success in running the annual Tribeca Film Festival in New York.

TROMA ENTERTAINMENT
http://www.troma.com
Best known for its outrageous horror-comedy titles, this fabled

distributor has focused its energies in the DVD market, although an occasional theatrical release rises up.

UNEARTHED FILMS
http://www.unearthedfilms.com
This DVD distributor describes itself as supporting "rare underground horror films, lost animated gems and psychotic action films."

VANGUARD CINEMA
http://www.vanguardcinema.com
This DVD distributor initially focused on films with a Latino theme, but it later expanded to a wider spectrum of indie features and global imports.

VCI ENTERTAINMENT
http://www.vcientertainment.com
This Oklahoma-based DVD distributor is primarily focused on classics and older curios, though on occasion it will allow contemporary titles to slip into its mix.

VIDEO DATA BANK
http://www.vdb.org
This niche distributor focuses on features by and about contemporary artists.

WATER BEARER FILMS
http://www.waterbearerfilms.com
This home entertainment distributor specializes in gay and lesbian titles.

WEINSTEIN COMPANY
http://www.weinsteincompany.com
Miramax founders Bob and Harvey Weinstein left the Disney fold in 2005 to pursue theatrical and DVD production and distribution in this corporate setting.

WELL GO USA INC.
http://www.wellgousa.com
A DVD distributor offering children's educational, fitness, special interest/instructional, documentaries, animations, music performance, Broadway shows and feature films.

WILD EYE RELEASING
http://www.wildeyereleasing.com
A DVD distributor with a taste for extreme horror and science-fiction.

WOLFE VIDEO
http://www.wolfevideo.com
This home entertainment distributor focuses primarily on gay and lesbian titles.

WOMEN MAKE MOVIES
http://www.wmm.com
This non-theatrical distributor, founded in 1972, describes itself as "a multicultural, multiracial, non-profit media arts organization that facilitates the production, promotion, distribution and exhibition of independent films and videotapes by and about women."

YORK ENTERTAINMENT
http://www.yorkentertainment.com
This DVD distributor spreads out films with a horror and sci-fi content, with an occasional joker in the pack (including *The Milton Berle Workout*).

ZEITGEIST FILMS
http://www.zeitgeistfilms.com
This theatrical and home entertainment distributor is primarily focused on global cinema; its American releases tend to be documentaries.

INTERVIEW
ANDREW GERNHARD, PRODUCER/DISTRIBUTOR

Andrew Gernhard is not shy when it comes to the aesthetic qualities of the films created by his company, Synthetic Cinema International, based in Rocky Hill, Connecticut. With titles like *Predator Island* (2005), *Werewolf: The Devil's Hound* (2007), *Blood Descendants* (2007), *Banshee!!!* (2008), *Assault of the Sasquatch* (2009) and *Opponent* (2010), the company is clearly not going to be mistaken for an art house outfit.

But what Synthetic Cinema International's canon lacks in art, it more than compensates in commerce: the company's films have played in theaters and television networks around the world and been available in all home entertainment distribution channels from a number of major distributors. The company is now seeking to expand into distribution on its own.

For Gernhard, success came about by understanding his potential audience and recognizing how to reach them.

Q: Can a no-budget indie film actually find a successful distribution today?

ANDREW GERNHARD: There was a time when no-budget films could make it. Now, distributors want high production values. We're trying to put higher production values into our movies, such as improved lighting and shot design, and we are adding some stars to the films.

When I go to Cannes, the first thing they ask is: "Who's in it? What is it shot on? And what genre is it?" What I found at Cannes is that there are a lot of great films, but they don't have stars. And there are also a lot of stars, but not in the right genre. We moved from horror to more sci-fi and action — action seems to sell like crazy, and we have a lot of Asian and German sales from that.

Q: When you begin a professional relationship with distributors, what are your first steps?

ANDREW GERNHARD: Whenever I sign with distributors, I say, "Feel free to edit it or change the name," because distributors know what will sell. Unfortunately, now, times are changing and they don't always know what will sell.

Q: What do you mean by that?

ANDREW GERNHARD: Distributors are hurting right now, from the biggest guys to the smallest guys. I've noticed some small guys have started their own labels. We're starting our own label. We've released stuff through Lionsgate, Universal, Maverick Home Entertainment, but the first film on our own label is *Banshee!!!* which debuted on the Syfy Channel and then went to video-on-demand and pay-per-view before going to DVD in March 2010. That film was made in 2007. Our next film is *Sasquatch Assault*, which was changed to *Assault of the Sasquatch* for marketing release purposes.

Q: Why did you change the name?

ANDREW GERNHARD: The new genre is video-on-demand. There is hardly any expense to the filmmaker or the distributor. The problem is that you want to make people want to see your film. We did *Sasquatch Assault*, but we changed it to *Assault of the Sasquatch* because our distributor said "A" is the first letter and when you go to video-on-demand, "A" is the first thing that pops up, so people are more inclined to rent it. We switched the title because we want people to see it.

Q: How do you determine what audiences want to see?

ANDREW GERNHARD: Go to Blockbuster Video and walk around. You have the major movies, you have the films that won a ton of awards, but there are no shot-on-video dramas, romances, comedies — basically any genre. The only thing that really sells are monsters and horror, but that market is shrinking up.

When video first came out on VHS, you could make a movie on anything, sell it, and become a millionaire. One of the reasons why is that if you wanted to get a movie on VHS, your choices were limited — if you went to the store, they would have six videos and you would pick one of them. As time passed, there were more movies and you started to become more selective.

We are now at a point that instead of going to a store and browsing to pick what is available, you find what you want either through video-on-demand or the Internet. We are moving to the point where you do not necessarily need to have the best content, but you need to have the content that people want to look at. Nowadays, we are dealing with studios making films versus indie filmmakers, which is shrinking down the market. And studios are making franchises now, even if it is only for direct-to-video channels.

Q: So how can an indie producer or distributor stand out?

ANDREW GERNHARD: We moved into more TV and video-on-demand stuff. We made the curve on DVD in 2005 to 2007, so now we are trying to make the curve on video-on-demand. The future is going to be online. *Banshee!!!* first came out on video-on-demand, then it went to download/DVD, then we paired *Banshee!!!* and *Sasquatch* on one Blu-Ray disc. We are trying to create a value: they are $14.99 on DVD, and Amazon always offers them as a discount. We want to make sure that everyone can get them and we try to put them on as many places as possible. We're on Netflix, Blockbuster, Overstock.com, eBay.

Werewolf: The Devil's Hound was released by Lionsgate in 2007 and became available on iTunes.

Q: But is this a better set-up for you?

ANDREW GERNHARD: We make money at point-of-purchase — we have a film on the shelf, people see it and buy it. Who is going to look up *Predator Island* on the Internet, unless you have banners and reviews or a high concept product?

Q: If you don't mind my saying, you make it sound easy to get films released.

ANDREW GERNHARD: People think you can just release movies. Frankly, Best Buy is not going to buy a movie from you. But it is those big sales that make a title commercially viable. We teamed up with a manufacturer/distributor who has major accounts that can make the films available through Baker & Taylor, VPD and other channels. If any store needs to order it, it is there. Big stores are not going to venture outside of their market if they can get all of the movies they want from middlemen like that, so why are they going to look for DVDs from you?

Q: If we can backtrack a bit, you said that it helps to have stars in your film. Why is that?

ANDREW GERNHARD: We've released a lot of films that are monster-based and horror-based, but that's not enough anymore. People need to feel comfortable with names. Whether it is Jeremy London, Brian Krause, Kevin Sorbo — they are looking for names to feel comfortable with. A lot of major stores will not buy if there are no names.

We hit the market when we released *Predator Island* (2005, released through Universal). *Blood Descendants*, and *Werewolf: The Devil's Hound* (2007, released through Maverick), and I can guarantee you that I could not sell them now.

Q: How did you handle the distribution of Banshee!!!*?*

ANDREW GERNHARD: *Banshee!!!* came out in America in 2010, but it was overseas for two years earlier. We had huge DVD sales in Germany, Japan and Thailand, and it was on TV in the U.K. It wasn't on TV in America until early 2010.

Q: How do you penetrate the global markets?

ANDREW GERNHARD: We usually have sales agents, but people now know our names and we are trying to capitalize on that. Plus, we have to do it ourselves — a lot of older companies have gone out of business, because the old style of business isn't there anymore.

Q: But that would say something about the value of your films, yes?

ANDREW GERNHARD: Our films are *not* masterpieces — *Predator Island* is a terrible film, but we sold about 52,000 units of this thing. DVD was unbelievable in 2005. At the same time, one of my friends made a drama that was unbelievable, it was 1,000 times better and won 50 film festivals, but Blockbuster passed on it. In the end, it was a drama with no stars.

Q: Since you mentioned festivals, what is your approach to the subject?

ANDREW GERNHARD: We don't go to the festival circuit. We've played in a couple of small festivals, but we require that we are not in competition because we don't work that way. If you are going to the festivals, you have to go to a lot to win a lot of awards. If you only go to a couple and win a few smaller awards, it is better not to go.

Q: Do you see Synthetic Cinema becoming a recognizable brand with wide recognition?

ANDREW GERNHARD: Realistically, we don't have a fan audience that says, "Oh, I saw the last three Synthetic Cinema films and I can't wait to see the next three!" Our audience comes from "I love this genre, I have to get this film because it is in that genre!"

311

LISTEN TO WHAT THE MAN SAYS

So, what are you going to do with all of the data from this chapter? This is what I hope you do:

1. Live by Mark Cuban's advice: "My suggestion however is for filmmakers to be brutally honest with themselves. Just because you wrote it, or will direct it, doesn't make it good." This has been said over and over in the book, and it is being said again: Before you approach any distributor, be honest with yourself about the film's quality and commercial viability. You will save yourself a lot of grief if you feel the film is not ready for release.

2. If you feel you are ready, go to the websites of the distributors here who release product that corresponds best with your movie. Go through the entire website, read every possible word. If you have specific questions about the company, email them or (if a phone number is listed on the website) call them. Calling is often better — the immediacy of a voice is more assuring than a screen of Times Roman font.

3. Then click about the Internet to determine how far these distributors reach. Can you find the company and its films listed in the right places? This is the only way to determine if the distributor is right for your film.

4. Check out the nontheatrical distributors listed here, especially if you made a documentary (non-fiction films are eagerly sought by nontheatrical distributors).

5. When you are finished with this book, get a book on film marketing. I would recommend Mark Steven Bosko's *The Complete Independent Movie Marketing Handbook* as a great starting point. The more you learn about that subject, the better you will be at the game.

THE FINAL WORD

Artists do not experiment. Experiment is what scientists do;
they initiate an operation of unknown factors to be
instructed by its results. An artist puts down what he knows and
at every moment it is what he knows at that moment.
— Gertrude Stein

Alas, our journey has come to an end, at least in regard to this book. Whether you opt to follow your dream into getting your film released, or whether you've been scared away from the film orbit, is entirely your decision.

But in parting, let's just put one last question forward to the film industry experts who've gathered to assist in this book.

The question: What advice would you give aspiring creative artists who want to get into the independent film business?

Eric Monder, critic, *Film Journal International*: Don't! It's suicidal.

Roger Weisberg, Academy Award–nominated filmmaker: My advice to novice filmmakers is to never take "no" for an answer. "No" is just the beginning of a conversation. Tenacity, passion, and vision are often more important qualities than experience when it comes to getting your film made and distributed.

Peter Hargrove, distributor, Hargrove Entertainment: Have a deliverable book completed with everything a distributor would ask for. This would include copies of all contracts signed with actors, writer, director, etc.; music cue sheets and music license agreements (or negotiated terms on their letterhead if not paid for yet); any and all releases for locations and logo'd/trademarked items (you can't use a Yankees baseball cap without getting the rights); laboratory access letters and a list of all elements (and where they are located); samples of poster designs (the distributor most likely will change it but putting your ideas down on paper shows you've thought through the marketing campaign); film festival bookings and press coverage; quotes from "names"; short and long synopses; full cast and crew credits (make sure from the talent that their IMDb listing is complete and updated); and a director's statement. And also have enough "action stills." We do not need static mug shots of actors or shots of the crew setting up or eating lunch.

John Farrell, filmmaker: Try some film festivals, but do not get too caught up in them. The cost of entries adds up, and I think there are too many fests now — and half seem like extended parties rather than serious venues where a newbie can get discovered. I would advise a new producer to also send samples/review cassettes to media/culture bigwigs in their own town and city — museum curators and small theater types who like to run new work, libraries (heck, even some big churches do); and then, of course, put up a solid website and consider self-distribution through places like Amazon — hence more exposure there. And now with iTunes going video — vodcasting — there's another way to promote short films and segments from longer features.

Greg Ross, distributor, Go-Kart Films: Have DVDs to sell on the festival circuit. We have noticed that people, after seeing films that they like, want to buy the DVDs. That's a great way for a filmmaker to sell some copies and make a few bucks.

Rory L. Aronsky, critic, *Film Threat*: Just get started. The risks are large and wide out there in the independent film business from flaky distributors, difficulty in raising funds, and tepid responses to your film, but just try. If you have an idea, it's most important to see how you can get started on it. Explore all facets of your story, think through all the characters if there are any, and see what you can do, what's best for your potential film. If you've got the drive, try it.

Eric Phelps, former development director, Atlanta International Film Festival: I think that I would encourage people to stay true to themselves and not write for the so-called market. In addition, I often told people who called asking about how to become a filmmaker to: learn how to use a camera, learn how to work with actors, and learn how to manage business affairs. If you want to direct people in films, it's *hard work* — not some glamorous thing. Often it seemed that the callers were more interested in being famous "rock stars" than they were in making films. Hell, I might just tell someone to stay away from it!

Christopher Munch, filmmaker: The festival climate has changed a great deal over the past decade owing to the glut of films in the marketplace. At the same time, there have sprung up many regional film festivals that seem to be little more than arms of the local chambers of commerce. The big festivals, for their part, are much bigger "star fuckers" than they used to be. This combination of factors has proven to be lethal for an emerging filmmaker whose work is not star-driven or otherwise attention-getting but who very much needs the exposure that a festival can provide. The newer "niche" festivals provide other opportunities for filmmakers, but their value in establishing a career is questionable. If I were starting out today, given what seems to be the unoriginality of much of the current programming and the ridiculousness of the entry fees that are charged by festival organizers, I would ask myself, "Is it worth it? What am I doing with my life? Why am I killing myself to make something of value when its public life is subject to the whims of festival programmers?"

Dennis Doros, distributor, Milestone Film & Video: The film-maker should really make sure that the distributor is in love with the film. Call other filmmakers in the distributor's catalogue to know what to expect and make sure they were happy. And choose a distributor who has a track record with the kind of film that you have made.

Kent Turner, editor, *Film-Forward.com*: The odds are against your film gaining a distributor, let alone having a theatrical release, so you better have confidence in what you're doing and know why you're doing it.

Leszek Drozd, filmmaker: In general, you need to prioritize: What are you doing that can be considered as wasting time versus what are you doing that can be considered as productive time? In other words, make a correct assessment of your priorities. That applies not only to the distribution aspect of the business, but also to everything regarding the movie business. Some filmmakers need five to ten years to understand what can be and should be done in six months. You can ask if I am one of them, and my answer is: "Probably, yes, I am!"

Josh Koury, programmer, Brooklyn Underground Film Festival: I feel it's important for filmmakers to understand their own film, where it stands, and how it applies to the film world. Is the work an experimental piece, a socially conscious documentary, a heavy-handed narrative/thriller, etc.? If you have lots of money and love rejection letters, please submit to every film festival out there. Normally, resources are limited, and it's best to research the festivals that would welcome your particular style of work. Investigate film festivals and see what type of work they've accepted. This can really help narrow down the festivals a filmmaker might consider submitting to. Ideally, the best thing to do would be to visit a film festival before submitting. Take a look at their program and familiarize yourself with the type of work they screen, and how they run the festival. If the filmmakers seem genuinely happy and excited about showcasing their work at this festival, then that's a good sign. Visiting every film festival is usually not an option, so it can also be very helpful to visit a film festival's Web archives. Take a good look at a film festival's previous programming before submitting. There are thousands of film festivals out there, so researching them will help find a good fit for your film.

Charles Pappas, film historian: Promise them anything but give them your movie. You are only as real as the backers who invest in you — and they need an illusion to feel comfortable with your concept. Fill the room with phrases like "*Speed* meets *Sideways*." They need to feel it is radically different — just so long as everybody else and his feng shui consultant have already done it.

Mike Watt, filmmaker: Do your research — I cannot stress this enough. There are a myriad of companies out there, but not all of them will give you a fair shake and not all of them have your best interests at heart. Talk to other indie filmmakers; find out what they thought of their individual deals. Take a hard look at the contracts offered — try and get a lawyer to look over it if you can. There are all sorts of hidden clauses in contracts. Some companies will buy the title — and all rights to that title — for a limited amount of time, usually five to six years, with an option of renewal. This means distribution and duplication, all marketing considerations, image rights, music rights, etc.

Christopher Bligh, writer, *Ain't It Cool News* **and** *DVDAuthority. com*: Get your voice out there, no matter what. It's always astonishing, because finishing a film is an astonishment in itself.

Doug Hawes-Davis, programmer, Big Sky Documentary Film Festival: I'd recommend having a sneak preview or small screening before you decide to release your film into the festival circuit or go after distributors. We get a lot of rough cuts that are nowhere near ready to be seen. It helps to get a lot of feedback and to make sure you feel strongly before you submit your film anywhere.

Tommy Lee Thomas, producer/actor: Have fun and learn from the experience. If the first few movies do not work out, try again. Do not let yourself feel like a failure if your movie does not show a profit. There are so many reasons why a movie may or may not make money. And never spend more money on your movie than you can afford to lose!

James Eowan, former senior vice president of operations and public relations, Seventh Art Releasing: The number one piece of advice I give all new filmmakers is to do your research before you make your film. Making the film is not enough for success. You need to be knowledgeable about films that came before that are similar to your own. Research where in the marketplace your film will fit. Be realistic and levelheaded about the options for your film. Make sure you create the elements that will be necessary once you move into distribution. Know your film's audience. Ultimately, exhaust all your resources to understand the full value of your film.

Antero Alli, filmmaker: My filmmaking passions are not enflamed by mainstream ambitions. I do not equate success with seven-figure nets or massive exposure. For whatever reasons, I have been immune to that virus peculiar to Hollywood standards and dreams of making movies as a glamorous event requiring fame and fortune as its big payoffs. I have seen how fame and fortune all too often act as epitaphs for the death of art, my central conceit for creating. Fame and fortune may indeed come to me, here or hereafter, but not because I want it or am seeking it out.

My approach to the process and the actual production is very workmanlike and not very glamorous. Glamour pales next to the great joy of working with foreboding talents and people I love and respect.

Steve Kaplan, distributor, Alpha Video: Understand the meaning of and difference between distribution and distributor/manufacturer. One simply distributes your product for a percentage. The other actually pays for the physical manufacturing of your film and therefore takes a bigger piece of the pie. Don't sell off *all* your rights (TV, international, etc.) unless you are compensated. Be wary of advances. This may be the only money you'll ever see!

Kamal Larsuel, editor, *3BlackChicks.com*: All I can say is what has been said before. Be persistent. Be creative in getting people to your movie. Use the Internet. Don't let rejection get you down.

Erica Jordan, filmmaker: Try not to judge the value of your work based on rejections from film festivals. Since they function as a business, they don't always represent independent work, often valuing a film's commercial appeal over artistic integrity. I think it's important to get your work shown in any venue, big or small. When your film does screen in small venues, it's important to network to bring in an audience since most small festivals don't have the publicity behind them to fill a venue in the way you might want. It is also important to continue making new work to stay in touch with what really moves you and continue to develop as a filmmaker.

Sue Early, managing director, Rehoboth Beach Independent Film Festival: Make sure you have a good story. It does not matter how large your budget is; if you have a good story it is what makes the film.

David Nagler, publicist: Start meeting a lot of people in the independent film community, especially if you're not particularly talented.

Larry Fessenden, filmmaker: Question authority. Try to be decent. Try to get in touch with the things that matter. Revere art — it is our best elixir. Anyway, that would be my message. But don't try to be "the next Larry Fessenden," because the current Larry Fessenden is just hanging by a thread!

Jordan Hiller, editor, *Bang It Out*: Find a great script. Most filmmakers are not David Fincher or Martin Scorsese. Most will have no vision when it comes to using the camera and conveying a mood or atmosphere. The best they will do is copy ideas they saw in different movies. A great script can make up for a lot. Filmmaking is storytelling and an independent needs to concentrate on story because there is no budget for special effects or big stars. The story, the script, the words are your stars… so don't even rent the equipment until you have in your hands a moving, involving, 90-page screenplay. Also, don't put your friends in the movie, even if they are willing to work for free, because if they can't act in the slightest it will ruin that great script you have in your hands.

Thomas Edward Seymour, filmmaker: Be prepared to fail with the first project. You may not, but the odds are certainly against you. I would say next that you should be prepared to make at least three films before you have the right to feel like you are being greatly wronged in not getting distribution or overnight success. I would say that your first few projects are the tools you will use to meet people, to improve your craft, to explore getting distribution, and to make friends with festival owners. I believe most real business relationships are formed with people who benefit from each other. For example, a theater owner benefits from a filmmaker because he has a product that the theater owner can use. I hate to say it, but meeting 20 filmmakers in a room who are all on the same level does almost nothing for anyone.

Edward Havens, former head of acquisitions, Troma Entertainment: I've had a few people get angry when we declined to acquire their film, but I wouldn't say it escalated to indignation or hostility. As for handling rejection, I can only recommend that filmmakers never give up. Just because 85 companies said no doesn't mean number 86 will as well. I would also suggest filmmakers ask acquisitions people why, in a polite, non-confrontational manner, the film was rejected. You might not get a lot of responses, but every once in a while you might come across that honest film lover who will be brutally honest about their pass. Only once has a filmmaker ever asked me why I was saying no to their film, and I explained exactly why. Sometimes, filmmakers are too close to their films and unwilling to accept any criticism, when that is exactly what they need.

Stephen J. Szklarski, filmmaker: If you are going to be an independent producer or filmmaker, make something that is meaningful and emotional. Thought-provoking content will get you noticed. There are many people out there looking, searching, and reaching for content.

David Foucher, editor, *EDGE Boston*: Make movies. The word "artist" and the word "business" are often non-collaborative. And it's easy to forget that it's not the studio executives or the distribution dealmakers who hold the true power. The audience does, and we all — filmmakers, financiers, critics — serve the same individuals. It is my job as a critic to determine what the great majority of people will enjoy seeing on the screen, so that they may spend their money more wisely when choosing which picture to experience. It is the filmmakers' job to entertain them.

Matthew Seig, former programmer, Two Boots Pioneer Theater in New York: What kind of a life do you want? What kind of a career are you looking for? What skills will you need other than filmmaking to realize your aspirations? How will the film in your mind advance these aspirations? The answers to those questions may lead you to a different film. A slick-looking film with nothing to say will not be noticed. A technically competent film that is unique in form or content will attract attention. If you really love movies and the important things in your life have been movies, be careful to gain some knowledge and insight into the world that comes from outside your experience with movies. If you want your film to be an homage to movies and TV, be careful to find a unique way of bringing your passion to your film.

Paul DeSimone, filmmaker: Being as professional as you can will help your movie. Don't be slack — try to do the absolute best job you can do. And budget yourself to make sure you can afford everything you're putting into the project.

Mark Pfeiffer, programmer, Deep Focus Film Festival: The earlier you can make your film available to festival programmers and distributors, the better off you'll be. Programming a festival is a slow, labor-intensive process, so it is to the filmmaker's advantage to make the right people aware of the film as soon as possible. For the time being we plan on curating the Deep Focus Film Festival rather than opening it up to submissions. I don't think that precludes filmmakers from requesting consideration for our festival, but we'll need to be informed of such films and given access to them. New filmmakers should keep in mind what they hope to gain by having their films play at festivals. Obviously everyone wants to secure distribution, but not all festivals are set up for such purposes. If the goal is exposure — getting your film shown to the public — then the opportunities open up quite a bit. Earning good word of mouth at several smaller festivals may be as beneficial as or more beneficial than trying to make a splash at a larger fest oriented around the film marketplace.

Christopher Null, editor, *FilmCritic.com*: Practice before you try to make a feature. Really hone your skills; learn the craft. Make some short films. Work on other people's crews. You have to know your stuff cold before you can make a movie, or do anything that requires such an investment of time, energy, and talent.

Ryan Dacko, filmmaker/writer: All in all, it doesn't matter about the quality of your actors, or the size of your budget, not even the originality of the story line. An independent filmmaker's success rides on how well he or she tells the story using the language of the cinema.

Darren Paul, marketing expert, The Night Agency: Be a millionaire, or be related to a millionaire. Think as much about the marketing of your film as you do about the making of your film. Shoot a low-budget DV feature and fly to Sundance. All will work out.

Keith Gordon, filmmaker: Remember — it's just a movie. It's not "you," it's something you did. Right now, it seems like the most important thing in the world. But it isn't. It's not as important as your mate, your kids, your dog, your health.

David Nelson, programmer/director, *minicine?*: As a DIY microcinema operator, I would have to respond by saying, "Get it out there however you can!" Certainly the microcinema network is a good place to start screening to an audience and showing distributors a film's potential.

Donald J. Levit, critic, *ReelTalk Reviews*: As with restaurants and boutiques, expect to see red ink for years, so keep a day job. Aspirants need to network like hell, get their dream works under as many noses as possible. You never know: The odds are less than slim, but you only need one bankroller and, overwhelmingly, the game is contacts and cash.

Stranger things have happened… or so legend has it!

❧

LISTEN TO WHAT THE MAN SAYS

The mathematician and philosopher Bertrand Russell once remarked, "The greatest challenge to any thinker is stating the problem in a way that will allow a solution."

The challenge at hand is this: How can an independent filmmaker get a movie into distribution? If anything, I hope this book provided something resembling a solution through the tools, tips, ideas, and stories collected here.

Making a film is certainly much easier than getting it seen. As many people pointed out in the course of the book, the odds of getting an independently produced film on a big screen can be discouraging. And not just for the first-time filmmaker — remember the challenge that Hal Hartley and Oscar-nominated documentary creator Roger Weisberg faced in getting their films into a projector?

Ultimately, what more can be said? Are you ready to go forward and get your film seen? If you are and you still feel nervous, that's okay — it goes with the territory. But keep moving and keep trying, because you can never experience the sensation of accomplishment if you fail to chase your dreams.

I can't make any guarantees that this book will aim you to the stage of the Academy Award ceremony. But if your film is great and you believe in yourself, you are (at the very least) pointed in the right direction.

The poet T. S. Eliot said it best: "Only those who will risk going too far can possibly find out how far one can go."

ABOUT THE AUTHOR

PHIL HALL is one of the most influential advocates of contemporary independent and underground cinema. He is the author of the critically acclaimed books *The Encyclopedia of Underground Movies: Films from the Fringes of Cinema* (published by Michael Wiese Productions in 2004) and *The History of Independent Cinema* (published by BearManor Media in 2009). He is a contributing editor for the popular online magazine *Film Threat* and his film journalism has appeared in the *New York Times, New York Daily News* and *Wired*. He is a member of the Governing Committee of the Online Film Critics Society, and has been a guest  commentator on film trends and issues for such media outlets as the *New York Post, Christian Science Monitor*, E! Online, National Public Radio, PBS and the Voice of America.

Hall also wrote the books *The New PR* (published by Larstan Publishing in 2007) and *What If They Lived?* (co-authored with Rory Leighton Aronsky and published by BearManor Media in 2011). He is a former book critic for the *New York Resident* weekly newspaper, and his column was nominated for the 2006 Pulitzer Prize.

THE COMPLETE INDEPENDENT MOVIE MARKETING HANDBOOK
PROMOTE, DISTRIBUTE & SELL YOUR FILM OR VIDEO

MARK STEVEN BOSKO

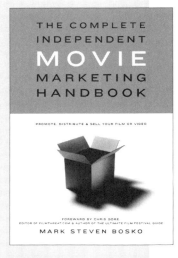

If you're an independent filmmaker looking for information on how to market, distribute, and find audiences for your movies and videos, you'll discover it here. This book is packed with street-smart savvy and real-world examples on how to promote and sell your productions. From landing a distribution deal and getting free media coverage to staging a low-cost premiere and selling your movie to video rental chains and over the Internet, this book is a must-have for any independent film or video maker looking to seriously launch and sustain a career in the entertainment industry.

"Get this book if you have a finished film you want to sell ! It's packed full with incredible ideas, gimmicks, and ploys to get little films out there and noticed. I wish we had this when we were doing Blair Witch."

> — Eduardo Sanchez, Co-Writer, Co-Director, Co-Editor, The Blair Witch Project

"The best book that I have read about grass-roots film marketing. Troma Entertainment actually uses the marketing secrets described in this excellent book, and has for nearly 30 years! They work!"

> — Lloyd Kaufman, President, Troma Entertainment Creator, The Toxic Avenger

"NOTICE TO ALL INDIE FILMMAKERS: You've shot a great indie film. You're proud of it. Your mother loves it. Now what? You need this book. Buy this book. Read this book cover to cover."

> — Elizabeth English, Founder & Executive Director, Moondance International Film Festival

"Mark Bosko's book is extremely well researched and replete with actual case histories and insightful observations and advice. If you are producing and marketing an independent film, Bosko's book should be on your must-read list."

> — Harris Tulchin, Harris Tulchin and Associates; Entertainment Attorney, Producer's Rep, Author, www.medialawyer.com

MARK STEVEN BOSKO has been promoting and distributing independent feature films for more than 10 years. In addition to performing virtually every job on a film production, he has worked professionally in public relations, marketing, and magazine publishing.

$39.95 · 300 PAGES · ORDER NUMBER 108RLS · ISBN: 9780941188760

SELLING YOUR STORY IN 60 SECONDS
THE GUARANTEED WAY TO GET YOUR SCREENPLAY OR NOVEL READ

MICHAEL HAUGE

BEST SELLER

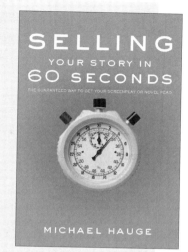

Best-selling author Michael Hauge reveals:
- How to Design, Practice, and Present the 60-Second Pitch
- The Cardinal Rule of Pitching
- The 10 Key Components of a Commercial Story
- The 8 Steps to a Powerful Pitch
- Targeting Your Buyers
- Securing Opportunities to Pitch
- Pitching Templates
- And much more, including "The Best Pitch I Ever Heard," an exclusive collection from major film executives

"Michael Hauge's principles and methods are so well argued that the mysteries of effective screenwriting can be understood — even by directors."

— Phillip Noyce, Director, *Patriot Games, Clear and Present Danger, The Quiet American, Rabbit-Proof Fence*

"... one of the few authentically good teachers out there. Every time I revisit my notes, I learn something new or reinforce something that I need to remember."

— Jeff Arch, Screenwriter, *Sleepless in Seattle, Iron Will*

"Michael Hauge's method is magic — but unlike most magicians, he shows you how the trick is done."

— William Link, Screenwriter & Co-Creator, *Columbo; Murder, She Wrote*

"By following the formula we learned in Michael Hauge's seminar, we got an agent, optioned our script, and now have a three-picture deal at Disney."

— Paul Hoppe and David Henry, Screenwriters

MICHAEL HAUGE is the author of *Writing Screenplays That Sell*, now in its 30th printing, and has presented his seminars and lectures to more than 30,000 writers and filmmakers. He has coached hundreds of screenwriters and producers on their screenplays and pitches, and has consulted on projects for Warner Brothers, Disney, New Line, CBS, Lifetime, Julia Roberts, Jennifer Lopez, Kirsten Dunst, and Morgan Freeman.

$12.95 · 150 PAGES · ORDER NUMBER 64RLS · ISBN: 9781932907209

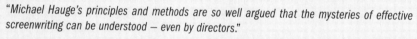

BANKROLL
A NEW APPROACH TO FINANCING FEATURE FILMS

TOM MALLOY

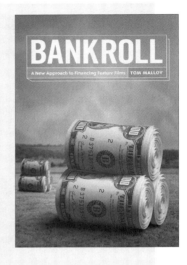

There is one golden rule in Hollywood: "He who has the gold makes the rules." Your film can have every other element in place, yet if it lacks financing, it's never going to happen. This book tells you how to get the gold.

Bankroll is the book that all filmmakers have been waiting for. This book deviates from the traditional business-oriented books that tell you how to get grants and explain in theory how studio deals work. *Bankroll* goes into the precise and practical details of how the author has raised over $10 million in the past four years for a number of feature films. By presenting a full and winning hand of different techniques, the book provides creative ideas and motivation that will get you the financing you need to make your movie happen.

"The simplest, most straightforward instructions I've ever read about how to finance your own film. This isn't an exposé of how studio moguls or bigwig indie producers do it; it's a step-by-step guide to how the hungry, scrappy (but no less savvy) do-it-yourselfers do it. Having read this, I now fully believe that I could go and raise $8 million for my own movie... tonight. (That may be a bit delusional, and easier said than done, but at least I know where to start.)"

> — Chad Gervich, TV Writer/Producer and Author; *Small Screen, Big Picture: A Writer's Guide to the TV Business*

"The most important part of independent filmmaking is finding the money. Without the money, nothing else can happen. This book tells you how to do it in simple, practical, and effective terms. I've read nothing else as informative on this first and most vital part of getting your film made. Kudos to Tom Malloy."

> — Tom Holland, Writer/Director, *Fright Night, Child's Play, Thinner*

"In refreshingly frank language, Tom Malloy tells it like it is... and like it isn't. Bankroll *could be the only book you'll ever need to read about independent filmmaking – this book is the real "deal." Tom's energy, enthusiasm and knowledge leap off the page – if this doesn't motivate and inspire you, nothing will!"*

> - Stephanie Austin, Producer, *Terminator 2, True Lies, Behind Enemy Lines*

TOM MALLOY most recently wrote, produced, and starred in *Love N' Dancing*, a west coast swing dance film directed by Rob Iscove (*She's All That*). Starring opposite Tom are Amy Smart, Billy Zane, and Betty White. He is also a nationally known motivational speaker for high school students (*www.TomMalloy.com*).

$24.95 · 224 PAGES · ORDER NUMBER 125RLS · ISBN 13: 9781932907575

GETTING THE MONEY
A STEP-BY-STEP GUIDE FOR
WRITING BUSINESS PLANS FOR FILM

JEREMY JUUSO

The only step-by-step guide on the market for how to write a film business plan. Tailored to artists unfamiliar with financial concepts, but detailed enough for those versed in high finance. Sure to become a staple in every filmmaker's toolkit.

Filmmakers interested in financing their own films have to start with a business plan. Few know how to put one together. *Getting the Money* gives a relaxed, step-by-step approach on how to do so. Of particular use are the financial sections where, for the first time, readers are guided on exactly what to do and exactly how to do it, using examples from sample plans. No more vague instructions that amount to hiring someone else. Once finished with the book, readers will have their own plan they can use to attract financing for their films.

"For the new filmmaker, you should consider this to be the definitive handbook to getting your movie financed. If you follow Jeremy's guidance, by the time you're finished, you will understand your movie from every financial angle necessary and your investors will love you for it. Then onward to the creative process."

> — Matthew Rhodes, executive producer, *An Unfinished Life*, starring Robert Redford and Morgan Freeman; producer, *Passengers*, starring Oscar nominee Anne Hathaway

"An amazing reference for anyone even thinking about writing business plans for films. Clear, concise, understandable — and a great overview of the nuts and bolts behind how an indie film makes money."

> — Arie Posin, director, *The Chumscrubber*, starring Carrie-Anne Moss, Rita Wilson, and Oscar nominees Glenn Close and Ralph Fiennes

JEREMY JUUSO graduated *cum laude* in economics from Harvard College. Upon graduation he accepted a Harvard fellowship and taught economics at a British boarding school to students applying to Oxford and Cambridge. Since England, he has worked at MGM's treasury and investor relations departments, the financial markets research firm *Bigdough.com* (now part of Ipreo Holdings), and the production company Fly High Films, where he currently serves as financial advisor and writes business plans for the company. Jeremy is also the founder of Jeremy Juuso Consulting, a firm specializing in the writing of film business proposals and educating investors on the basics of the movie business (*www.jeremyjuuso.com*).

$26.95 · 240 PAGES · ORDER NUMBER 132RLS · ISBN 13: 9781932907643

THE PERFECT PITCH – 2ND EDITION
HOW TO SELL YOURSELF AND
YOUR MOVIE IDEA TO HOLLYWOOD

KEN ROTCOP

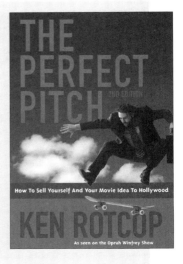

If you want to sell ANYTHING in the world, including yourself, you've got to learn how to create the Perfect Pitch. A good pitch can mean the difference between seeing your name on a lucrative studio contract or a rejection form letter.

This book not only covers every facet of pitching; Rotcop also shares fascinating stories about plagiarism, how to get an agent, gimmicks to bring to pitch meetings, how to get a studio job, and what to do if Brad Pitt and Angelina Jolie want to star in your screenplay.

"Before you can get someone to read your screenplay you have to know how to pitch them on the idea. Ken Rotcop is the master at teaching writers how to pitch. Remember, it's all in the pitch!"
— Oprah Winfrey, *The Oprah Winfrey Show*

"A short, yet fact-filled manual to help level the playing field. Being an old hand at pitching and knowing both sides of the field, Rotcop has a lot of good advice to offer, though some of it is just good common sense. Still, pitching is a skill, which needs to be developed, and this book certainly provides the reader with sufficient ideas and examples to start practicing on their own killer pitch!"
— *Screen Talk* Magazine

"The pitch is an executive's first impression of you. He must decide whether he likes your story, likes you, and sees infinite possibilities to become rich. All within two minutes! Rotcop's sure-fire tips on pitching will show you how to gently grab the executive by the throat and not let go until he agrees to read your script."
— *Creative Screenwriting* Magazine

"Forget about snappy dialogue, characterization and plot. It's the pitch that gets a script read and a movie deal done. If it were not for Ken Rotcop, most new writers would be out of the loop."

— John Lippman, *Wall Street Journal*

KEN ROTCOP produces Pitchmart,™ Hollywood's biggest screenplay pitch event. His screenwriting workshop was the subject of a feature-length documentary, *Talk Fast*, which has won various film festival awards. Most recently STARZ network produced a two-part series on Ken Rotcop, *Pitching Guru*.

$19.95 · 216 PAGES · ORDER NUMBER 92RLS · ISBN: 9781932907520

SAVE THE CAT!®
THE LAST BOOK ON
SCREENWRITING YOU'LL EVER NEED!

BLAKE SNYDER

He's made millions of dollars selling screenplays to Hollywood and now screenwriter Blake Snyder tells all. "Save the Cat!®" is just one of Snyder's many ironclad rules for making your ideas more marketable and your script more satisfying — and saleable, including:

· The four elements of every winning logline.
· The seven immutable laws of screenplay physics.
· The 10 genres and why they're important to your movie.
· Why your Hero must serve your idea.
· Mastering the Beats.
· Mastering the Board to create the Perfect Beast.
· How to get back on track with ironclad and proven rules for script repair.

This ultimate insider's guide reveals the secrets that none dare admit, told by a show biz veteran who's proven that you can sell your script if you can save the cat.

"Imagine what would happen in a town where more writers approached screenwriting the way Blake suggests? My weekend read would dramatically improve, both in sellable/producible content and in discovering new writers who understand the craft of storytelling and can be hired on assignment for ideas we already have in house."
> – From the Foreword by Sheila Hanahan Taylor, Vice President, Development at Zide/Perry Entertainment, whose films include *American Pie, Cats and Dogs, Final Destination*

"One of the most comprehensive and insightful how-to's out there. Save the Cat!® is a must-read for both the novice and the professional screenwriter."
> – Todd Black, Producer, *The Pursuit of Happyness, The Weather Man, S.W.A.T, Alex and Emma, Antwone Fisher*

"Want to know how to be a successful writer in Hollywood? The answers are here. Blake Snyder has written an insider's book that's informative — and funny, too."
> – David Hoberman, Producer, *The Shaggy Dog* (2005), *Raising Helen, Walking Tall, Bringing Down the House, Monk* (TV)

BLAKE SNYDER, besides selling million-dollar scripts to both Disney and Spielberg, was one of Hollywood's most successful spec screenwriters. Blake's vision continues on *www.blakesnyder.com*.

$19.95 · 216 PAGES · ORDER NUMBER 34RLS · ISBN: 9781932907001

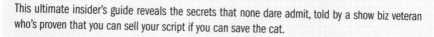

THE WRITER'S JOURNEY - 3RD EDITION
MYTHIC STRUCTURE FOR WRITERS

CHRISTOPHER VOGLER

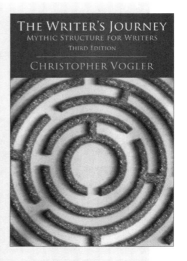

BEST SELLER
OVER 180,000 COPIES SOLD!

See why this book has become an international best seller and a true classic. *The Writer's Journey* explores the powerful relationship between mythology and storytelling in a clear, concise style that's made it required reading for movie executives, screenwriters, playwrights, scholars, and fans of pop culture all over the world.

Both fiction and nonfiction writers will discover a set of useful myth-inspired storytelling paradigms (i.e., "The Hero's Journey") and step-by-step guidelines to plot and character development. Based on the work of Joseph Campbell, *The Writer's Journey* is a must for all writers interested in further developing their craft.

The updated and revised third edition provides new insights and observations from Vogler's ongoing work on mythology's influence on stories, movies, and man himself.

"This book is like having the smartest person in the story meeting come home with you and whisper what to do in your ear as you write a screenplay. Insight for insight, step for step, Chris Vogler takes us through the process of connecting theme to story and making a script come alive."
> – Lynda Obst, Producer, *Sleepless in Seattle, How to Lose a Guy in 10 Days*;
> Author, *Hello, He Lied*

"This is a book about the stories we write, and perhaps more importantly, the stories we live. It is the most influential work I have yet encountered on the art, nature, and the very purpose of storytelling."
> – Bruce Joel Rubin, Screenwriter, *Stuart Little 2, Deep Impact,*
> *Ghost, Jacob's Ladder*

CHRISTOPHER VOGLER is a veteran story consultant for major Hollywood film companies and a respected teacher of filmmakers and writers around the globe. He has influenced the stories of movies from *The Lion King* to *Fight Club* to *The Thin Red Line* and most recently wrote the first installment of *Ravenskull*, a Japanese-style manga or graphic novel. He is the executive producer of the feature film *P.S. Your Cat is Dead* and writer of the animated feature *Jester Till*.

$26.95 · 448 PAGES · ORDER NUMBER 76RLS · ISBN: 9781932907360

THE MYTH OF MWP

In a dark time, a light bringer came along, leading the curious and the frustrated to clarity and empowerment. It took the well-guarded secrets out of the hands of the few and made them available to all. It spread a spirit of openness and creative freedom, and built a storehouse of knowledge dedicated to the betterment of the arts.

The essence of the Michael Wiese Productions (MWP) is empowering people who have the burning desire to express themselves creatively. We help them realize their dreams by putting the tools in their hands. We demystify the sometimes secretive worlds of screenwriting, directing, acting, producing, film financing, and other media crafts.

By doing so, we hope to bring forth a realization of 'conscious media' which we define as being positively charged, emphasizing hope and affirming positive values like trust, cooperation, self-empowerment, freedom, and love. Grounded in the deep roots of myth, it aims to be healing both for those who make the art and those who encounter it. It hopes to be transformative for people, opening doors to new possibilities and pulling back veils to reveal hidden worlds.

MWP has built a storehouse of knowledge unequaled in the world, for no other publisher has so many titles on the media arts. Please visit www.mwp.com where you will find many free resources and a 25% discount on our books. Sign up and become part of the wider creative community!

Onward and upward,

Michael Wiese
Publisher/Filmmaker

FILM & VIDEO BOOKS

TO RECEIVE A FREE MWP NEWSLETTER, CLICK ON WWW.MWP.COM TO REGISTER

SCREENWRITING | WRITING

And the Best Screenplay Goes to... | Dr. Linda Seger | $26.95
Archetypes for Writers | Jennifer Van Bergen | $22.95
Bali Brothers | Lacy Waltzman, Matthew Bishop, Michael Wiese | $12.95
Cinematic Storytelling | Jennifer Van Sijll | $24.95
Could It Be a Movie? | Christina Hamlett | $26.95
Creating Characters | Marisa D'Vari | $26.95
Crime Writer's Reference Guide, The | Martin Roth | $20.95
Deep Cinema | Mary Trainor-Brigham | $19.95
Elephant Bucks | Sheldon Bull | $24.95
Fast, Cheap & Written That Way | John Gaspard | $26.95
Hollywood Standard – 2nd Edition, The | Christopher Riley | $18.95
Horror Screenwriting | Devin Watson | $24.95
I Could've Written a Better Movie than That! | Derek Rydall | $26.95
Inner Drives | Pamela Jaye Smith | $26.95
Moral Premise, The | Stanley D. Williams, Ph.D. | $24.95
Myth and the Movies | Stuart Voytilla | $26.95
Power of the Dark Side, The | Pamela Jaye Smith | $22.95
Psychology for Screenwriters | William Indick, Ph.D. | $26.95
Reflections of the Shadow | Jeffrey Hirschberg | $26.95
Rewrite | Paul Chitlik | $16.95
Romancing the A-List | Christopher Keane | $18.95
Save the Cat! | Blake Snyder | $19.95
Save the Cat! Goes to the Movies | Blake Snyder | $24.95
Screenwriting 101 | Neill D. Hicks | $16.95
Screenwriting for Teens | Christina Hamlett | $18.95
Script-Selling Game, The | Kathie Fong Yoneda | $16.95
Stealing Fire From the Gods, 2nd Edition | James Bonnet | $26.95
Talk the Talk | Penny Penniston | $24.95
Way of Story, The | Catherine Ann Jones | $22.95
What Are You Laughing At? | Brad Schreiber | $19.95
Writer's Journey – 3rd Edition, The | Christopher Vogler | $26.95
Writer's Partner, The | Martin Roth | $24.95
Writing the Action Adventure Film | Neill D. Hicks | $14.95
Writing the Comedy Film | Stuart Voytilla & Scott Petri | $14.95
Writing the Killer Treatment | Michael Halperin | $14.95
Writing the Second Act | Michael Halperin | $19.95
Writing the Thriller Film | Neill D. Hicks | $14.95
Writing the TV Drama Series, 2nd Edition | Pamela Douglas | $26.95
Your Screenplay Sucks! | William M. Akers | $19.95

FILMMAKING

Film School | Richard D. Pepperman | $24.95
Power of Film, The | Howard Suber | $27.95

PITCHING

Perfect Pitch – 2nd Edition, The | Ken Rotcop | $19.95
Selling Your Story in 60 Seconds | Michael Hauge | $12.95

SHORTS

Filmmaking for Teens, 2nd Edition | Troy Lanier & Clay Nichols | $24.95
Making It Big in Shorts | Kim Adelman | $22.95

BUDGET | PRODUCTION MANAGEMENT

Film & Video Budgets, 5th Updated Edition | Deke Simon | $26.95
Film Production Management 101 | Deborah S. Patz | $39.95

DIRECTING | VISUALIZATION

Animation Unleashed | Ellen Besen | $26.95

(Cinematography / Directing)

Cinematography for Directors | Jacqueline Frost | $29.95
Citizen Kane Crash Course in Cinematography | David Worth | $19.95
Directing Actors | Judith Weston | $26.95
Directing Feature Films | Mark Travis | $26.95
Fast, Cheap & Under Control | John Gaspard | $26.95
Film Directing: Cinematic Motion, 2nd Edition | Steven D. Katz | $27.95
Film Directing: Shot by Shot | Steven D. Katz | $27.95
Film Director's Intuition, The | Judith Weston | $26.95
First Time Director | Gil Bettman | $27.95
From Word to Image, 2nd Edition | Marcie Begleiter | $26.95
I'll Be in My Trailer! | John Badham & Craig Modderno | $26.95
Master Shots | Christopher Kenworthy | $24.95
Setting Up Your Scenes | Richard D. Pepperman | $24.95
Setting Up Your Shots, 2nd Edition | Jeremy Vineyard | $22.95
Working Director, The | Charles Wilkinson | $22.95

DIGITAL | DOCUMENTARY | SPECIAL

Digital Filmmaking 101, 2nd Edition | Dale Newton & John Gaspard | $26.95
Digital Moviemaking 3.0 | Scott Billups | $24.95
Digital Video Secrets | Tony Levelle | $26.95
Greenscreen Made Easy | Jeremy Hanke & Michele Yamazaki | $19.95
Producing with Passion | Dorothy Fadiman & Tony Levelle | $22.95
Special Effects | Michael Slone | $31.95

EDITING

Cut by Cut | Gael Chandler | $35.95
Cut to the Chase | Bobbie O'Steen | $24.95
Eye is Quicker, The | Richard D. Pepperman | $27.95
Film Editing | Gael Chandler | $34.95
Invisible Cut, The | Bobbie O'Steen | $28.95

SOUND | DVD | CAREER

Complete DVD Book, The | Chris Gore & Paul J. Salamoff | $26.95
Costume Design 101, 2nd Edition | Richard La Motte | $24.95
Hitting Your Mark, 2nd Edition | Steve Carlson | $22.95
Sound Design | David Sonnenschein | $19.95
Sound Effects Bible, The | Ric Viers | $26.95
Storyboarding 101 | James Fraioli | $19.95
There's No Business Like Soul Business | Derek Rydall | $22.95
You Can Act! | D. W. Brown | $24.95

FINANCE | MARKETING | FUNDING

Art of Film Funding, The | Carole Lee Dean | $26.95
Bankroll | Tom Malloy | $26.95
Complete Independent Movie Marketing Handbook, The | Mark Steven Bosko | $39.95
Getting the Money | Jeremy Jusso | $26.95
Independent Film and Videomakers Guide – 2nd Edition, The | Michael Wiese | $29.95
Independent Film Distribution | Phil Hall | $26.95
Shaking the Money Tree, 3rd Edition | Morrie Warshawski | $26.95

MEDITATION | ART

Mandalas of Bali | Dewa Nyoman Batuan | $39.95

OUR FILMS

Dolphin Adventures: DVD | Michael Wiese and Hardy Jones | $24.95
Hardware Wars: DVD | Written and Directed by Ernie Fosselius | $14.95
On the Edge of a Dream | Michael Wiese | $16.95
Sacred Sites of the Dalai Lamas– DVD, The | Documentary by Michael Wiese | $24.95